TELEVANGELISM
POWER AND POLITICS ON GOD'S FRONTIER

Jeffrey K. Hadden
Anson Shupe

HENRY HOLT AND COMPANY
NEW YORK

Published by Henry Holt and Company, Inc.,
115 West 18th Street, New York, New York 10011.
Published in Canada by Fitzhenry & Whiteside Limited,
195 Allstate Parkway, Markham, Ontario L3R 4T8.

Library of Congress Cataloging-in-Publication Data
Hadden, Jeffrey K.
Televangelism: power and politics on God's frontier
Jeffrey K. Hadden, Anson Shupe.—1st ed.
p.   cm.
Bibliography: p.
Includes index.
ISBN 0-8050-0778-4
1. United States—Church history—20th century.   2. United States—
Politics and government—1981–   3. Television in religion—United
States.   4. Evangelistic work—United States—History—20th century.
5. Evangelists—United States.   6. Evangelicalism—United States—
History—20th century.   7. Fundamentalism.   8. Conservatism—United
States—History—20th century.   9. Robertson, Pat.   I. Shupe,
Anson D.   II. Title.
BR526.H23   1988
269′.2—dc19   87-30556
                                                                            CIP

First Edition

Designed by Jeffrey L. Ward
Printed in the United States of America
1   3   5   7   9   10   8   6   4   2

ISBN 0-8050-0778-4

Contents

Acknowledgments

This is a book about televangelists and their followers and how together they are creating a cultural revolution in America. In some respects, M. G. "Pat" Robertson's quest for the presidency has made our task more difficult. The animosity and fear so many Americans feel toward televangelists cloud their ability to objectively evaluate the emerging political strength of the New Christian Right. The fact that we do not share the hysteria many people feel toward evangelical Christians makes us suspect. Scores of people have probed to learn if we are closet evangelicals and private supporters of Robertson's candidacy. We always assure them that we are both unreconstructed 1960s liberals out of the liberal Protestant church tradition—although that doesn't necessarily allay their fears.

If Robertson's candidacy has complicated our task, it surely will help call attention to the issues we are addressing. Whatever distance Robertson may finally go in the 1988 presidential sweepstakes, his success will surprise most people, and serious people in every sector of society will have to ask why he did so well. We believe this book provides a foundation for answering that question, although the questions we address are much broader.

We are sociologists by training, but our quest to understand the emergence of the conservative Christian movement in America has taken us down many paths and across traditional academic boundaries. Immersion in American religious history was an indispensable part of our task. To Martin Marty, who first showed us more than twenty years ago the practical value of history for understanding contemporary America, we owe continuing gratitude. Razelle Frankl's tracing of the roots of modern televangelism to 19th-century urban revivalism provided a critical link for our understanding of the phenomenon. Joel Carpenter's writings have shown us the continuity of the evangelical movement through most of this century. This project has also taken us onto the turf of political science to a greater degree than either of us had heretofore ventured. Our thanks to Luther Haggard for guidance here.

Our own scholarly orientation to understanding the rise of the New Christian Right is a conceptual field known as resource mobilization theory. Mayer N. Zald and John N. McCarthy have pioneered this approach

to social movement theory, and they have also helped us better understand how religious sentiment is channeled into social movements. Many other scholars and colleagues have contributed to our understanding of the relationship between conservative faith and politics in America. We would like to acknowledge especially: Nancy Ammerman, Ben Armstrong, Jim Castelli, David W. Clark, Bob Dugan, George Gallup, Jr., Barbara Hargrove, James D. Hunter, Benton Johnson, Jeremy Rifkin, Tom Robbins, W. Clark Roof, Rodney Stark, and Paul H. Virts.

Jerry Falwell and Pat Robertson are the two key figures in the emergence of the New Christian Right in America and, naturally, they figure centrally in this book. Without their cooperation and help, our task would have been much more difficult. Both have given generously of their time for many interviews. Our thanks to them and their respective staffs.

Since we are among a very few scholars who systematically study religious broadcasting, we have been interviewed by literally hundreds of print and broadcast journalists covering, at one time or another, the ever unfolding story of televangelism during this past decade. If we have been able to provide them with the perspective of the independent observer, we are grateful for the opportunity. But we are also very much in their debt for valuable insights, probing questions, and healthy skepticism, which have challenged our thinking. We consider these people our colleagues in the continuing effort to better understand the role of religious broadcasters in American life. Special gratitude is extended to: Ed Briggs of *The Richmond Times-Dispatch*, Bruce Bursma of *The Chicago Tribune*, Russell Chandler and John Dart of *The Los Angeles Times*, Drew Digby of *The Lynchburg News and Advance*, Jim Jones of *The Fort Worth Star-Telegram*, Helen Parmley of *The Dallas Morning News*, and Cecile White of *The Houston Chronicle*.

We fully recognize that our thesis is controversial. Indeed, many of our colleagues, including some here acknowledged, have told us bluntly that we have taken leave of our senses. Hence, it is especially important to underscore our sole responsibility for any shortcomings in the analysis. But to the extent we are right, those here acknowledged each have our gratitude for sharpening our thinking about the issues we address.

Jeffrey K. Hadden   Anson Shupe
Charlottesville, Virginia   Fort Wayne, Indiana

TELEVANGELISM

1

Getting Saved
from the Televangelists

*He would combine in one association all the moral or-
ganizations of America—perhaps later, the entire world.
He would be the executive of the combination; he would
be the super-president of the United States, and some
day the dictator of the world.*
                                            —Sinclair Lewis,
                                              Elmer Gantry

Elmer Gantry was as loathsome a
character as has ever been born in the mind of an American writer.
The hypocritical, slick-talking Gantry consumed great quantities of
whiskey, seduced church secretaries, and removed the choir robes of
countless virgins, all without the slightest qualm of conscience; he
stole from little old ladies and lined his pockets with offerings from
the collection plate. The tough-talking evangelist Sister Sharon Fal-
coner, another Sinclair Lewis character, said Gantry was ". . . an un-
grateful dog that bit the hand that took [him] out of the slimy
gutter, . . . a liar, a ignoramus, a four-flusher, and a rotten preacher."[1]

A social critic whose satirical account of a simpler America won
Lewis the Nobel Prize for literature in 1930, the controversial nov-
elist's special targets were those who, in the name of religion, preyed
upon America's innocent and uneducated—preachers of an old if dis-
honored American evangelical-fundamentalist tradition.

Like the contemporary American humorist Garrison Keillor, the
creator and until mid-1987 host of the popular radio program "A Prairie

1

Home Companion," Sinclair Lewis hailed from a small town in Minnesota. But, unlike Keillor, who romanticized and celebrated the people and folkways of backwoods and main streets of small-town America, Lewis rejected his midwestern roots in favor of the secular culture of sophisticated city life. Whatever the validity of Lewis's lessons and their relevance today, it is important not to lose sight of two critical facts:

First, Sinclair Lewis hated religion, and he hated the religious more than he hated folk lawyers, physicians, hypocrites, conformists, and all provincials. If anyone in America detested fundamentalist religion more in his time, it surely was newspaper editor H. L. Mencken, to whom Lewis dedicated *Elmer Gantry*. In his coverage of the Scopes "monkey" trial, Mencken portrayed prosecuting attorney William Jennings Bryan and his fanatical fundamentalist friends as poor, ignorant vestiges of an archaic people outside the mainstream of American life.

Lewis's *Elmer Gantry* told "mainstream" America about how these fundamentalist ignoramuses were victimized by vulturous vipers clad in holy vestments. The first sentences of Lewis's novel introduce the reader to both the character of his preacher and the mind of the creator: "Elmer Gantry was drunk. He was eloquently drunk, lovingly and pugnaciously drunk."[2] And in the closing scene of Lewis's pamphleteering attack upon evangelical preachers, Gantry extricates himself from yet another scrape—this one another "inexcusable intimacy" with a church secretary. On his knees before a sanctuary packed with people shouting Hallelujah to assure the Reverend Doctor Gantry that they believe in his innocence, the hypocritical preacher turns heavenward and prays:

> O Lord, thou hast stooped from thy mighty throne and rescued thy servant from the assault of the mercenaries of Satan! . . . Let me count this day, Lord, as the beginning of a new and more vigorous life, as the beginning of a crusade for complete morality and the domination of the Christian church through all the land. Dear Lord, thy work is but begun! We shall yet make these United States a moral nation![3]

And the second fact about the Elmer Gantry character? It is all too easily forgotten in Lewis's seductive caricature that Elmer Gantry

never existed. He is a fictional character drawn by a writer who hated evangelicalism.

Yet Lewis's stereotype survives just as certainly as do Mencken's frivolous fundamentalist fools. But today the evangelical's message also survives, albeit in television studios, instead of from hastily constructed wooden tabernacles; only the site of the heavenly hoax has changed.

The conniving and lecherous televangelists featured in many a contemporary television drama are fictional too. But everybody, especially those who know nothing about religious broadcasting, "knows" that these video vicars are but mirror images of those who appear on Christian networks.

Few evangelicals today have read *Elmer Gantry*, but Sinclair Lewis's sinister novel seems to be required reading for anyone who wants to produce a made-for-television movie or an episode of a soap opera or mini-series that features a TV preacher. An ABC television movie entitled "Pray TV" left viewers with little doubt that the message was about *preying* and not *praying*. Portrayals of televangelists in such series as "Murder, She Wrote," "Mike Hammer," and "Spenser for Hire," among others, are straight out of *Elmer Gantry*.

This Gantryesque imagery in today's fictionalized televangelism centers on money and power to stagger the imagination; to protect their turf and hide their lecherous lifestyles, the characters portrayed have no qualms about living on the edge, even outside of the law. Lying is not a defensive measure to save one's hide. It is, along with sweetness and slick talk, a means to whatever ends are desired. And, it is assumed, every high-rolling TV preacher must have a carefully concealed Swiss bank account as insurance against the possible future discovery of his fraudulent religious racketeering.

Exaggerated stereotypes portrayed to America through the mass media carry the day outside the Bible Belt. And, like all significant stereotypes, part of the success of the image rests on the viewer's unfamiliarity with the person or group being portrayed. The negative stereotype so fits "mainstream" America's preconceptions that a large proportion of those who have never switched the dial to a religious program are convinced that the caricature is literally true to life.

* * *

For more than 200 years, America's great evangelists have been colorful and controversial. And a few of them have been rascals. But most have been honest men and women, doing the best they could by the means available to them to preach the gospel. Still, the Gantry caricature obtains, and the worst characteristics of the "bad apples" are lumped together and applied indiscriminately to all televangelists.

At least this is the way it seemed to the knowledgeable few studying the video vicars who bring religion into the comfort of our living rooms.

But then came the stormy month of March 1987, which seemed to confirm that Sinclair Lewis was right after all. It began with God's promise that this would be Oral Roberts's last month on earth if Oral's followers did not produce $8 million in "ransom money." While Islamic Jihad routinely holds hostages in the name of Allah, this was a first: God Almighty, in Christian guise, had become involved in holding a hostage for ransom.

The media were having so much fun with the Roberts story that they almost missed the announcement that Tammy Faye Bakker, star of the PTL (Praise The Lord or People That Love) Network's live daytime drama, "The Jim and Tammy Show," had entered the Betty Ford Center for drug rehabilitation.

Then, just as reporters were descending upon Tulsa, Oklahoma, to report on the countdown to see whether Oral would raise enough money to buy more time, a sex scandal involving Tammy Faye's husband, Jim Bakker, began unfolding at their headquarters in Heritage USA, the Christian retreat–cum–theme park at Fort Mill, South Carolina (just south of Charlotte, North Carolina).

Poor Oral. For years this Pentecostal preacher, who began his ministry in a tent on the sawdust trail of revivalism, had described his wrestlings with the Devil in lurid detail. With his vast modern communications machinery, Oral was having a devil of a time persuading his followers that God was holding him hostage; he looked straight into the television cameras and told his viewers that God was not fooling around. Roberts sent out millions of direct-mail letters to advise people of the gravity of the situation—your money or my life.

But the bucks were not coming in fast enough to meet God's ultimatum. So Oral took a calculated risk. He reasoned that if he could get the attention of the secular media in America, they would write about his plight. He believed that many of his followers who had

strayed would, upon learning how serious the situation was, respond to his clarion call for help.

His strategy worked splendidly. Oral and son Richard Roberts, who has his own television program, complained that they didn't appreciate the cynical spin the secular press was putting on the story. But privately they knew that the secular media's coverage would get the attention of backsliders from their ministry. After all, publicity is the money game's name; it wouldn't be long before the postman started delivering bags and bags of money.

All fund-raising campaigns lead toward a crescendo. Like a giant fireworks display, everything builds toward the grand finale. Managed properly, the final thrust can push a fund-raising campaign well over its stated objectives.

Just as Oral was moving toward his triumphant grand finale, the scandal broke at Heritage USA. Before Oral could utter, "Something good is going to happen to you," something horrible happened to his fund-raising campaign. The media abandoned him. A hundred reporters grabbed their notebooks and tape recorders and cameras and headed for the Tulsa airport to catch the next flight to Charlotte.

Oral's fund-raising scam was a Sunday school picnic compared to what would unfold at Heritage USA. For the next several months, the press experienced a jubilee of unceasing morsels of unholy conduct that produced spellbinding print and broadcast copy.

"An irresistible spectacle," *Newsweek* called it on June 8, in their second cover story of the scandal in as many months.[4] "The thrill of watching a Jim and Tammy Show," claimed *Washington Post* TV critic Tom Shales, "is something comparable to the thrill of a Judy Garland show late in Garland's career, when some members of the audience showed up just to see if she'd make it through the night."[5]

Cartoonists and satirists had a field day. Doug Mirletts's cartoon strip "Kudzu" featured an iconoclastic character named The Reverend Will B. Dunn. Will's TV ministry was ruined when he got entangled with Tammy Faye in the "Mascarascam." "Church Lady," a regular on the "Saturday Night Live" TV program, asked a stammering actor portraying Reverend Bakker about his infamous encounter with the church secretary in a Florida hotel, "Were her naughty parts engorged and tingling?"[6]

But the commentary wasn't all in fun: ". . . [B]eneath the little-girl

sweetness and outrageous wigs and false eyelashes," wrote Jean Seligmann, "Tammy Faye Bakker is as shrewd as Imelda Marcos—and
probably just as unrepentant about her excesses."[7]

From the beginning, it was live soap opera, unlike anything that
had ever happened in the history of broadcasting. The sex, the hypocrisy, the pillaged coffers of PTL, the unholy name-calling among
some of the biggest stars of televangelism; investigations of PTL by
the Internal Revenue Service, the FBI, the U.S. Postal Service, the
South Carolina Tax Commission, Congress, and others—all were sordid elements of a seemingly endless, sleazy, real-life soap opera. And,
unlike most religious donnybrooks in American history, this story
developed its own momentum and just wouldn't go away.

For sheer entertainment, this was better, juicier, than any episode
of "Dallas" or "Dynasty," and it was a story that would never have
made it past the network censors. Because it was "news," tens of
millions of Americans were able to watch it on prime time and read
about it in *USA Today*. Detroit *Free Press* cartoonist Bill Day portrayed a family in front of the TV as the announcer warns, "Before we
do the religious news, we urge all children to leave the room."[8]

By any standard of soap sleaze, it was a spectacular first-class drama.
This was not Burt Lancaster portraying Elmer Gantry; it was life
imitating art. Elmer Gantry was alive and well.

Some accused the mass media of perpetuating a circuslike spectacular, and there is some evidence that they did. By June of 1987 ABC's
"Nightline," for example, had devoted eleven full programs to the
scandal. The ratings soared. Almost from the beginning of the story,
USA Today and the *Washington Post* assigned at least two reporters
full-time to cover it. Yet the media didn't create the characters or
write the script; they merely provided the set for the action.

Jim and Tammy Faye Bakker, once the stars of the PTL Network's
"Jim and Tammy Show," with no more than a million viewers, were
suddenly propelled into superstardom. The story emerged principally
from the Bakkers' antics—what they did before the scandal broke, as
well as their unrepentant obsession with picking up the fantasy where
it had left off before their "exile" to their plush desert residence in
Palm Springs, California.

The Bakkers seemed unaware of or unconcerned about the havoc
they were bringing down upon the entire enterprise known as religious

broadcasting. They were too self-centered to care. From the very moment of their departure from PTL, Jim Bakker's sweet words were accompanied by bitterness, defiance, and a determination to blame others for their downfall. In his televised statement of resignation on March 19, 1987, Bakker decried the *Charlotte Observer* for twelve years of incessant attacks and a new "campaign to defame and vilify me." And of his sexual encounter with the former church secretary in 1980, he said he was "wickedly manipulated by treacherous former friends . . . who victimized me with the aid of a female confederate."[9]

When the Bakkers made their first public appearance after resigning, Jim expressed concern for the well-being of Heritage USA and the PTL Network, forgave all their enemies for what they had done, and said he and Tammy Faye didn't want to be part of a circus. These seemingly selfless expressions were again sandwiched between self-righteousness and preoccupation with their own well-being. Shades of Elmer Gantry:

> We've been accused of so many things that we've just decided to let our accusers do what they would like. We're just going to forgive them. We're going to go on, and we're going to love.[10]

Jim Bakker acted as if everything could be washed clean by saying, "We forgive them who have accused us." Convicted felons and others serving time in prison understand this type of theology, but it is unlikely that the federal authorities investigating illegal aspects of the Bakkers' high-rolling wheeling and dealing are likely to consider this a satisfactory recompense.

And as for their sincere concern for the fate of Heritage USA and PTL, Bakker told reporters, "We hope they will give us our royalties. We have $8 million or $9 million out there we have never received."[11]

Jim Bakker repeatedly pleaded that he and Tammy did not want to be part of a circus, yet their antics were the main event in the center ring. When Jerry Falwell entered the picture, the Bakkers pursued guerrilla warfare tactics to make Falwell's task of putting PTL and Heritage USA back on a stable course almost impossible.

The Bakkers' return to their home in South Carolina on the eve of the new PTL board's filing for "Chapter 11" (bankruptcy) was a cynical, even pathetic act of defiance and duplicity. Instead of slipping in

quietly to recover their personal possessions, the Bakkers returned to create another media event. Cameras were present when Tammy Faye dropped to her knees to kiss the pavement in front of their home. And loyalists obviously had been tipped off that they would make a brief appearance at the Heritage Grand Hotel.

Art Harris and Michael Isikoff, *Washington Post* reporters who covered the story from the beginning, described the scene:

> As hundreds of largely adoring devotees sang hymns, shouted adoration and thrust gifts, a black 450 Mercedes sedan eased to a stop at the luxury Heritage Grand Hotel here today. One smoke-tinted window rolled down. A man's gold Rolex popped into view. Down came the other window. Long red fingernails appeared.
>
> Jim and Tammy Faye Bakker were back—if only briefly—to survey their lost kingdom occupied by rivals. Blowing kisses, waving to the crowd, they climbed from the back seat. "We love you!" shouted Jim Bakker.
>
> It was a wild, festive homecoming. . . . And though it lasted but a moment, it brought a new level of drama to the Bakkers' bizarre saga of sex, sin and salvation.[12]

Bakker also used the occasion of their return as an opportunity to announce that he and Tammy Faye would be back on television within thirty days. But no specific details. Just stay tuned for the next episode.

All good television soaps have multiple plots and story lines that interlock. Details of one subplot are played out for a while, and then, before the audience tires, the story shifts to another theme. That's the way it happened with the new "Jim and Tammy Show."

There were many significant underlying themes to give the PTL scandal a cheap theatrical appeal guaranteed to keep it in the news for months. The 1987 unholy wars of televangelism brought together most of the leading figures in syndicated religious programming. Even Robert Schuller, whose theology is light years and Crystal Cathedral a continent away from the Bakker action, became involved early on when PTL counselor Norman Roy Grutman commented that people who live in glass houses should not cast stones—seemingly implicating Schuller as a culprit in the alleged "hostile takeover."

The first and grandest theme tying all the other subplots together

was the fairy-tale life of the central characters themselves. The main scene for most of the action was a fantasy world called Heritage USA, which Jim and Tammy Faye created from the dimes and dollars of those who sent their savings and Social Security checks. The sad part of the Bakker fairy tale began on March 19 when a tearful Jim told his television audience how a very mean man was about to usurp Jim and Tammy's kingdom. The ammunition possessed by this mean man (who was shortly to be identified as televangelist Jimmy Swaggart) was information about an itty-bitty affair Jim Bakker had had with a church secretary years before.

Details of the takeover plot unfolded gradually; Swaggart was about to blow the whistle on Bakker to the church elders of the Assemblies of God Church. This would lead to an investigation that would result in Bakker's being stripped of his ordination. The shame brought by all of this was not deserved, of course (God and Tammy had both forgiven Jim years before). A little-known clause in the Heritage USA charter bequeaths the entire kingdom to the Assemblies of God in the event that Jim and Tammy are not able to reign. Swaggart, being the most powerful preacher in the Assemblies of God alliance, thus would be the one to move in and take over.

A white knight named Jerry Falwell agreed to take the kingdom into custody to protect it from Swaggart's evil intentions. Two months later, when Bakker advised Falwell that he was ready to return home, Jerry replied, "Not now nor ever." Jim and Tammy brushed back the tears and told "Nightline's" Ted Koppel and 23 million Americans— who had stayed up late to see this dramatic episode—how they had been tricked by Falwell.

Bakker now claimed that Falwell, the man from Liberty Mountain, had become a thief in the night rather than a white knight. It was Falwell all along, they said, not the honky-tonk preacher from the Louisiana bayou, Jimmy Swaggart, who was the real villain. Falwell, with his slick-talking New York lawyer, had tricked Jim and Tammy Faye into believing that the only way they could save their kingdom was to relinquish it to Jerry—temporarily.

Exhausted and bewildered, Jim and Tammy Bakker had tearfully given up their magic kingdom with its Rolls-Royces and furs and gold-fixtured dressing rooms and presidential suite and credit cards and daily starring roles in their own "Wheel of Fortune."

Ted Koppel had warned Jim and Tammy at the beginning of the "Nightline" program "not to wrap themselves in the Bible." By the end of the program, it was Koppel who had been wrapped in the mesmerizing melodramatic tragicomic fantasy the couple had spun.

Playing to Koppel and the huge television audience with words that sounded ever so sweet and loving, Jim Bakker now declared war against Falwell. They just wanted to come home to Heritage USA, but if Jerry Falwell wouldn't let them, they might start a new Shangri-la in the California desert near their Palm Springs hideaway.

Koppel advised them that this might be difficult in light of reports from Heritage USA that the mail was running overwhelmingly in support of Falwell's measures to save the spiritual Disneyland. "If the people don't want us back, if they want Jerry Falwell, then they should support Jerry Falwell," said an emotional Bakker. ". . . But if they don't, they should support Jim and Tammy Bakker."[13] The Bakkers seemed genuinely unable to grasp the reality of the tragedy that had befallen them, to say nothing of its impact on others.

A second significant subplot in this unholy religious soap involved evidence of personal misconduct, mismanagement, and pillaging of the PTL treasury. Thus, there were two dimensions to the scandal: the Bakkers' personal "moral" lives, and their mismanagement and misuse of Heritage USA resources. And just when it seemed that all the sordid details had oozed out, new disclosures and allegations of offenses emerged.

In the beginning, there was only the sexual indiscretion, when Jim Bakker, in a moment of mental exhaustion and loneliness, succumbed to the advances of a young seductress. The way Bakker told the story to Jerry Falwell, he was so ashamed that he became impotent and was unable to consummate the liaison. The hush money he paid to the woman, a church secretary, was for the sake of the PTL ministry, Bakker said.

Within hours, newspaper reporters were in hot pursuit of tips about other alleged incidents of personal misconduct. Lots of people were talking, but nobody wanted to speak on the record.

Then, on the eve of a meeting of the newly constituted PTL board headed by Jerry Falwell at Heritage USA, rumors suggested that Jim and Tammy Faye might return to retake possession of their fiefdom, and this prospect led the Reverend John Ankerberg, host of a debate-

format TV show broadcast from Chattanooga, Tennessee, to tell what *he* knew.

Ankerberg used first "The Larry King Show," then "Nightline," to talk generally about the sexual escapades, the mismanagement of PTL resources, and the exorbitant salaries and bonuses paid to the Bakkers and their closest cronies. Ankerberg was not explicit, but he told enough to intrigue the media. After six weeks of intensive investigative reporting, the alleged details out-Gantryed Elmer Gantry: infidelity, homosexuality, prostitution, alcoholism, even wife-swapping among top managers at PTL.

While confessing that all have sinned and come short of the glory of the kingdom of God, the Bakkers were not about to answer the litany of allegations. "Ninety-nine percent of what they [the media] have printed or said about Jim and Tammy Bakker bears no truth whatsoever," Tammy told a gathering of reporters in April outside their Palm Springs retreat.[14]

The Bakkers declined to meet their accusers. Jerry Falwell offered them that opportunity; so did the elders of the Assemblies of God, which conducted their own inquiry. When Bakker declined to appear before his district presbytery to face charges, the Assemblies of God dismissed him for "conduct unbecoming to a minister." Reverend G. Raymond Carlson, general superintendent of the church, said the "alleged misconduct involving bisexual activity" weighed heavily in the decision to unfrock Bakker.[15] Carlson noted further that the word *alleged* was used because Bakker did not wish to defend himself.

For many people, allegations of misappropriating PTL resources for their own personal use and the payment of huge salaries and bonuses were far more serious charges than the allegations of sexual misconduct.

The Bakkers had appointed a rubber-stamp board of directors to oversee their management practices. In return for acquiescing to Jim and Tammy's whims, several of these board members received tens of thousands of dollars in fees, bonuses, and contributions to their own projects.[16]

In 1986 the Bakkers were paid $1.9 million; since 1984, a total of $4.8 million had been paid to them. In addition, PTL monies were used for expensive homes, a palatial suite at the Heritage Grand Hotel, automobiles, lavish wardrobes, vacations, and parties. The Bakkers'

closest associates were privy to their high living at the expense of PTL partners. They, too, were well paid. Reverend Richard Dortch, the Assemblies of God minister who many thought had brought some order and organization to the rapidly growing Heritage USA operations, was paid $240,000 in 1985 and $350,000 in 1986. He received approximately $270,000 during the first three months of 1987 before Falwell sacked him. David Taggart, a twenty-nine-year-old "personal aide" to Bakker, received $360,000 in 1986; Jim Bakker's personal secretary received $160,000.

And then there were "consultants." James Taggart, interior decorator and David Taggart's brother, was paid $10,000 a month, but, according to the new PTL management, he had performed no services "for months."[17] Peter B. Teeley, press secretary to George Bush until 1984, was paid $120,000 for eighteen months to serve as a Washington "liaison"; apparently there were no written records of any services performed.[18]

When the Bakkers departed, the financial records of the organization were in shambles—as they probably had been for years. No fewer than forty-seven separate checking accounts were found in the first days of the Falwell takeover. "The books are a mess," proclaimed Harry Hargrave, the Dallas-based consultant Falwell hired to become PTL's new chief executive officer.[19]

Noted Jerry Nims (Falwell's CEO for the "Old Time Gospel Hour" in Lynchburg), who came in to help dig out, "This was a business organization that was totally out of control."[20] Added Nims, "For these folks, there were no rules. You're not talking about people nudging over the line. There was absolutely no line. . . . It was fiscal sin."[21]

Early on, it appeared that $92 million was missing. As the financial records of Heritage USA were consolidated and audited, much of this money was accounted for, but then evidence of unpaid bills began to grow. By early June, outstanding debts were estimated at $70 million owed to 1,400 creditors, and $23 million of this debt was delinquent.

Independent of the struggle between Jim Bakker and Jerry Falwell was the unsightly scene of other members of the Protestant cloth taking sides and launching verbal missiles at one another. In addition to the principals of the electronic church, there emerged a large cast of walk-on characters seeking a moment of glory in front of the camera.

One subplot involved Swaggart, who had been accused of complicity in the "diabolical plot" to take over the Bakker ministry. A member of the Assemblies of God, Swaggart stepped forward and said that he had initiated a church inquiry into Bakker's personal conduct, but that it was "absurd and ridiculous" to suggest that he wanted to take over PTL.

Expressing distress about the state of affairs in religious broadcasting, he countered:

I'm ashamed, I'm embarrassed. The gospel of Jesus Christ has never sunk to such a level as it has today. We've got a dear brother in Tulsa, Oklahoma, perched up in a tower telling people that if they don't send money that God's going to kill him, then we got this soap opera being carried out live down in South Carolina all in the name of God.[22]

In another interview on "The Larry King Show," Swaggart claimed that Bakker's downfall represented a "very glad day, because this cancer has been excised that I feel has caused the body of Christ untold reproach."[23]

These comments aroused Oral Roberts's ire, and he blasted Swaggart while defending Bakker. The backbiting among major evangelical figures flared intermittently for months.

David R. Gergen, editor of *U.S. News & World Report*, commented:

Amidst all the squabbling [among] television evangelists, one man distinguished himself: The Rev. Billy Graham. He kept quiet.[24]

As weeks became months, Gergen's accolades to Graham seemed increasingly appropriate.

While Graham stood aloof in Olympian silence, few seemed ready to express appreciation to Jerry Falwell, who had committed himself to taking the muck of the Bakker scandal in both hands and doing what he could to salvage an electronic ministry in which a large national audience once held almost absolute faith. His attempt to stabilize a situation riddled with sleaze and lurid revelations, to cool tempers of colleagues inflicting injury upon themselves, their ministries, and the God they claim to serve, would receive little positive recognition.

Falwell is no fool. He recognized immediately the ramifications of the Bakker scandal for all religious broadcasters. In this sense, he acted out of self-interest. In taking on the challenge, he knew he would risk his own reputation and endanger his "Old Time Gospel Hour" TV program and his rapidly growing Liberty University. His fundamentalist allies blamed him for fraternizing with apostates, while the Pentecostal movement charged him with interference. Meanwhile, the media, in pursuit of the hottest, juiciest religious scandal of the twentieth century, scrutinized his personal life and his ministry.

Until the scandal broke, most Americans knew Jerry Falwell as the loudmouthed, slick-talking, troublemaking Baptist preacher who helped to create the right-wing Moral Majority organization. The image of Falwell as troubleshooter and peacemaker was both ironic and incongruous.

Cynics believed that Falwell stood to profit from taking over the PTL, that he would become the giant of the God-biz industry by consolidating two major ministries. They ignored—indeed, were unaware of—the long history of intramural hostility between fundamentalists and Pentecostals.

Of course, Falwell received criticism both from his own fundamentalist camp and from Bakker's Pentecostal allies. The organization of a PTL Partners Association represented only a remnant of the once-loyal Bakker supporters, but their presence at Heritage USA won them repeated media exposure.

When Bakker charged that Falwell tricked and double-crossed him into relinquishing his ministry, the story was treated as yet another morbid sequence in the ongoing drama. For all the information that had been uncovered regarding the Bakkers' misdeeds, press coverage gave little hint that the Bakkers' accusation might have any less credibility than Falwell's.

Suspicion that the preacher from Liberty Mountain might have sinister motives surfaced anew as his "natural" adversaries engaged in another round of Falwell-bashing. One commentator claimed, relying on credible sources, that Jim Bakker had "gained possession of a tape recording of a meeting in which Mr. Falwell and his closest associates . . . planned and plotted how they would topple Jim Bakker."[25]

In the fallout from the scandal, there are two central issues that

could have profound, lasting importance for American culture and the future of evangelism in America.

The first is the outcome of the criminal inquiries. On June 1, 1987, the U.S. Justice Department announced that it would coordinate a multiagency inquiry into the alleged wrongdoings at Heritage USA.[26] Mail fraud, tax evasion, conspiracy to defraud, and the tax-exempt status of PTL and Heritage USA were among the announced subjects of inquiry. In late September of 1987 a federal grand jury began the long and arduous task of hearing testimony on the multifaceted allegations of misdeeds. And in October the House Ways and Means subcommittee on oversight, headed by Congressman J. J. Pickle (a Democrat from Texas), launched an inquiry into the financial accountability of religious organizations and the role of the IRS in overseeing them.

The real significance of these inquiries was not the consequences for Jim and Tammy Bakker or the empire they created, but the First Amendment and the fragile line between church and state. Public indignation over the PTL abuses was likely to provide a forum in which government agencies would gain a relatively free hand in probing any religious organization. At issue in the inquiries is not only the tax-exempt status of PTL and Heritage USA, but, ultimately, the tax-exempt status of all religious organizations.

Further, efforts to guard against future abuses by religious broadcasters could result in regulations that would restrict all broadcasters. Liberal churches and secular organizations that oppose evangelical religious broadcasting could be given the power to restrict religious broadcasting.

The dilemma for the liberal churches is that whereas they would like to check the evangelical monopoly of the airwaves, they stand in opposition to government interference in religious matters.

The struggle between those who would regulate religion and the religious organizations that are poised to ward off government regulation could touch off one of the major constitutional battles for the balance of this century. If this happens, we are likely to see a realignment to bring most religious traditions in America into a single coalition.

The first evidence of this possible coalition was manifest in the mid-1980s, when the Justice Department indicted and subsequently convicted the Reverend Sun Myung Moon for tax evasion and conspiracy.

While not supporting Reverend Moon's unique blending of Christianity with eastern religious traditions, various religious groups of nearly every ideological and theological persuasion filed *amicus curiae* briefs, arguing that the Justice Department had arbitrarily encroached on domains protected by the First Amendment.

The second significant issue is the impact of the scandals on all religious broadcasting. So serious are the scandals that they have shaken this powerful enterprise to its very foundations. There can be no question that the scandals have damaged all television ministries, as public opinion polls make abundantly clear. A national poll conducted by the *Los Angeles Times* in July 1986, and then repeated after the scandals erupted, found that every television preacher lost ground in terms of public approval.[27] A March 1987 *New York Times* poll found that 65 percent of the American public had an unfavorable opinion of most television evangelists. Among nonviewers, 73 percent had an unfavorable opinion, 6 percent had a favorable opinion, and 21 percent had no opinion.[28] Of those nonviewers who had an opinion, 92 percent are unfavorable.

A *USA Today* poll found 90 percent of Americans disapproving of the fund-raising techniques of TV preachers. Of those expressing an opinion, 98 percent said they didn't believe God gave Oral Roberts a deadline to raise $8 million. And 71 percent said TV evangelists in general are out to enrich themselves.[29]

This negative image of televangelists did not emerge overnight. The *Los Angeles Times* poll demonstrates solid negative sentiment *before* the scandals broke. But certainly the scandals damaged the credibility of contemporary religious broadcasters, and, stereotypes to one side, the negative sentiment was by no means limited to nonviewers. In the *New York Times* poll, of those who reported having contributed to TV evangelists, 35 percent expressed generally unfavorable views about TV evangelists. The *USA Today* poll found about one-quarter (26 percent) who had previously contributed would not be likely to contribute again.

The ministries themselves subsequently reported sharp declines in contributions. Three months after the scandals broke, Oral Roberts, whose "Donate or call me home" campaign kicked off the tumultuous month of March 1987, claimed his ministry's revenues were off $1.5 million per month. Jerry Falwell reported income losses of $2 million

monthly, while Jimmy Swaggart reported a monthly decline of $2.5 million.

On June 5, M. G. "Pat" Robertson announced on "The 700 Club" program that the Christian Broadcasting Network was laying off 470 employees, 200 of them permanent, full-time workers. Since news of the Bakker and Roberts scandals had broken in March, Robertson told his viewers, CBN's revenues were down $12 million, and they were forecasting revenue losses of $28 million by year's end. These losses were over and above revenue declines CBN had expected to occur as a result of Robertson's reduced schedule on "The 700 Club."

Robertson stated, "In the history of American Christianity we have never seen anything like this. The scandal has hit the evangelical world like a bombshell."[30] Before the scandals broke, he was making headway in his bid for the Republican nomination for the presidency. Now Pat Robertson's presidential aspirations were whiplashed by his televangelist colleagues. The Los Angeles Times poll, for example, showed a sharp rise in the percentage of Americans who reported that they would be disinclined to vote for Robertson if he were a presidential candidate.[31] In July 1986, about half had said they were not likely to vote for Robertson; that rose to 70 percent in late March of 1987. The USA Today poll in mid-1987 found 52 percent saying that the controversy had hindered Robertson's presidential aspirations, whereas only 3 percent thought the scandal would help.[32]

But presidential campaigns have a long history of taking unexpected twists and turns. Witness the swift demise of Democratic front-runner Gary Hart in the spring of 1987. It happened so quickly that it almost appeared as misdirected pious indignation intended for the wayward shepherds of televangelism.

Or witness the dramatic and quick discovery of the peanut farmer from Plains, Georgia, after his unexpected showing in the Iowa caucuses.

An important outcome of the prolonged public attention devoted to Oral Roberts's "donate-or-I-die" campaign and the Heritage USA scandal is that many Americans who previously lumped all conservative Christians together under the label of fundamentalists came to understand that these people, as with other groups, are a complex and diverse lot. Anyone who watched a befuddled Ted Koppel on ABC's "Nightline" try to grapple with the distinctions among funda-

mentalist Baptist Jerry Falwell, Pentecostal Jimmy Swaggart, and the more mainline Robert Schuller could see that an important educational process was at work. The more that Americans learn about the diverse styles and beliefs of the televangelists, the more they will begin to discriminate among them. Such sophistication, however modest, can only benefit Robertson's presidential aspirations. If Robertson is to have a shot at the GOP presidential nomination, he must break out of the negative mold into which all televangelists have been cast. The irony is that the religious television scandals may have provided Robertson with the opportunity to separate himself from all the others.

On October 1, 1987, Pat Robertson officially entered the presidential race. The announcement came just two weeks after Robertson beat both George Bush and Robert Dole in a much publicized Republican straw poll in Iowa. And four days later, Robertson's operatives in Michigan successfully beat back a Bush effort to change the rules for the selection of that state's delegates to the Republican National Convention. Barring some extraordinary development that would seriously erode Robertson's strength, this seemed to assure him control of forty-four of the seventy-seven Michigan delegates to the Convention.

Between Pat Robertson and Jesse Jackson, America is in for the wildest primary season of the twentieth century, perhaps ever. The two preachers will dominate their respective parties, either as serious candidates or as power brokers.

Another bizarre chapter in the melodramatic soap opera starring Jim and Tammy Bakker? No. Not at all. It is a logical culmination of a process that has been unfolding for years. The growth of evangelical political strength in America is not well understood because few people have been paying attention.

Although evangelical Christians are splintered in dozens of directions theologically, common political objectives are creating a powerful new ecumenical force among them. That force stands ready and waiting to be transformed into power in American politics.

Jim and Tammy Faye Bakker have lived a fantasy life that, in the spring of 1987, became theater for our amusement and entertainment. It was a great sideshow, but the main event is yet to come.

As the 1988 presidential primary process gets underway in earnest, Pat Robertson's candidacy stands to be a far more spectacular story than the PTL scandals. And it won't be a fantasy. It will be a race to

decide who runs America and who determines the shape of American politics through the balance of this century.

Whether or not Pat Robertson wins the Republican nomination for the presidency, the process of politicizing conservative Christians will continue. And remember, these people vote. By the end of this century—just twelve years away—they seem destined to become the single most powerful political force in the United States.

2

"God Bless Our President . . ." and Other Revolutionary Ideas

---

I've always thought that a providential hand had something to do with the founding of this country, that God had His reasons for placing this land here between two great oceans to be found by a certain kind of people.
—Ronald Reagan, Statue of Liberty
Relighting Ceremonies

On April 29, 1980, a crowd estimated at a quarter to a half million poured onto the Mall in Washington, D.C., for a marathon prayer meeting that its organizers called Washington for Jesus. Those who were on the Mall at 6 A.M. and remained until the final benediction after 6 P.M. heard forty-seven speakers, scores of prayers, and almost as many religious and patriotic songs. One by one, the speakers came forth to confess a long litany of national sins and to repent on behalf of a yet-unrepentant secular nation. Each of the early speakers presented slightly different emphases and oratorical styles, but as the damp and dreary morning gave way to a sunny afternoon, the words seemed to blur. The audience had become mesmerized.

The gathering then took on a festive, Woodstock-like quality—it was a religious happening unlike any that had occurred before in America. The speakers' platform was usually the focal point of the gathering, but at times dozens of spontaneous prayer groups and off-

podium speeches captured the attention of significant numbers of the assembled.

Undergirding the sermons, prayers, and speeches was an unmistakable historical sense. The date of April 29 was selected for an important reason. It was April 29, 1607, that the first permanent settlers planted a cross in the sand at Jamestown, Virginia, and prayed that this new land might arise and prosper with "His blessing and to His glory."

April 29 was the eve of another monumental date in American history. In the anguish of the War Between the States, 256 years after the Jamestown settlers reaffirmed their covenant with God, President Abraham Lincoln proclaimed April 30, 1863, as a day of National Humiliation, Fasting, and Prayer.

"We have been the recipients of the choicest bounties of Heaven [God's gift of dominion]," wrote Lincoln, ". . . but we have forgotten God [man's failure to keep the terms of the covenant]." Lincoln's confession on behalf of the torn and battered nation continued:

. . . we have vainly imagined, in the deceitfulness of our hearts, that all these blessings were produced by some superior wisdom and virtue of our own. Intoxicated with unbroken success, we have become too self-sufficient to feel the necessity of redeeming and preserving grace, too proud to pray to the God that made us![1]

In a manner and form that is completely consistent with numerous Old Testament confessions, Lincoln's proclamation moved from confession to pleading for God's forgiveness:

It behooves us, then, to humble ourselves before the offended Power, to confess our national sin, and to pray for clemency and forgiveness. . . . All this being done, in sincerity and truth, let us then rest humbly in the hope, authorized by the Divine teachings, that the united cry of the Nation will be heard on high, and answered with blessings, no less than the pardon of our national sins and restoration of our now divided and suffering country to its former happy condition of unity and peace.

On April 29, 1980, the words of Abraham Lincoln's Proclamation for a National Day of Humiliation, Fasting, and Prayer reverberated

off the granite monuments of America's capital city, as did the words
of numerous Old Testament prophets; they challenged the assembled
to renew the vows of Lincoln and the first settlers of this land so that
the godly character of America might be restored.

> Righteousness exalteth a nation, but sin is a reproach to any
> people (Proverbs 14:34).

The day's most frequently cited verse of Scripture—virtually the theme
of the rally—came from an Old Testament covenant story. Solomon
asks God what is to be done to restore his favor. God replies:

> If my people which are called by my name, shall humble them-
> selves, and pray, and seek my face, and turn from their wicked
> ways; then will I hear from heaven, and will forgive their sin, and
> will heal their land (2 Chronicles 7:14).

Speaker after speaker intertwined words of the Old and New Tes-
taments with American history and the contemporary malaise as if
they were interlocking experiences. In America and in the Bible, the
theme repeats itself: (1) God's covenant, (2) man's disobedience to the
covenant, (3) confession and repentance, (4) redemption and restoration.

Dr. William R. Bright, founder and president of Campus Crusade
for Christ International and co-chairman of the Washington for Jesus
rally, set the tone of confession and repentance early in the morning:

> It's no mystery. We've turned from God and God is chastening us.
> Laugh if you will. The critics will laugh. And they'll make fun. But
> I'll tell you, this is God's doing. You go back to 1962 and 3 and
> you'll discover a series of plagues that came upon America. First,
> the assassination of President Kennedy. The war in Vietnam accel-
> erated. The drug culture swept millions of young people into the
> drug scene. The youth revolution. Crime accelerated over 300 per-
> cent in a brief period of time. Racial conflict threatened to tear our
> nation apart. The Watergate scandal. The divorce rate accelerated.
> There were almost as many divorces as marriages. And there was
> an epidemic of teenage pregnancies, an epidemic of venereal dis-

ease, an epidemic of drug addiction, an epidemic of alcoholism. And now, we are faced with a great economic crisis. . . . God is saying to us, "Wake up! Wake up! Wake up!". . .[2]

Bill Bright's chronicle of recent American history intermingles transgressions against God with the evidences of God's chastening. A rational scholar might well criticize Bright for lack of conceptual clarity. What is cause and what is effect?

What is important about Bright's statement is his forceful communication of the gnawing conviction that something has gone terribly wrong with America. What is wrong is the result of sin, of disobedience of God's covenant with America. There is also, in the words of Bright and others, the steadfast belief that America is not just one among nations; it is instead the nation with a providential mission in God's grand scheme of things. And finally, a certain faith is expressed that repentance can again restore the covenantal relationship and set America on the path God intended when He led His people of faith to the shores of this continent.

The national media ignored Washington for Jesus, or gave it brief notice. Almost everyone who did cover it noted that the rally failed to produce the million participants forecast by its organizers—supposedly evidence that the meeting was not a success. They also gave nearly as much attention to a hastily organized counter-rally, which attracted only a few hundred. But the media did not mention that it was the largest crowd ever to assemble on the Mall—larger than for any of the civil rights marches on Washington during the 1960s, larger than several antiwar protests during the 1960s and 1970s, larger than the crowd that attended a mass with Pope John Paul II on the same site a few months earlier. The event was telecast over the satellite network of the Christian Broadcasting Network, PTL Network, and Trinity Broadcasting Network, putting several million more faithful in touch with this historic moment.

Bill Bright was undaunted by the media's lack of attention and generally negative tone. He looked out upon the throng of people and proclaimed April 29, 1980, to be "the most important day in this nation's history apart from its founding."[3] Televangelist Pat Robertson, co-chairman of the event, agreed that something important was happening: "I believe this is an historic moment for our nation."[4]

Washington for Jesus was the brainchild of John Gimenez, a self-proclaimed "holy roller" preacher from Virginia Beach, Virginia. Earlier in his life, Gimenez, the son of a Puerto Rican Methodist minister, was overwhelmed by the dark side of Spanish Harlem in New York City. He pimped to support an addiction to heroin, and his life in the underworld rewarded him with prison terms at Auburn, Elmira, Sing Sing, and Riker's Island.

In 1966 Gimenez had a life-changing experience under the guidance of evangelists Mom and Pop Rassaddo of the Damascus Church in the Bronx. A year later he married Anne Nethery, a traveling evangelist. In 1968 Pat Robertson invited them to Virginia Beach to be guests on "The 700 Club." They stayed on, founding the Rock Church a few blocks from CBN headquarters, never returning to New York. With John and Anne Gimenez as co-pastors, the Rock Church has grown to more than 5,000 members. They have founded eighteen additional Rock Churches, one as far away as Oklahoma, and in 1986 they launched the Rock Church Network, a seven-day-a-week, twenty-four-hour network targeted at Hispanics.

The idea for a mass rally in Washington came to Gimenez in 1978, while he was preaching at a conference in California. When he returned to Virginia, he shared the idea with his friend Pat Robertson, who agreed to be national chairman of the effort.

John Gilman, an independent filmmaker who is a member of Gimenez's Rock Church and the former producer of "The 700 Club," agreed to be national coordinator for the event. With Robertson's guidance, they soon lined up the support of many of the leading charismatic religious figures in America.

Although all of the principals for the planning of this event were *charismatic* Christians, they concluded that this gathering was important to exclude noncharismatics. (More about these vast tinctions later.) But how could they accomplish this, since the se\ major branches of conservative evangelical Christianity have engaged in an ideological war for the better part of this century? story unfolds.

In the spring of 1979, while traveling in Asia, Bill Bright, v not a charismatic, felt he was being led by God to organize a p conference in 1980 to pray for the nation. He shared this with of his televangelist friends at a small gathering in Texas.

When Gilman learned of this, he flew to California to enlist Bright's support for the Washington for Jesus rally. Bright was not immediately certain that this rally was the event God was leading him to schedule, but after talking with Gimenez and Robertson, he was confident that the plans were inspired by God, and he agreed to join Robertson as co-chairman.

Bill Bright is not nearly as well known outside evangelical circles as Billy Graham, but for those who have worked in the evangelical Christian movement over the past three decades, there is no name other than Billy Graham's that is more recognizable and respected. Bright's energetic sponsorship would greatly expand the rally's theological base.

Bill Bright is a man of vision, ambition, boundless energy, and determination. The Campus Crusade for Christ, which he founded at UCLA in 1951, is an organization that has spilled over the boundaries of college and university campuses in America to become a worldwide ministry in 150 countries. In addition to its emphasis on evangelizing youth, Campus Crusade for Christ International has scores of ministries to prisoners, inner-city ghettos, hospitals, business and professional organizations, and diplomatic communities.

Bill Bright's grand-scale vision has inspired all 16,000 members of his worldwide staff to raise money to cover their own salaries. He believes he can evangelize the world. If the *Guinness Book of World Records* kept track of soul-saving spectaculars, Bright's name probably would be in the book before Billy Graham's. His "prayer target" is to introduce at least *one billion* people to Christ by the year 2000.

One of Bright's major projects is a combination evangelistic meeting and training workshop that he calls "EXPLO." Each takes several years to prepare, and the first, EXPLO '72, climaxed in Dallas with 180,000 persons attending a final rally. EXPLO '74 registered 323,000 in Seoul, Korea, with several times that number (it was claimed) attending one of the evening sessions. Bright returned to Seoul in 1980 to attract 2.7 million Christians (believed to be the largest gathering in history) to one rally.

Bright is reaching out to the vast rural areas of the Third World with a film on the life of Jesus. The film's sound track has been translated into ninety languages of a 271-language target—making the words

understandable to "almost all of the world's population," as Bright puts it.

People don't normally think of Bill Bright as a televangelist. He doesn't have a syndicated program, nor does he regularly telecast specials as Billy Graham does. Yet few preachers are more skilled in the art of modern communications. EXPLO '85 was a technological spectacular. Utilizing eighteen communications satellites, his global training conference was simulcast at more than ninety sites in fifty-four nations from a satellite hookup in London; most of the sessions of this four-day videoconference were simultaneously translated into thirty languages.

EXPLO '85 was the largest international closed-circuit satellite videoconference in history, involving 20,000 technicians under the direction of communications specialist Michael Clifford of Scottsdale, Arizona, who claimed the project was more technically complex than the 1984 worldwide Olympics telecast. Spokespersons for the event stressed that they were not simply putting on a onetime video-wonder for the record books. With their experience and technological know-how, they plan to stage a greatly expanded EXPLO '90.

The financial support for televangelists consists of tens of thousands of $15-to-$25-per-month pledges. Bright, however, has learned how to work a different crowd, and in 1980 dreamed up a billion-dollar fund-raising campaign. His target: "History's Handful," a thousand donors who would each give or raise at least a million dollars. A few months into the campaign, he had pledges of $170 million. One intimate breakfast for 500 in Houston netted $15 million. Not a bad morning's work.[5]

Had the Washington for Jesus rally occurred anywhere else, Bright might have claimed the goal of a million was achieved and few would have been the wiser. But the secular media were present, and the National Park Service estimated the crowd on the Mall at about one-fourth of that size. Given that the rally lasted twelve hours, with a number of people coming and going during the day, the total number of participants may have approached the half-million figure claimed by the organizers.

Whatever the number, it was no small achievement. Large demonstrations do not occur spontaneously. Anyone who was involved in the civil rights marches of the 1960s or the antiwar protests a few

years later knows how essential it is to tap into hundreds of organizations to bring out a crowd. But what of these Christians on the Mall? Where did they come from, and why?

The answers are evident in the personalities and the messages of the speakers who paraded to the microphone to speak and preach and pray. The roster of sponsors and speakers was a *Who's Who of the Electric Church*. Bill Bright and Pat Robertson were joined by Ben Armstrong, Jim and Tammy Faye Bakker, Paul Crouch, Ben Haden, Rex Humbard, D. James Kennedy, Carl Richardson, James Robison, Robert Schuller, Lester Sumrall, Charles Stanley, George Vanderman, and many more. There were some conspicuous absences, including Billy Graham, Oral Roberts, and Jerry Falwell. But most of the stars of the electric church were present.

The crowd was there because powerful radio and television preachers from all over America used their programs and publications to invite their constituencies to Washington. They then tapped into the infrastructures of their multifaceted communications organizations to help get people aboard buses and airplanes and private vehicles en route to Washington.

Washington for Jesus was as firmly anchored in American history as any assembly in the nation's capital might be. Late-twentieth-century secular Americans may choose to be ignorant of the role of religion in shaping this nation's history. But by trivializing the importance of religion in history, they blind themselves to an understanding of how religious forces are again shaping the nation. If they remain ignorant of the past and fail to grasp the significance of the contemporary religious surge in America, they will certainly render themselves impotent in the struggle to determine the shape of things to come.

This is not a mistake that Ronald Reagan has made. Early on, politician Ronald Reagan saw the pragmatic benefits of courting evangelical Christians. His alliance with the New Christian Right began on August 22, 1980, when he addressed a gathering of preachers in the Reunion Arena in Dallas. It was 104 degrees outside as he spoke to the National Affairs Briefing. On that occasion, candidate Reagan had to wait ninety minutes beyond his scheduled appearance while a bunch of long-winded preachers, including Jerry Falwell, got in their licks to a capacity house of 15,000.

Had Governor Reagan been a Bible scholar, he might have wondered, as he watched and waited, if he were in King Nebuchadnezzar's fiery furnace with Shadrach, Meshach, and Abednego. He thought it was a friendly crowd, but televangelist James Robison, the man who warmed up the crowd for him, told them not to commit themselves to a candidate, and they loved it. And with all the introductions and offerings and other carryings-on, no one seemed the slightest bit interested in hearing Reagan. Certainly they weren't particularly respectful of his grueling schedule, his age, or his position.

Undaunted, Reagan stepped to the podium and displayed a classic example of his extraordinary sense of timing. Departing from his prepared remarks, he began:

A few days ago I addressed a group in Chicago and received their endorsement for my candidacy. Now I know this is a nonpartisan gathering and so I know you can't endorse me, but I only brought that up because I want you to know that I endorse you and what you are doing.

Those words worked their magic, as the enthusiastic evangelicals leapt to their feet with wild applause and exuberant shouts of "Amen!"

For liberals, including the press, Reagan's popularity with evangelical Christians has been an enigma. And his religious values are perhaps the least-understood dimension of his persona. To the extent that secular journalists have tried to understand his religious character, they have been prone to interpret it as cynical. After all, he doesn't go to church often, his contributions to charity are nil, he is divorced, he doesn't interact with his children much, and so forth.

While Reagan in his personal life and behavior may not be a paragon of evangelical piety and virtue, not to recognize how his worldview is anchored in religious precepts is to miss one of the most important aspects of the man. Whether or not religious principles have always undergirded Reagan's worldview is an open question. But it is clear that he sees religious significance in, and has offered religious explanations for, many of his policies in public office.

Ronald Reagan has been accused of merely "throwing crumbs" to the New Christian Right. But that is not the way the New Christian

Right leadership sees it. From that electrifying moment in the Reunion Arena, they have never questioned Ronald Reagan's support.

Some of their more sophisticated leaders understand very well that the most important support Reagan can offer is the legitimizing of their agenda and their organizations. During his campaign and his first term in office, Reagan addressed the National Religious Broadcasters on five occasions. No other interest group received that kind of attention.

President Reagan is doing much more than merely acknowledging gratitude for past support. By arousing their enthusiasm, by reassuring people who have not traditionally been politically active that it is all right for Christians to get involved in the political process, Reagan is mobilizing evangelical Christian participation in politics. And there is no more profound multiplier effect in American politics than 3,500 religious broadcasters disseminating the social and political agenda of the New Christian Right on their respective radio and television programs.

Ronald Reagan's popularity with evangelical Christians also tells us something very important about the changing character of this large sector of American society. While stereotyped as dogmatic and aloof from the world, evangelicals have become increasingly this-worldly and pragmatic. Reagan's agenda and theirs have been close enough that they haven't been interested in quarrelling about the fine details of his personal beliefs and behavior. What matters to evangelicals is that Ronald Reagan has been instrumental in "turning America around."

In the quarter century before Reagan became president, America achieved technological advancements that were beyond the human imagination only a generation earlier. Americans had taken giant strides to erase inequities and injustices inherited from their ancestors. And they had grown increasingly conscious of their planet, their place on it, and the environmental requirements of planetary good-citizenship.

But, ironically, for all of the accomplishments and good intentions, America seemed to stumble. In a series of tragedies that sorely tested their character, her people suffered the pain of assassination, the agony of defeat in war, the frustration of impotence in world affairs, and the disgrace of failed leadership.

Domestically, the evidence of lasting progress in eliminating discrimination against minorities and women seemed ambiguous at best;

poverty stubbornly resisted prescription for eradication; drug use and crime seemed out of control. The list of ills and frustrations, at home and abroad, seemed to grow.

However Ronald Reagan may be remembered, he most certainly will be recognized for his role in transforming Americans' attitudes toward themselves, their institutions, and their country. He stressed that patriotism—even chauvinism, properly understood—is a virtue, and that it's OK to feel good about, and look out for, oneself.

If Reagan's nuclear arms control initiatives serve as a secure foundation for progressive steps toward real disarmament, this achievement will certainly be his most enduring legacy. But Reagan's restoration of confidence and pride in America will also likely be as important a legacy as any president could hope to convey.

Reagan's finest hour may well have been on the Fourth of July weekend of 1986, midway through his second term in office. For America, the weekend was an orgy of self-celebration, with festivities that in intensity and spectacle exceeded anything in the nation's 210-year history, eclipsing even the Bicentennial.

Patriotic speeches; a six-hour procession of historic tall sailing ships and international naval vessels plus a flotilla of 30,000 pleasure boats; fireworks in an intensity and duration never before produced anywhere; and, of course, star-studded entertainment: It was quite a bash.

The manifest occasion was the centennial of the Statue of Liberty, which had just undergone two years of refurbishing. But beneath the stated purpose of the celebration was a deeper meaning: Americans had begun to refurbish their own spirits and to feel good about America again. "The pride is back," rang out a television commercial for an American-made automobile. And, indeed, it was.

The restoration of the Statue of Liberty had been surrounded by controversy from the outset, and the very logic and structure of mass-media news coverage assured the critics and naysayers a voice. From the decision to turn over the restoration of Liberty Island to free enterprise, to the gaudy carnival merchandising of Statue of Liberty paraphernalia, to the firing of Lee Iacocca as chairman of the federal commission overseeing the restoration, to the $5,000 admission tickets to the opening ceremonies on Governor's Island, critics disparaged the project as a sham and a cheapening of the Statue and what she stood for.

But on Liberty Weekend, Americans were not much in the mood for such negativism, or for rhetoric about the indispensability of liberty and justice (and the absence of the latter under the Reagan administration). This was a day when Americans came together. The projected 8 million souls never descended on Manhattan in person, but no one complained or suggested that the shortfall meant the festivities were not a resounding success. One didn't need a yacht or an expensive window seat in a skyscraper restaurant to be a part of the action. A twenty-five-cent ride on the Staten Island Ferry brought tens of thousands right into the middle of the action. And the most spectacular seats of all were in America's living rooms; hours of breathtaking sights and sounds for a few cents of electricity. People who chose to spend big bucks for a grand time of conspicuous consumption were more a source of amusement than of scorn or envy. It's a free country. To each his own.

For that moment, at least, Americans were not concerned about vast income discrepancies. Nor were they concerned about the illegal immigrants from Haiti being held in detention centers, nor about the hundreds more that U.S. immigration officials would turn back from the Mexican border that weekend—halting, temporarily at least, their efforts to join the huddled masses who had come to America generations earlier. The Fourth of July in 1986 was a time to forget problems and differences. It was a time to celebrate and a time for Americans to rediscover their heritage.

Presiding over the festivities in New York Harbor was Ronald Reagan. This moment had to be one of the grandest of his long life and several careers. He had hosted a couple of impressive inaugural parties, but nothing like this. Nor had he ever starred in a movie with such a grand concept and set. He watched the tall ships proudly and, on several occasions, addressed his countrymen with all the self-confidence of a commander-in-chief firmly in control of things.

Ronald Reagan is a master communicator because he understands and utilizes symbols and myths as well as anyone who has occupied the office of the presidency in this century. His words had begun lifting Americans' spirits and restoring their confidence in their country long before they gathered together via the marvel of television as well as in New York Harbor, to pay respects to Miss Liberty and celebrate 210 years of nationhood. Now he had the most potent of symbols to

work with, the Statue of Liberty, and the mythology he invoked employed a skillful intertwining of both secular and sacred creation myths.

"I've always thought that a providential hand had something to do with the founding of this country," he said, moments before he tripped the switch to relight Miss Liberty's torch. No pope, no victorious general, no Shakespearean actor could have timed better the delivery of his best lines.

God intended that America be a special place in His scheme of things. That is the myth. America is the Promised Land and those who find their way here are surely his Chosen People. The idea that there is something providential about the American experience is as old as America itself—older, actually. By choosing to intertwine the secular and the religious symbols and myths of American culture, Ronald Reagan transformed a secular commemoration of a limited aspect of the nation's collective experience into a civil-religious ceremony of enormous significance.

Myths are the stories that people tell about their origins, their ancestors, and their heroes. Myths both appeal to and reflect the consciousness of people by embodying their ideals and by giving expression to their most profound and deeply held sentiments. Myths create, sustain, and reinforce meaning in human cultures.[6]

Anthropologically speaking, myths cannot be judged as true or not true. Rather, they stand as raw data bearing witness to the sentiments and values of a people. Some myths are intended to be understood as lighthearted, others clearly bear evidence of transcendent sacred meanings. They tell a people what is right and wrong, sacred and profane.

No known society lacks a rich array of mythological motifs that manifest themselves in many forms.[7] To strip away myths systematically, or to declare them illegitimate or inferior, is to create a vacuum—a culture without meaning. But, as Richard John Neuhaus has argued so brilliantly in *The Naked Public Square*, a vacuum is a temporary condition. If old myths are destroyed, new ones will rush in to fill the vacuum.[8]

The festivities of Liberty Weekend represented a bold attempt to rekindle some old creation myths. And President Reagan, the architect of America's new pride, knew exactly what he was doing. The recounting of the long and often dangerous sea voyages that brought

immigrants to these shores served as a powerful reminder of the origins of this country. Many millions of us can claim direct ancestry to those who entered the country through New York Harbor, passing the Statue of Liberty en route to Ellis Island. The weekend's broadcasts focused on this powerful symbol of who Americans are and what the nation is all about. Oscar Handlin, the historian-biographer of the roots of white Anglo-Saxon Americans, began his classic work, *The Uprooted*, with these words: "Once I thought to write a history of the immigrants in America. Then I discovered that the immigrants *were* American history."[9]

Ronald Reagan's proclamation that "We are all boat people" is, of course, an exaggeration, but it is not all that far from the truth. Some 200 million Americans trace their ancestry to European soil, another 21 million to Africa, and 3.5 million to Asia. Native Americans account for only about 7 million. Thus, a huge proportion of Americans can identify with the immigration experience.

The Statue of Liberty, then, is a symbol of the national myth of origin. Of course, the ancestors of many who witnessed the festivities came to this country before Lady Liberty stood proudly in the harbor, and others had relatives who came to the country through another port of entry. But these facts do not diminish the power of the creation myth to instill a sense of common origin and identity. While millions are indeed directly linked to the Statue, millions of others regard the Statue as a symbol of their immigrant origins.

Similarly, not all came to America in poverty, and some did not even come willingly. But millions did, and so the imagery of the poor and huddled masses seeking a new start is also a part of the creation myth, with the Statue of Liberty a symbol of humble origins and of hope.

The power of the Statue of Liberty to evoke sentiment is further enriched by the fact that a very large proportion of American soldiers who went to fight World War I and World War II passed through New York Harbor going and/or returning. Miss Liberty gave meaning to that ordeal then. And the public rededication of the Statue renews that meaning.

But what does all of this matter? What purpose is served when a collectivity is able to identify with these symbols? Quite simply, the ability to sense a common identity transforms a collectivity into a

bonded group. In this case, it was not just a group but a nation. In addition to the sense of belonging, there is an awareness of a common past and an identification with that past. [10]

The earliest Americans likened their experience to that of the Is-raelites: They were a Chosen People who made a covenant with God. America was their Promised Land. The Calvinist Puritans explicitly thought of themselves as the New Israelites, but they were by no means the only ones who drew upon Old Testament imagery to give meaning to their experience.

Reagan's assertion of America's providential nature was not an ad lib or an irrelevant passing reference. It was the core content of his civil-religious sermon. "We are the keepers of the flame of liberty," he proclaimed; "We hold it high tonight for the world to see. A beacon of hope. A light unto the nations."

How similar are these words to those that John Winthrop, first governor of the Massachusetts Bay Colony, preached to the Pilgrims aboard the Mayflower before their landing in 1630:

. . . wee must Consider that wee shall be as a Citty upon a Hill, the eies of all people are uppon us . . . if our heartes shall turne away [from God] soe that wee will not obey, . . . wee shall surely perishe out of the good Land whither wee passe over this vast Sea to possesse. [11]

Except for the occasional stern pronouncement on the evils of communism, Reagan's language tends to be milder than a Winthrop sermon, so that on Liberty Weekend, rather than threaten Divine judgment for failure to keep the covenant, he merely reminded Americans that they have a duty to be true to it:

We dare to hope . . . that we will understand our work as Americans can never be said to be truly done until every man, woman, and child shares in our gift—in our liberty.

Clearly there is a strongly secular character to this mandate. What is usually overlooked is the fact that this secular language is, nevertheless, anchored in transcendental meaning and purpose. Witness, for example, George Will's suggestion of America's mission to spread

liberty around the globe. In a column written for a special issue of
Newsweek devoted to the Statue of Liberty rededication, the First
Family's favorite pundit wrote:

> American nationalism is a worthy passion. It is morally sound and
> important to the betterment of the world. Am I saying American
> nationalism is better than other nationalism? Yes. Patriotism is
> love of country. Nationalism is "patriotism plus." It is the belief
> that one's country is not just lovable, it is invested with special
> merit and charged with a special responsibility—a moral mission
> in the world. Americans have always believed, and at the end of
> this turbulent century should believe more than ever, that the
> light cast by the Statue of Liberty's torch is supposed to fall upon
> other shores too.[12]

When Reagan in his Liberty Weekend speech linked the secular
meaning of America as a land of immigrants with the religious meaning,
he contributed to the resacralization of the American creation myth.
And in doing so, he placed the New Christian Right's understanding
of the American experience on center stage for one of the most significant ceremonies to take place in this country for many years.

Words arouse sentiments, and with sentiments aroused, persons of
faith have risen and changed the world. Reagan understands this. If
he has not been more active in pushing the social and moral agenda
of the New Christian Right, it is because he knows that its supporters
have not been sufficiently aroused to pursue that agenda effectively.
But he has been extremely active in encouraging the development of
a solid support base for the evangelical program. One cannot possibly
understand or account for the rapid movement of religious broadcasters into the political arena during the 1980s without examining
the role of Ronald Reagan in legitimizing both their causes and their
involvement in politics.

Largely unnoticed by the media and, hence, the general public,
Reagan's first term in office saw evangelicals enjoying unprecedented
access to the presidency and the White House, with theological liberals
and moderates virtually locked out. Reverend Jerry Falwell replaced
the more establishment evangelical Billy Graham as the White House's
unofficial chaplain. No president during this century has so completely

snubbed the established liberal religious leadership of this nation as has Ronald Reagan. His embrace of the New Christian Right has, in effect, rewritten the book on who is "The Establishment."

On August 23, 1984, just hours before his acceptance of the Republican party's nomination for a second term, President Reagan addressed 17,000 supporters at a prayer breakfast in the Reunion Arena in Dallas. The occasion was, in fact, a reunion for Reagan and the New Christian Right. Their alliance had begun four years and a day earlier when candidate Reagan had addressed the gathering of preachers at the National Affairs Briefing from that very same podium.

It is difficult to recall a single memorable line from Reagan's acceptance speech later that same day, but not so the prayer breakfast speech. His words proclaiming the inseparability of religion and politics had an instant impact:

The truth is, politics and morality are inseparable. And as morality's foundation is religion, religion and politics are necessarily related.

Back in 1980, the leaders of the Washington for Jesus rally had vociferously denied that their prayer meeting on the Mall in Washington had anything to do with politics. But the social ills they identified and the substance of their prayers made engagement in politics inevitable. On the other hand, those who believe that a political agenda was the primary objective miss the significance of the event as a spiritual and ecumenical moment. Pat Robertson did not. In *America's Dates with Destiny*, he notes:

Many times during that incredible day, I sat on the platform watching men and women of faith from all across the nation as they prayed. They were every color, every class, every denomination imaginable. They were chief executive officers of large corporations, and they were unemployed, blue-collar workers. They were old and young, rich and poor, well-dressed and shabby. But they were one, and their prayer for the nation was one prayer. And God was hearing and would answer their prayer. April 29, 1980, was the beginning of a spiritual revolution.[13]

Today, even more so than in the emotion and high drama of that moment, there is a growing conviction among conservative Christians

that the Washington for Jesus rally was a turning point in American history. God heard their prayers, and he recognized that not just a faithful remnant but a growing, rejuvenated, repentant movement was seeking a return to the covenant. During the years of the Reagan administration, they believe, the country turned around and was now resetting its course.

To paraphrase the lyrics of a song from *Hair*, Broadway's embodiment of the 1960s counterculture, April 29, 1980, was the dawning of the Age of the Christian Right. But, more important, it was the dawning of a new conservative ecumenical movement. Without the latter, the former would never be possible.

In the chronicles of time, we often fail to take note of events when they occur—events that are seen later as historic. Someday, historians may well agree that Washington for Jesus was a watershed in American history. And, if so, this dawning of a cultural revolution passed virtually unnoticed by the overwhelming majority of Americans. But the several hundred thousand happy warriors for Jesus, who may not have been aware of the political implications of their actions, were sure that God Almighty had taken notice.

And from the stage erected in front of the old Smithsonian Castle, Pat Robertson certainly took notice of the crowd. It stretched as far as he could see toward the Washington Monument to his left and the United States Capitol on his right. Happy, shouting, singing, praying Christians all, proclaiming that they were reclaiming Washington and the nation for Jesus. Pat Robertson was confident that God was present, and he must have sensed that this could be the start of Something Big.

3

The Electronic Communications Revolution and the Rise of the New Christian Right

> *There is no dedicated group of viewers who are emotionally committed to an anchorman. On the other hand, there are millions of viewers who are personally committed to one or another of the electronic churchmen. Thus, they will sit in front of a screen and listen to a lengthy interview, and even try to understand. This puts a major educational tool into the hands of Christian leaders—a tool which the humanists cannot match on television because of the "least common denominator" principle which governs the Nielsen rating wars.*
> —Gary North,
> *Backward Christian Soldiers*

The electronic communications revolution is a technological megatrend that is reshaping not just America, but our entire planet. Its marvels of instant global communications inundate us with massive quantities of new information and images in alluring new packages, challenging and even overrunning traditional values as it alters lifestyles around the world. It is transforming our allegiances. Yet few recognize its impact; still fewer understand.

More than two decades ago, media prophet Marshall McLuhan said,

"The extension of any one sense alters the way we think and act—the way we perceive the world."[1] In the past, the limitations of each individual's perception were largely physical (distance) and biological (the senses of sight, sound, speech, touch, and smell). There were real, concrete boundaries to our world.

But we are no longer bound by physiology. The expansion of the world open to our senses began with the telegraph; gathered speed exponentially with the advent of the telephone and radio; came into its stride with television, transistors, microchips, videotape, and computers; and is now roaring ahead—its momentum undiminished—with laser technology.

"Societies have always been shaped," wrote McLuhan, "more by the nature of the media by which men communicate than by the content of the communication."[2] Thus the critical link between mass media and social movements emerges—a link that has enormous implications for religion in the twentieth century.

The invention of the printing press in fifteenth-century Europe paved the way for both the Renaissance and the Protestant Reformation. Samuel F. B. Morse's telegraph, steam-powered railroads, and high-speed printing presses all developed within a few decades of each other in the mid-nineteenth century, together helping to improve the communication of interests, grievances, and dissent, and contributing to movements around the world for mass democratic politics.

In this century, likewise, modern electronic communications act as a catalyst for social movements. In the first two decades following World War II, television played a major role in mobilizing black Americans for the civil rights movement. Despite control over books, newspapers, and libraries, southern whites could not stop even illiterate blacks from seeing nightly television broadcasts of civil rights activity on "The Huntley-Brinkley Report."[3]

Nor could the Pentagon, with all its image-making propaganda machinery, contain or stifle the news of unrest over the escalating Vietnam conflict during the 1960s. There is even good reason to believe that the archetypal American demagogue, Senator Joseph McCarthy, was in large measure brought down by television coverage of his Senate hearings.[4]

It is a fundamental truth of our era that leaders who don't know

how to use the mass media effectively see their movements stop dead in the water. By focusing attention on certain causes and crusades to the exclusion of others, by identifying one movement as "newsworthy" or another as hopeless, mass media can lend or withhold the publicity needed to attract members, achieve respectability, or stave off ignominy.

Almost without our recognizing it, this communications revolution is reshaping American religion. And American religion, in turn, is using this same electronic communications technology to reshape the country—and beginning to reach out to reshape the world.

How could this be? The answer is simple. Evangelical Christians have developed the most sophisticated communications system on this planet. They did so in full view of the American public, but nobody was paying attention. Radical social activist Jeremy Rifkin is among the few who were taking note. In *The Emerging Order*, a 1979 book that deserved much more consideration than it received, Rifkin documents the development of evangelical political power in America and concludes:

Of one thing there is little doubt, the evangelical community is amassing a base of potential power that dwarfs every other competing interest in American society today. A close look at the evangelical communications network . . . should convince even the skeptic that it is now the single most important cultural force in American life.[5]

But skeptics remain aloof from the evidence. And while they continue to snarl at any suggestion of ascending political power among evangelicals, those who would change America are going about the business of mobilizing their resources, unmolested by the ideological opponents of the New Christian Right.

Media manipulation is the key to understanding the realignment now underway in American religion and culture. Men and women who have learned techniques of media management, regardless of their educational backgrounds or formal credentials, are the ones whose causes, interests, and movements will succeed. Thus, the most profound social and cultural upheaval in twentieth-century America—

perhaps in our entire history—is intimately intertwined with the larger transformation in communications from print to electronics.

To be without historical perspective is to lack any basis for sorting out the significant from the mundane in day-to-day events. But modern mass media foster culture without history. They put within our reach cultural artifacts beyond the dreams of pharaohs and kings and emperors. These are available to hundreds of millions of us at the flick of a switch for a minuscule charge for energy. Yet, without history, these artifacts are simply relics. And news without historical context is nothing but a set of images to amuse, confuse, persuade, and otherwise clutter our minds until another set replaces it moments later.

So superficial are the images of mass media that any reporter good enough to be holding down a job can, from knowledge base zero, in a few moments or at worst a few hours, produce visual or printed images that meet socially accepted standards for presenting the news.

Deadlines—the five o'clock news, the evening edition, the weekend supplement that must be pulled together by Friday evening—demand this breakneck assemblage of the complex patchwork of events into a straightforward, simplified narrative called news. Reality that cannot be so packaged is either radically truncated into a "story" (distorted but digestible) or left alone by editors and producers.

The producers of news are not unaware of the problem. Notes Eleanor Randolph, feature writer for the *Washington Post*:

> Today's television writers are close to being caption writers. They are told to "write to the pictures," advice that sounds good, given the nature of the medium, but that can vastly limit their opportunity to explain and educate.[6]

And James T. Wooten, ABC correspondent formerly with the *New York Times*, observes:

> There is the danger that you give the viewer the illusion that he or she is well-informed, when you keep shortening and shortening and abbreviating until appearance of information is merely that and that alone.[7]

In-depth and feature coverage tends to be only slightly more demanding for the writer and provides little additional information for

the reader or viewer. Further, the impact of repeated "depth analysis" tends not to be cumulative. For example, from 1981 through 1986 the authors performed a simple experiment. We videotaped fourteen "depth" segments on Islamic Jihad from network television newscasts. Except for an expanding chronicle of events attributed to "Jihad," a viewer learns little more from watching all segments than from careful study of a single segment selected at random. Image-rich, the episodes were information-poor.

Analysis of the scores of stories that have been printed and aired about the New Christian Right since it first became highly visible during the 1980 presidential campaign probably would produce a similar conclusion.

Mass media do not expand our knowledge about particular subjects so much as select certain issues and events upon which to focus our attention. But that focus is highly transient. Whatever else, the images in the box must sustain interest so that the viewer doesn't switch channels. To guard against boredom, the images must be fast paced, virtually ensuring their superficiality.

But pace is not the only reason that there has been little analysis of significant religious developments—including the New Christian Right and the cultural revolution being fomented by disgruntled evangelicals. Media personnel generally do not consider religion a significant force in social change, making serious coverage therefore unnecessary.

The typical mass-media commentators—print journalists, television's roving reporters and anchorpersons, and most editors—are also captive to a secular mindset that is predisposed to exclude religion from news except when it is bizarre or sensational. Compare, for example, media attention devoted to covering the Jonestown cult suicides in 1978 or the Jim and Tammy Faye Bakker debacle with lack of media analysis of major currents of religious change. Pope John Paul II has been the subject of much news because of his unprecedented globetrotting, but there has been relatively little analysis of the meaning or implications of the pope's aggressive leadership.

Nor is the typical communicator well equipped to assess what information about religion may cross his or her desk. There are only about 250 religion newswriters in the United States. To the extent that religion is covered, the majority of journalists find themselves

covering it between reporting assignments on natural disasters, crime sprees, traffic accidents, garden shows, and county fairs. And when a significant religious story does break, editors tend not to assign their religion reporters. For example, of the 270 members of the press corps registered at Heritage USA for the news conference following the second meeting of PTL's Falwell board, only five were members of the Religious Newswriters Association, the professional organization of religion writers in the secular media.

Not surprisingly, news coverage of religion tends to be superficial and lacking context. Reporters are ill prepared to probe beyond the surface of events. One result is that mass-media communicators tend to portray religion in a skeptical or even negative light, particularly if the newsmakers in question do not reflect establishment thinking. Faced with new religious developments, reporters tend to display a mixture of professional cynicism, ignorance, bemusement, and an off-hand dismissal of the possible widespread or profound implications of religious change. At best, religiously grounded social movements tend to be misinterpreted when they run up against such journalistic narrowness.

This is precisely what has happened in the story of how the wedding of modern communications technology and Christianity is transforming American religion. The media frequently picture men such as Reverend Jerry Falwell or Pat Robertson as amusing cranks, fanatics, megalomaniacs, or shrewd showmen. They have been caught unaware—a professional sin worse than lack of objectivity—by the surge of new and different religiosity. Thus, they have misconstrued what is happening.

The electric church and the multibillion-dollar enterprise of televangelism did not arrive overnight, born full-blown like the goddess Athena from the head of Zeus. Television preaching has organizational and strategic roots more than two centuries old. Out of the religious revivals that swept the American colonies that historians call the Great Awakening and the great nineteenth-century urban revivals arose new groups to plan, promote, and stage evangelistic crusades. These groups were different from existing churches and denominations. They were totally independent and autonomous. But they crossed sectarian

boundaries and drew their support from Christians who belonged to a wide variety of churches. They were *parachurches*.

The modern electric empires of the Pat Robertsons, the Jerry Falwells, the Robert Schullers, and the Jimmy Swaggarts are the direct descendants of these parachurches in both organizational form and substance. The original parachurch revivalists devised successful strategies for manipulating conversions and staging huge, impressive public crusades. They build massive organizations and improved methods to raise money and mobilize believers by the tens of thousands.

Most important, the skills and managerial savvy they accumulated was not lost. Indeed, it was preserved and passed down through generations of evangelists.

Three giants of parachurch revivalism stand out in particular: Charles Grandison Finney, Dwight L. Moody, and Billy Sunday. These three men honed the skills for swaying large audiences into highly sophisticated techniques. They each made separate contributions to the growth of the parachurch phenomenon, but they also represent a cumulative process. Each of them (and dozens of lesser revivalists) built upon the wisdom of his predecessors.

Charles Grandison Finney (1792–1875) has been widely acclaimed as "the father of modern revivalism." Trained as a lawyer, Finney literally wrote the book on the subject. His *Lectures on Revivalism of Religion*, first published in 1835, stood for generations as a how-to manual for conducting effective revivals.[8]

Finney saw evangelism and conversion as rational, logical outcomes of a deliberate process. Conversion, Finney argued, "is not a miracle or dependent on a miracle in any sense. . . . It is purely a philosophical result of the right use of constituted means."[9]

Finney thus turned the revival idea on its head: Man was responsible for producing revivals of spirit rather than the Holy Spirit for sending a revival to man.

Finney's strategies for working a crowd's emotions included lengthy meetings to produce fatigue; long, mesmerizing intercessory prayers; sermons instilling fear and hope alternately; and personal harangues at those wavering on the brink of conversion.

Just as important, Finney took great care to lay the groundwork beforehand. His assistants would recruit lay workers in the local churches and organize motivational prayer sessions. These workers would then

post placards, take out newspaper advertisements, pass out handbills on street corners, and go door-to-door before Finney even arrived for the scheduled revival. He then arranged with local ministers to receive and sign up as members the "awakened sinners" who answered his altar calls.

Finney developed the first theory and rationale for mass evangelism and pioneered their use in practice. He created the first significant evangelistic parachurch.

But it was Dwight L. Moody (1837–99) who turned Finney's new principles into established, routine techniques. A successful businessman-turned-evangelist, Moody expanded Finney's rational model of revivalism with a marketing perspective. He went far beyond Finney in creating a complex division of labor in his parachurch to ensure the smooth planning and execution of revivals. He also improved on the public relations techniques that Finney had begun.[10]

Moody "sold" local businessmen and ministers on the benefits of a revival in their communities. He persuaded businessmen to underwrite the costs of the revivals. To ministers he held out the prospect of new members and renewed commitment among the old ones.

Even as Moody involved influential people in elaborate planning and participation, he maintained organizational and financial autonomy from any church or denomination. Meanwhile, his parachurch spun off institutions such as The Moody Bible Institute. Moody had learned his lessons well from Finney's manual of a generation earlier.

When Billy Sunday (1862–1935), the third "giant" precursor of modern-day televangelists, passed away of a heart ailment, he was hailed by one of his contemporaries as "the greatest evangelist since Martin Luther."[11] A former professional baseball player converted by a street-corner missionary, Sunday undoubtedly was the most colorful preacher in American history. In contrast to Finney's logical argument or Moody's calm, persuasive style, Sunday was all emotion. His behavior often bordered on the outrageous. But it was great entertainment.

Sunday was a showman. He would skip, gyrate, slide, and do cartwheels. He would stand on chairs, peel off layers of clothing as he worked himself up into a lather, and do burlesque-style imitations. He was bombastic, loud, abusive, rancorous.

Sunday was also a shrewd administrator. He had more than twenty

full-time specialists in his parachurch organization. One economics professor of the era claimed that Sunday's organization was one of the five most efficient businesses in the United States. When Sunday died, he was enormously wealthy. He may have been uncouth, but Billy Sunday added the roles of entertainer and celebrity—he liked to hob-nob with leading businessmen and politicians—to the urban evangelists' repertoire. From Billy Graham to Pat Robertson, the latter-day televangelists were to follow in his footsteps.

In sum, with the advent of electronic technology, evangelistic preachers already had an organizational form and strategy for ministry to follow. Without the developments in staging revivals and building parachurch networks in the nineteenth and early twentieth centuries, religious broadcasters would not wield the influence in American life that they do today. And the prospects for preachers launching national moral-political crusades, perhaps even a presidential campaign, would have been extremely remote.

The marriage of this particular organizational form to the emerging technology was possible because of another unique feature of broad-casting in the United States—its emphasis on free enterprise, which has shaped radio and television broadcasting more decisively in this country than in any other nation. Broadcasting is regulated, but the Federal Communications Commission gives networks and local stations a great deal of liberty in setting their own policies and procedures.

It is assumed, first of all, that broadcasters have a right to pursue profit. As long as they devote some small proportion of their broad-casting to the "public interest," and their programming is not judged grossly offensive, stations and networks can more or less broadcast whatever they wish.

Almost from the inception of regularly scheduled broadcasting in the 1920s, religious programming has been considered to be "in the public interest." Most stations and networks offered religious groups some airtime on a sustaining (i.e., free) basis. From the beginning, the demand for free airtime exceeded the supply, so broadcasters had to develop policies governing access.[12]

The first national radio network was the National Broadcasting Company (NBC), formed in 1926. From the outset, NBC offered no commercial time for religious broadcasting and allocated what free time

it chose to offer through the Federal Council of Churches (later the National Council of Churches).[13]

The Columbia Broadcasting System (CBS), formed in 1927, did offer commercial time out of financial necessity, but it switched to gratis time in 1931 as a way to get rid of the demagogic Catholic priest Father Charles E. Coughlin.[14] Thereafter, CBS used a combination of an in-house advisory board and the Federal Council to select persons to appear on the CBS "Church of the Air." By 1934, the Federal Council of Churches' Department of National Religious Radio, with twenty-four cooperating denominations, had some oversight over six regularly scheduled network programs.[15]

The Mutual Broadcasting System was the only network to offer commercial time without restriction from 1935 to 1944.[16] Two of its more notable programs were Charles E. Fuller's "Old-Fashioned Revival Hour" and "The Lutheran Hour," featuring Walter A. Maier and sponsored by the Missouri Synod of the Lutheran Church.

In 1944, the *Christian Century*, the leading liberal Protestant periodical, published an attack on "religious racketeers" for allegedly using radio as a medium for exploitation. The author accused Mutual of tolerating programs such as "The Lutheran Hour" because they were financially lucrative and called for the termination of all paid religious broadcasting, or, failing this, a "ruling from the Federal Communications Commission against the sale of time for religious broadcasting."[17]

At the same time, James DeForest Murch, a towering figure of evangelical Protestantism, accused Frank R. Goodman, chairman of the Department of National Religious Radio of the Federal Council of Churches, of leading a campaign to squeeze evangelicals off the air. Goodman, he claimed, had "signed up fifty or more radio stations 'with ironclad contracts obliging them to use the Federal Council–approved programs and no other.' "[18]

Officials of the Federal Council of Churches have always denied that they pressured networks to develop programming under their aegis to the exclusion of evangelicals. But the evidence is clear that evangelical Protestants did not share in the free airtime granted by the networks and, further, that there existed a campaign to pressure Mutual into a "no commercial time" policy.

In March 1944, Mutual announced changes in their paid-time broad-casting that severely curtailed access. Among the restrictions adopted were: (1) a limit of broadcasts to thirty minutes, (2) a prohibition against the use of airtime to solicit funds to pay for the broadcasts, and (3) broadcasting on Sunday mornings only. The reason for this policy change? Ralph Jennings, in the most comprehensive study of radio religious broadcasting, concludes: "Strong criticism from mainstream Protestantism as cases of alleged abuses mounted."[19]

Evangelicals understood what was happening and had been mobi-lizing to fight back. The first major step toward developing cooperation among evangelicals had been taken two years earlier, at the National Conference for United Action among Evangelicals, which in turn spawned the National Association of Evangelicals (NAE). Evangelical broadcasters took a prominent role in the meeting,[20] whose keynote speaker was Harold Ockenga, pastor of the Park Street Church in Boston. Setting the mood for the formation of NAE, Ockenga's heart-stirring address returned several times to the theme of discrimination in access to the airwaves. Referring to a meeting he had had with the president of NBC, he concluded that in the absence of a united evan-gelical organization, there was "absolutely no opportunity of sharing equally in the broadcasting facilities of that great company."[21] "We are discriminated against," Ockenga asserted, "because of the folly of our divided condition."[22]

In April 1944, just a month after Mutual announced its policy changes, 150 evangelical broadcasters met in Columbus, Ohio, and formed the National Religious Broadcasters.[23] Their first official act was to retain a Washington-based communications attorney to provide "counsel in the preparation of a Constitution and Bylaws and a general policy and program."[24] They met again in Chicago in September for a constitu-tional convention.

With the creation of the National Religious Broadcasters, the tide began to turn for evangelicals. NRB launched an aggressive public relations program and adopted a Code of Ethics, which they consid-ered a "veritable Declaration of Independence from radio racketeers." They called on the Federal Communications Commission to help ame-liorate the unequal distribution of airtime. They also petitioned the networks to reconsider their policies.

At least some results were achieved in short order. That same year,

Mutual allocated six-and-a-half hours of free time to NAE.[25] NBC's Blue Network, which would become the American Broadcasting Company (ABC), also offered time to NAE on a restricted basis.

After an early burst of success, NRB lost some of its thrust and vitality, a typical pattern for social-movement organizations. Perceiving extensive victory in a few visible successes, participants lose their zeal, lower their financial contributions, and ignore appeals to redouble their efforts. As a result, a movement organization becomes vulnerable at the very moment its supporters appear to have won, or are about to win.

Liberal Protestants, now reorganized as the National Council of Churches, did not fail to note this vulnerability. As television expanded rapidly in the early 1950s, the NCC pursued an initiative to ensure their exclusive representation with the networks. CBS, leery of earlier conflict with evangelicals, added the Southern Baptists to its consortium of liberal Protestants, Catholics, and Jews, a conciliatory gesture not particularly appreciated by the NRB, since the Southern Baptists were not members. The other networks also developed interfaith programming, but evangelical Christians were basically excluded.

An exception was Billy Graham, whose phenomenal popularity enabled him to cut through the liberal church monopoly and acquire network time, both gratis and purchased. But the rank-and-file NRB evangelicals were effectively locked out, a situation unchanged even today; rather than deal with the networks, evangelical broadcasters must contract with individual stations.

Meanwhile, new opposition to paid religious broadcasting developed at the state level, a campaign endorsed by the Broadcasting and Film Commission of the National Council of Churches.[26] These renewed hostilities with the liberal Protestants and the failure to break into network television reinvigorated the National Religious Broadcasters. Beginning in 1956, under the leadership of James Murch, NRB took new organizational initiatives. The most important step was bringing their annual meetings to Washington, D.C. Murch explained the rationale:

> I felt that our position would be immensely strengthened if we could take our national convention to the Nation's Capital. This was the seat of the Federal Communications Commission and the

lawmakers who could assure our constitutional rights to freedom
of religion and freedom of speech on the airwaves. It was also the
seat of the industry's National Association of Broadcasters and the
leading trade journal of the industry, *Broadcasting* magazine.[27]

Being in Washington paid such high dividends that the NRB has
never since met elsewhere. The organization has established lobbying
and liaison relationships with all the groups Murch hoped to contact,
and more. There is an annual Congressional Breakfast that, with more
conservatives in Congress, has been increasingly well attended. The
group enjoys good relations with the Federal Communications Commission and holds an annual luncheon in its honor. The counsel who
represents the NRB before the FCC is Richard Wiley, former chairman of the FCC. The presidents of the National Association of Broadcasters and each of the networks have accepted invitations to speak.
And in recent years, the convention has benefited from the appearance
of Ronald Reagan. In a word, the NRB has learned its way around
Washington.

An important benefit of being in Washington came early, during
the battle with the National Council of Churches. James Murch called
on Sol Taishoff, editor and publisher of *Broadcasting* magazine, to
plead NRB's case for the purchase of airtime.

"Why can't you Protestants settle your disagreements amicably and
make some sort of compromise on broadcasting policies?" fired Taishoff.

"Well, you see," said Murch, "there are several kinds of Protestants
and we are unwilling to give up our differing convictions for the sake
of unity. May I illustrate? There are several kinds of Jews—Orthodox,
Reformed and Conservative. . . ."

"With a hearty laugh," reports Murch, "Sol threw up his hands and
immediately retorted, 'You don't need to argue your case any further.
I know what you are talking about. You certainly have equal rights
before the law and the sale of time is the easiest way to guarantee
those rights.' "[28]

Broadcasting became a champion of NRB's campaign to purchase
airtime.

The success of the National Religious Broadcasters and its constituent members has been a gradual process. But if there was a single

turning point, it was a 1960 FCC policy directive that ruled that no important public interest is served by differentiating between gratis airtime and commercially sponsored programming.

To grasp the significance of this ruling, one needs to look back to the Communications Act of 1934, which authorized the FCC to grant broadcasting licenses. A license is, in effect, a monopoly to use a scarce commodity—namely, a specific airwave. Simply put, it has always been presumed that stations "owe" some proportion of their broadcast time to the "public interest" in exchange for this monopoly. From the beginning, religious broadcasting was designated as one way of fulfilling that obligation.

The implication of the 1960 ruling was that local stations could sell airtime for religious programs and still get "public interest credit" in the eyes of the FCC. Two important developments followed. First, the ruling buoyed the commitment of evangelical broadcasters to buy commercial time, and fierce competition ensued. Second, this competition enhanced the value of the time slots, with the result that many local stations, which previously had adhered to network policy not to sell airtime for religious broadcasting, decided to cash in on the new demand.

While evangelicals were buying their way onto the air in unprecedented numbers, a technological innovation expanded the number of stations on which they could appear—the invention of videotape. Because film was expensive, filmed programs were shown on one station, then mailed to another, and so on, around the country. Program content had to be planned carefully to keep it from appearing badly out of date. Videotapes could be mass produced and aired during the same week all across the country. Programming could now be scheduled to correspond to the calendar; Easter services could be broadcast on Easter, Christmas services on Christmas, and so on, thus greatly enhancing a program's appeal.

The FCC policy directive was devastating for programs that had been carried on a sustaining basis. Why should local stations give free airtime to religious programs when syndicated broadcasters were bidding against each other to buy time? As a business proposition, it made no sense. Station managers dropped sustaining-time programs produced both by their own network and by individual denominations.

The collective impact of these market decisions shows up dramat-

ically in a 1979 report by the Communications Committee of the U.S. Catholic Conference.[29] In 1959, just before the FCC ruling, 53 percent of all religious broadcasting in America was paid-time programming. By 1977, that proportion had increased to 92 percent.

As a result, religious broadcasting since the mid-1970s has been firmly in the hands of evangelicals and fundamentalists who manage parachurch organizations. It is they, more than the mainline denominations, who can afford to commit huge percentages of their annual revenues to purchasing airtime and the hardware necessary to produce programs. Unhampered by denominational bureaucracies or any other "normal" church apparatus, the parachurch televangelists have drawn their sustenance from the mass audience, and, in turn, have been able to cater almost exclusively to it.

That some televangelists would one day utilize the airwaves to communicate a political message should not have come as a surprise. Indeed, from the earliest days of broadcasting, politics has never been very far removed from the agenda of some religious broadcasters. Late in his career, for example, Billy Sunday had become political. Father Charles E. Coughlin, probably the most successful broadcaster of the 1930s, and certainly one of the most controversial, was overtly political. In the early postwar era, the most visible were right-wing fundamentalists Carl McIntire and Billy James Hargis. In 1955, Carl McIntire claimed to be broadcasting on 600 radio stations.[30] In 1961, Tulsa-based Hargis claimed to be on over 200 radio stations in forty-six states and a dozen television stations.[31]

The strident messages and flamboyant personalities of these men contributed to the stereotyping of all religious broadcasters. In comparison with their predecessors, today's politicized televangelists are distinct moderates. But part of the legacy they have inherited is the popular conviction that they are all political radicals or right-wing fanatics—a conviction held by many Americans who have never seen or heard an evangelist of either era. The Elmer Gantry stereotype made an easy transition from canvas tent and sawdust floor to radio and television studios.

But if modern religious broadcasters appear more polished and seem more moderate than some of their predecessors, collectively they have become a potent force in molding conservative Christians into a social movement. The primary reason is that their programming, mostly or

entirely undiluted by secular commercial interruptions, can create a religious context into which all their messages, as well as viewers' interests and concerns, can be packaged.

In other words, all topics—not just sin and salvation—can be brought under a religious umbrella. A host of social problems—from abortion to the problems of the Social Security Administration to 250 U.S. Marines dead in Beirut—can be interpreted in biblical terms of cause and effect. However simplistic the resulting perspective may seem to nonviewers or nonbelievers, supporters of such electronic ministries receive a coherent social ideology.

And what critics of televangelism demean as the "continual begging" for money does more than simply raise the revenues needed to continue broadcasting. Contributions go to a cause, and the contributors are bearing witness to that cause every time they give.

In order to appreciate the importance for a conservative social movement of the worldview imparted by televangelists, one needs to look at the consequences of the lack of any such context in secular television.

The electronic communications revolution has created a marvelous paradox. Via television, radio, computers, and satellites, messages can be transmitted instantaneously and simultaneously to any number of points on earth; yet the speed of transmission has decontextualized the content of any single message. The flood of information in the mass media tends either to go unnoticed or to overwhelm us if we try to consume it.

One thing is clear. The greater the attention the media devote to a topic, the greater are the chances that public sentiments will crystallize around it. This occurs because the normal flood of competing topics is temporarily reduced to a trickle; information becomes manageable. And it is then that television becomes a powerful communications tool.

The usual breakneck pace of news in the electronic media is one important reason that conservative Christians in this country have had to wait until recently to be mobilized for social and political change. Television, in particular, has dealt with many moral and political topics, but without much context and certainly not from an explicitly Christian perspective. This has worked against the consolidation of evangelical sentiment and opinion regarding national and international issues.

Until now, evangelicals who did insist on interpreting their world along Christian lines (putting a biblical slant on issues such as prayer and curriculum content in public schools, national economic policies, or the U.S. military presence in the Middle East) found themselves estranged from the secular news establishment. It is difficult to maintain a coherent Christian worldview when the mass media offer no worldview at all.

Some Christians have responded simply by tuning out current events. Others have swum against the current, trying to reassert Christian values in the public forum (and getting labeled as eccentric or intolerant for their efforts). Still others have worked quietly, sharing their thoughts with like-minded friends and waiting patiently.

Waiting for what? The answer is now clear: some way—some platform, some party, some candidate—to crystallize their sentiments without having to depend on the secular media.

That is the essence of Pat Robertson and the growing political movement composed of the followers of televangelism. This movement is now well under way, thanks in substantial measure to the electronic communications revolution and the televangelists' mastery of it.

4

We're Mad As Hell and We're Not Going to Take It Anymore!

I want you to get up now out of your chairs and go to the window! Open it and stick your head out and yell, "I'm mad as hell and I'm not going to take it anymore!"
—Howard Beal, Anchorman,
Network

I t was a glorious, if berserk, moment in Paddy Chayefsky's screenplay for *Network*. The rain-soaked, suicidal anchorman of a national nightly news program bellowed out the quintessential rage and frustration of America's urbanites: The country is out of the common person's grasp or control. Individuals are at the mercy of imponderable social forces and unfeeling social institutions that use them as faceless cogs. They've—we've—lost all self-determination.

Probably unknown to Chayefsky, his fictional anchorman-turned-"mad prophet of the airwaves" was speaking to and for the millions of conservative Christians as well. Ironically, many evangelicals and fundamentalists had long since stopped watching commercial television or attending Hollywood movies before *Network* reached their local theatres in 1976. But if they did see the film, their spirits must have known that Howard Beal spoke for them.

In the past several years, evangelicals and fundamentalists have also

begun to shout, "We're mad as hell and we're not going to take it anymore!" But whereas Howard Beal symbolized raw frustration and despair, these conservative Christians are confident that they have what it takes to turn the country around. And they intend to do so.

What brought out millions of previously unregistered "born-again" voters in the 1970s and 1980s? What made fundamentalist Jerry Falwell dissatisfied with merely preaching "the pure saving gospel of Jesus Christ" and inspired him to found the Moral Majority in 1979? Why did so many evangelicals and biblical inerrantists think they could resurrect their old antievolution creation theory and buck the scientific establishment?

In short, what new sentiments and attitudes suddenly galvanized evangelicals into a conservative social and political movement? What made them unwilling "to take it anymore"?

In one sense, these questions are misleading. Evangelicals have always battled both personal sin and social evil. If many groups were reluctant to commit themselves publicly to social reform for a good bit of this century, they never completely lost their zeal for changing the world by changing individuals, i.e., winning souls for Christ. And now that they are back with a vengeance, hindsight suggests that there was every reason to believe their retreat from the public arena would only be temporary.

In the past decade, a series of developments has aroused the sleeping evangelical giant. Evangelicals have witnessed public schools purging their very existence from textbooks on American history and banning their God from the classroom; they have endured journalists and editors treating them as archaic kooks; and at the hands of mainline Protestants they have experienced the ultimate insult—they have been ignored.

In the 1970s the evangelicals were as they had always been—not some shrinking remnant of crazies, but tens of millions, as the polls would show. They were a large part of the Silent Majority that Richard Nixon and Spiro Agnew used to talk about in the 1960s, although Nixon and Agnew never dreamed that so many of their constituents came from a distinctly religious interest group.

Contrary to media perception, says Richard John Neuhaus in *The Naked Public Square,*

. . . the country did not change its mind in "going conservative" in the late seventies. Rather, millions of people who had disagreed with societal directions all along found new ways to make their disagreement politically effective. . . . [M]illions of fundamentalists and conservative evangelicals came in from the political cold.[1]

Like all Americans, evangelicals shared the national sense of "malaise" that President Jimmy Carter spoke of during the dark days of double-digit inflation and the Iranian hostage crisis. Unlike others, however, they thought they knew what had caused it, and that made them angry. Following World War I and the Scopes trial, the liberals had taken control of the dominant institutions of society. More immediately, the liberal model for America, with its naive faith in science, its welfare state, and its abandonment of biblical values, had broken down.

In Jeremy Rifkin's words, they knew that "the liberal superstructure had cracked."[2] Worse yet, the liberal economists, politicians, and educators who had led the country into this mess could not see the futility of their philosophies or the bankruptcy of their "solutions." And, further, they refused to step down from their positions in the institutions that had the power to turn the situation around.

Meanwhile evangelicals looked around and saw crime rates up, prisons overcrowded, and the criminal justice system throwing good money after bad; sexual hedonism hampered only by epidemics of AIDS and venereal diseases, with rampant drug abuse filling in where promiscuity left off; divorce, spouse and child abuse, homosexuality, and single-parent families at all-time highs; a welfare system that creates a permanent "underclass" subsidized by taxpayers; a fetish for science (or scientism) and technology at the same time that privacy, personal liberty, and environmental quality are on the decline; bloated state and federal bureaucracies that have become less efficient, less fiscally responsible, and less honest; an entertainment industry that continually escalates its commercial formula of explicit violence and sex; a public school system unable to discipline students or teach them at any level but that of the lowest common denominator; and a foreign

policy that appeases terrorists and responds ineptly to Third World bullying and Communist expansionism.

True, liberals suffered under the same social conditions, but for them it was different. Neoconservative Lutheran Richard John Neuhaus makes a very astute distinction between "sins of omission" and "sins of commission."[3] For liberals, he notes, a conservative government's faults are more often seen as "sins of omission." Liberals may complain, for instance, that a conservative administration does not provide enough aid for the poor or foreign aid to Third World nations; that it does not exert enough effort to save whales, eagles, baby seals, or other wildlife; that it does not strenuously enough advance minority rights—things "that liberals think it is the business of government to do."

But for conservatives—and evangelicals are overwhelmingly conservative politically—a liberal government's sins are more likely (and resentfully) seen as "sins of commission":

> . . . government does many things they think it should not do and forbids them to do things they think they should be free to do. They are notably outraged by governments that . . . advance changes in sexual and family mores—areas that could hardly be more value-laden. . . . [T]hey resent deeply programs such as school busing and "affirmative action" aimed at mandatory racial integration. They react vociferously to government actions that get in the way of praying in schools, owning handguns, hiring whom they want, and living where they please. In sum, in very everyday ways they feel assaulted by liberal government as liberals do not feel assaulted by conservative government.[4]

If the general failure of liberal big government—and, indeed, of liberal society itself—led many evangelicals to mobilize, at times specific issues spawned social movement organizations. Christian Voice is a classic example. It began when a ballot proposition put to California voters in 1978 would have expanded legal protection for homosexuals. When fundamentalist pastors became involved in a campaign to defeat it, the Internal Revenue Service stepped in to warn them that if they persisted, their churches' tax-exempt status would be reexamined. As

a result, they founded Christian Voice as a vehicle to continue their fight.

A number of Supreme Court rulings in the early 1960s convinced many conservative Christians that the federal government had needlessly and callously intruded itself into the community, and, by extension, the family. Prominent among them were *Engel* vs. *Vitale* in 1962, which ruled that a nondenominational prayer prepared by the New York Board of Regents violated the First Amendment's establishment clause, and *Abington School District* vs. *Schempp* in 1963, which judged the same of Bible readings in a public school.

Issues such as school prayer hung in a kind of "free-floating" readiness, waiting to be linked to others, such as the availability of abortion-on-demand following *Roe* vs. *Wade* in 1973, or IRS enforcement of minority quotas in parochial schools, or government harassment over the tax-exempt status of Christian schools. No one single factor sounded the clarion call to battle, but as one issue mounted on top of another, evangelicals gradually decided that they had had enough.

And, once they were aroused, the issues that caught their attention and concern multiplied. The agenda of these newly politicized evangelicals became, as one analyst put it, "maddeningly multifaceted." To the wide range of areas noted above, add dogmatic defense of free enterprise, a sometimes-confusing but unyielding support for Israel, a lobby for a stronger national defense, and even the closure of the U.S. Department of Education.

As Neuhaus observes, "If your goal is to 'turn the country around,' you can hardly limit your concern to one or even to a dozen issues."[5] But at the same time, so many issues and so many associated causes needed to be simplified for popular consumption and mass mobilization. However much leaders argued that these were all interrelated, they could not keep their adherents' attention scattered across such an immense field of social problems. Many evangelicals lacked the stamina, and others the minimal formal education, to comprehend fully so many separate controversies.

As in all significant social movements, they had to establish two simple things—a cause and an effect, a perpetrator and a victim—on which to focus their efforts. So the evangelical leadership reduced the complexities of modern American society and the sources of this "malaise" to the familiar biblical symbols of good and evil. First they chose

the hallowed family as the focal point around which virtually all other issues could revolve. Then they marked "secular humanism" as their villain.

The family has become the evangelical master issue of the 1980s. The New Christian Right has made use of sociological wisdom even as it condemns sociologists. The family is the basic unit of human societies, they note. And no culture has ever survived without the family. They also tie the family to the greatness of America. Writes televangelist James Robison in his book *Attack on the Family*:

> . . . all that America has become—a strong, thriving nation, full of creativity, variety, and uniqueness—owes itself to the foundational influence of marriage and the family. . . . The family has also proved itself the most effective economic institution the world has ever known.[6]

It follows, therefore, "that anyone who wanted to destroy the American way of life would single out marriage and the family as first-priority targets."[7]

And beware, the country is filled to overflowing with sinister forces who are out to destroy America. Robison promises in his introduction to "reveal in stark detail" the handiwork of those who seek to "destroy the home and the American way of life."[8] One's first impression upon encountering Robison, or many other writers of the New Christian Right, is that one is in for a new round of McCarthyism or Red-baiting. Not so. They do speak disparagingly of "the collectivists," but collectivists are never identified as Communists, and, furthermore, they are seen as only a minuscule part of the problem. The real enemies threatening to destroy the family and bring down the country in one swoop are the Secular Humanists.

The family, notes Donald Heinz, is a primary symbol with powerful emotional significance. It stands as "a means to recover a lost meaning as well as a lost past."[9] What's more, all other issues can be subsumed under the "pro-family" label: the teaching of evolution, prayer in schools, abortion, traditional roles for women, sex and drugs, pornography, and so forth.

While each of these issues has a family-centered dimension, another critical element of the evangelical perspective is the belief that these

problems represent a loss of freedom. Freedom, say evangelicals, is not genuine unless it is matched with responsibility and discipline— biblically grounded discipline. Freedom apart from biblical values becomes promiscuity, abuse, and chaos. Evangelicals argue that the secular, relativistic type of freedom that liberals espouse has given American society nothing but fleeting, superficial pleasure and many long-term headaches. Their biblically grounded conception of freedom is thus the foundation for their attacks on the liberal drift of social mores and Supreme Court decisions over the past quarter-century.

Evangelicals decry the steady erosion of the sanctity of life since *Roe* vs. *Wade* in 1973, which has resulted in millions of abortions and a growing acceptance of euthanasia. It has hampered legal restrictions on the availability of contraceptives to teenage girls, leading in turn to widespread venereal disease and teenage pregnancy. It has even helped promote the entertainment industry's fascination with Rambo-like death and destruction.

Close to abortion on the evangelical list of evils is the systematic assault on women's traditional roles. From elementary school through the university, educators encourage students to reconsider traditional roles; the federal government actively promotes their destruction as the courts strike down discriminatory restrictions and legislators subsidize day-care programs; and the media fuel the fire with favorable coverage of everything from women's liberation to androgynous entertainers such as Boy George.

The women's liberation movement is credited by evangelicals with pushing large numbers of women into the work force while simultaneously neglecting their families. The consequences include day-care "orphans," a severe breakdown in patriarchal authority in the home, lax discipline of children, a decline in the national birthrate, and a rising divorce rate.

The family breakdown, in turn, spurs the government to try to correct the problems that it has been substantially responsible for creating; and increasing government involvement leads to the creeping danger of totalitarian government.

John W. Whitehead is an evangelical lawyer and intellectual leader in the New Christian Right Movement. Founder of the Rutherford Institute, a nonprofit organization concerned with educational and litigational issues relating to the First Amendment, Whitehead has

written two books that are widely circulated and influential in the movement: *The Second American Revolution* and *The Stealing of America*.

In the latter, Whitehead argues forcefully that one important consequence of the breakdown of the family is that it loses its traditional capacity to serve as a buffer between the individual and the state. The result is that the state becomes a surrogate family, ultimately exacting a heavy price in human liberty. He states:

> The assertion of governmental authority over areas of life once considered to be under individual and private control means that the American state has become more than government. It is making claims and is acting as if it possesses the attributes of deity.[10]

The state usurps the rights that were once sacred within the family, and in so doing destroys the biblically sanctioned fabric of family life. For example, in the 1976 case of *Planned Parenthood* vs. *Danforth*, the Supreme Court ruled unconstitutional a Missouri statute requiring a husband's consent before a married woman can obtain an abortion. In this single ruling the Court managed to abrogate the sanctity of the life of the infant-to-be, the woman's responsibility to live with the consequences of her sexuality, the husband's authority over his wife, and his rights of parenthood. Whitehead musters case after case as evidence of how, in his view, the liberal drift of American society is responsible for a host of threats to the family.

Whitehead pins much of the blame on the decisions of the U.S. Supreme Court. In *The Second American Revolution*, he accuses the Court of usurping powers it was never meant to have and thereby creating an imbalance of constitutional power.[11] By violating the Founding Fathers' system of checks and balances, the Supreme Court justices have become de facto the nation's supreme legislators and policymakers.

Whitehead refers to the justices as "social engineers" and "an imperial judiciary," calling their body a "legiscourt" fostering "statism"— the belief that government is the total solution to society's problems. His thinking about the Supreme Court has been profoundly influential among New Christian Right leaders, including Pat Robertson and

Herbert Titus, dean of the Christian Broadcasting Network University's School of Law.

Part of the credo of the New Christian Right is the tenet that Americans have forgotten the importance of religion in the founding of the nation. Whitehead has gone further by documenting how the Supreme Court justices have lost sight of the grounding of our country's laws and Constitution in the Judeo-Christian values of the Bible. He argues that the Court has substituted relativism for a permanent set of standards, the prevailing attitudes of the justices themselves forming the basis of their rulings. Law has ceased to be anchored in higher principles. The law is now only what the justices say is law, a development stemming from a kind of encroaching Darwinism. Lawyers once learned their practice according to the texts of Blackstone, who assumed absolute biblical principles unaffected by prevailing mores. Then, in the nineteenth century, an evolutionary view of law crept into the profession, thanks to Christopher Langdell, dean of the Harvard Law School. Langdell utilized the case method of teaching basic legal principles and doctrines as products of an evolving process, which can be read in the opinions written by judges over many years. The problem with this, asserts Whitehead, is that the cultural basis for their opinions will change, like fads and trends. He refers to these new principles for deriving law as "sociological law."

Thus, the Supreme Court, caught up in the liberal climate of twentieth-century America, has moved away from the values on which this country was founded. Warns Whitehead, "This [has] meant that what a judge said was law, and not what the Constitution said."[12] Law, in other words, has become hostage to current vogue. Or, as conservative writer Herbert Schlossberg puts it, "There is no principle of justice that transcends the expediency of the hour."[13] At the same time, the Supreme Court justices are not even proper evolutionists. They have become crusading "activists" hastening the process of social change:

> Instead of waiting patiently for the natural flow of evolution, the courts have become active in their development of the law. Judicial activism is now a recognized fact. The courts make law. The written Constitution has little value except as a shibboleth used by the courts to justify their intrusions into the lives of people.[14]

Conservative Christians are angry at the Supreme Court, something Pat Robertson recognizes. His much-publicized criticism of the Court in the fall of 1986—that in an elected constitutional democracy the unelected justices cannot have the final word on law—reflected a strong segment of popular opinion. In a 1986 interview, he elaborated:

> In the Christian community there is rage against the Supreme Court that is so intense you cannot believe it. The people I deal with, the evangelicals, despise the Supreme Court. I use that word advisedly. I mentioned once to a group that I was going to the funeral of one Supreme Court justice, and they all started to applaud. I said, "No, this is one of the good ones that died." It's that kind of feeling. There is antipathy, tremendous antipathy. And when the people who are the most law-abiding in the society feel that the Supreme Court is their enemy, then you've got something significant.[15]

The Court is seen as the source, the author of the secular, liberal drift away from morality in modern society. Robertson noted further:

> There is the feeling that the Supreme Court has trampled our schools, religious liberties, and our method of government in an egregious fashion. The Court has stood the Constitution on its ear.[16]

Whether or not one accepts the logic of Whitehead's or Robertson's arguments about the errors of the Supreme Court, conservative Christians have constructed a plausible story line. It neatly explains the process that has undermined the sacred institution of the family and indicates where changes are needed. Since evangelicals and fundamentalists have long felt the family was under siege by godless forces, sophisticated analyses like Whitehead's explain the why and the how of it.

Thus, in many ways this "pro-family" position serves an important social purpose. It gives evangelicals a target, helps focus their anger toward the government, and links government policies to the trends that most upset them.

Some of these links are frankly dubious, such as the claim that the

Supreme Court's liberal rulings on pornography have been responsible for increased incidences of rape, child molestation, and divorce. But their scientific standing is not what is important. What *is* important is that the family has become a rallying symbol for protest.

Now back to the arch-villain, secular humanism.

Until recently, many liberals had no idea they were Secular Humanists, and there are still many more who have yet to find out. For many, a first encounter with the concept has a familiar, and perhaps flattering, ring—something akin to "humanitarian." But evangelicals do not use the term to flatter. Secular humanism, or simply humanism, is, in their view, the underlying godless principle eroding the moral foundation of America. It is the source of all critical social problems, from government bureaucracy to pornography.

The concept of secular humanism seems to have appeared first in a legal context in the 1961 Supreme Court case of *Torcaso* vs. *Watkins*. Torcaso had been appointed to the office of notary public by the governor of Maryland but refused to affirm an article in the state's constitution that required profession of "belief in the existence of God." Torcaso's plea was upheld in a decision written by Justice Hugo Black: "Neither a State nor the Federal Government can constitutionally force a person 'to profess a belief or disbelief in any religion.' "

University of Chicago historian Martin Marty notes that constitutional scholar Leo Pfeffer argued before the Court that the Maryland Constitution was invalid because it stated a preference for theistic faiths over nontheistic faiths, "such as Buddhism, Taoism, Ethical Culture, Secular Humanism and others." In his written opinion, Justice Black cited Pfeffer. Therein, contends Marty, "a new name for a nonexistent denomination was born full-blown from the mind of one justice."[17] Etymologist William Safire also traces the legal use of the concept to the Torcaso case, but he attributes use of the term to an *amicus curiae* brief written by Joseph Blau, professor emeritus of religion at Columbia University.[18]

The concept apparently entered the vocabulary of the New Christian Right through an article written by John Whitehead and John Conlan and published in the *Texas Tech Law Review* in 1978. They argued a point that has since been repeated again and again by conservative Christians: The Supreme Court has determined that secular humanism is a religion.[19]

A parenthetical reference to secular humanism in a Supreme Court decision, even though the reference appears in a unanimous Court decision, hardly gives secular humanism a legal status. Nevertheless, from thousands of pulpits all over America, one hears expressed with supreme confidence that the Supreme Court has ruled (or determined) that secular humanism is a religion.

As sociologist James Davison Hunter testified in 1986 during a lawsuit brought by 642 Alabama parents against their local school board for teaching humanism, this nontheistic perspective has, furthermore, all the earmarks of a religion. It deals with spiritual themes: the nature of the universe (or cosmology), the origin of the human race, human values, and the goals of life. It even possesses that familiar characteristic of many religious groups—the belief that its views on such profound matters are superior to other groups' ideas.[20]

The Alabama suit was brought by Mobile parents concerned that "the religion of secular humanism" was being unconstitutionally promoted in public school textbooks, while religion's important place in American history and in the founding of the nation was suppressed. Moral choices and common civics were presented to young students in texts that relativized ethics and/or tried to present situational and ethical material in a value vacuum.

Both liberal and conservative interest groups leaped into the fray. John Buchanan, chairman of People for the American Way (alternately referred to as PAW or "People For") helped arrange legal representation for the Alabama school board. Pat Robertson's National Legal Foundation provided counsel to the Christian plaintiffs.

The Department of Education, meanwhile, commissioned New York University psychologist Paul Vitz to analyze typical public school textbooks, and his results clearly buttressed the Mobile parents' case. Vitz found that many history texts failed to mention Reverend Martin Luther King's religious commitment as a civil rights leader. In one social studies book, thirty pages were devoted to discussing the Pilgrims without once mentioning religion. Vitz concluded:

Serious Judeo-Christian motivation is featured nowhere. References to Christianity or Judaism are rare and generally superficial. Protestantism is almost entirely excluded, at least for whites. In contrast, primitive and pagan religions, as well as magic, get

considerable emphasis. Patriotism is close to nonexistent in the sample. Likewise, any appreciation of business success is grossly unrepresented. Traditional roles for both men and women receive virtually no support, but feminist portrayals regularly show women engaged in activities indistinguishable from those of men. Finally, clear attacks on traditional sex roles, especially traditional concepts of manhood, are common.[21]

Meanwhile, People for the American Way mounted its own textbook review and reached a similar, if much more moderate, conclusion: "The texts too often are static descriptions of dynamic processes, ignoring questions of belief and value at the heart of people's 'lives and fortunes and sacred honor.' "[22] At an April 1987 conference on "Values, Pluralism and Public Education" sponsored by People for the American Way, the organization's founder, Norman Lear, spoke eloquently about the need to inculcate values, many of them shared with religion, in public schools. Essentially, the conference attempted to coopt the conservatives' original outcry against what Richard Marquand in the *Christian Science Monitor* called, "the often pallid condition of moral and ethical instruction in schools."[23]

In early April 1987, federal district judge William Brevard Hand ruled in favor of the Mobile parents—asserting that secular humanism is indeed a religion—and banned forty-five textbooks in Alabama's largest school district. School officials elsewhere in the state hesitated, as the decision was immediately appealed (but eventually overturned), but in Mobile, at least, the school system began collecting the textbooks.

Ironically, in the original 1961 *Torcaso* vs. *Watkins* case, it served the interests of humanists for secular humanism to be recognized as a nontheistic alternative religion. In Alabama, as sociologist James Hunter points out, humanists wanted it the other way as well. In his opinion, "Current efforts to redefine Humanism as something other than religion should be viewed with a measure of skepticism."

Just four months earlier, in a similar case in Greenville, Tennessee, conservative Christian parents objected to their children being exposed in public schools to such things as Roman Catholicism, the Renaissance, Shakespeare, and the Wizard of Oz—all influences, the parents claimed, of secular humanism and paganism. The federal dis-

trict judge ruled in their favor, awarding the parents $50,521.29 for expenses they incurred in placing their children in other schools.

Author Tim LaHaye defines humanism as "man's attempt to solve his problems independently of God."[24] John Whitehead says humanism is the idea that men and women can "begin from themselves" without reference to the Bible and can derive by reason alone standards to judge all matters.[25]

Whitehead and Conlan draw heavily upon two documents known as the *Humanist Manifestos I & II* to prove the existence of this nontheistic religion. The first *Manifesto* was released in 1933 and bore the signatures of eleven prominent educators, including John Dewey and Harry Elmer Barnes. The group's spokesperson was John H. Dietrich, a Unitarian minister from Minneapolis.[26] Theirs was a pragmatic philosophy, as reflected in the following statement from the *Manifesto*:

We find insufficient evidence for belief in the existence of the supernatural . . . as nontheists we begin with man not God . . . no deity will save us; we must save ourselves.[27]

The American Humanist Association was organized in 1941 and has traditionally drawn its leadership from the Unitarian-Universalist church, while remaining organizationally distinct. Its updated *Manifesto*, published in 1973, received little attention until it became the object of scrutiny by the New Christian Right.

The American Humanist Association's periodical, *The Humanist*, had a circulation of 17,000 in 1986.[28] Given that most periodicals have somewhere between a few hundred and a few thousand library subscriptions, organizational memberships are usually somewhat smaller than the circulation of their publications. By any measure, the AHA can hardly be considered a very large organization, nor is it a particularly visible or active group.

But according to the New Christian Right, this is the organization that has quietly infiltrated key institutions and effectively taken over America.

Writes Tim LaHaye in *The Battle for the Mind*:

Much of the evils in the world today can be traced to humanism, which has taken over our government, the UN, education, TV, and most of the other influential things of life.[29]

Tim LaHaye is not well recognized outside evangelical circles, but evangelicals know him well. Among other things, he is a prolific writer with approximately two dozen books to his credit. The *New York Times* and other publications that take note of best-sellers don't include the sales of Christian books in their listings; if they did, Christian books would predominate. As it is, the Christian book market is a subterranean one, but it is very big. And Tim LaHaye's name is never absent from the Christian Booksellers Association's best-seller list for very long.

One of LaHaye's big blockbusters was *The Battle for the Mind*. Published in 1980, just as the New Christian Right was first receiving national attention in the secular media, it popularized and detailed how secular humanism has penetrated and taken over American culture. LaHaye followed up with *The Battle for the Family* in 1982 and *The Battle for the Public Schools* in 1983.

In 1984 LaHaye moved his operations from Southern California to Washington, D.C. From an office with an impressive panoramic view of the U.S. Capitol, LaHaye runs the American Coalition for Traditional Values (ACTV), which seeks to engage Christians in the electoral process and to work for the reestablishment of traditional values as public policy. On the executive committee and board of ACTV are such prominent televangelists as Jimmy Swaggart, Jim Bakker, Kenneth Copeland, Jerry Falwell, Rex Humbard, D. James Kennedy, James Robison, Charles Stanley, and Jack Van Impe.

Down the hall, LaHaye's wife and frequent collaborator, Beverly LaHaye, heads a new organization called Concerned Women for America (CWA), which approaches public policy from a conservative woman's perspective. The LaHayes claim that CWA is the largest women's organization in America, with twice as many members as the National Organization for Women (NOW). In all probability, CWA's numerical claims are, like Jerry Falwell's, to a certain extent illusory, but there can be little question about the LaHayes' central role in warning evangelicals of the dangers of secular humanism.

Sociologist Donald Heinz's analysis of what evangelicals mean by

the term comes up with two basic tenets. First, humanism rejects any supernatural conception of the universe; there is no reality beyond this life. Second, humanism affirms "that ethical values are human and have no meaning independent of human experience." He adds that "secular humanism is characterized by godlessness, moral relativism, and permissiveness regarding decency issues."[30]

Humanism, in other words, is the absence of God, or of truths revealed in His Word, not only in institutions such as schools or government but also in individuals' daily lives. It is believing that we are accountable for our actions only to each other. It is believing that all truth is relative. For this reason, Mel and Norma Gabler, the fundamentalist textbook watchdogs in Longview, Texas, whose Educational Research Analysts organization has given that state's education officials so many headaches, oppose New Math. That some integers could have infinite or nonabsolute values is a potentially dangerous notion for a child reared in a home of religious absolutes.

Where did humanism come from? The answer depends on how far back in history you want to go. Herbert Schlossberg finds the danger of humanism first appearing in Genesis, with the serpent who tempted Eve to eat the forbidden fruit by telling her it would give her knowledge and power equal to that of God.[31] It promised her that she "would be wise apart from God." Like pride, the Fall was really a form of self-worship.

Some evangelical writers trace the roots of humanism to such medieval philosophers as Thomas Aquinas or Francis Bacon. Others start with the Renaissance, when Europeans began to rediscover classical (i.e., pagan) writers. Others focus on a *Who's Who* of more recent thinkers, such as Descartes, Locke, Voltaire, Comte, and Rousseau. Still others implicate modern theologians such as Reinhold Niebuhr or intellectuals such as Aldous Huxley.

Evangelicals are also capable of seeing one continuous pattern stretching from the Creation to today. Tim LaHaye reminds his readers that Michelangelo's statue of David is a prime example of humanism. He believes the glorification of the body is contrary to God's command that Adam and Eve wear skins. "Ever since," LaHaye says,

. . . there has been a conflict concerning clothes with man demanding the freedom to go naked. The Renaissance obsession

with nude "art forms" was the forerunner of the modern humanist's demand for pornography in the name of freedom.[32]

Regardless of its origins, the concept of secular humanism is critical
to the emerging cultural revolution. It explains how America came to
be in its present predicament, and how it can get out. It defines the
enemy, and suggests how the enemy should be confronted. Humanism
is the liberal, secular drift that has characterized mainstream culture
in the twentieth century and permeated its institutions. It is found in
the public schools, the courts, television, movies, theatre, and literature. The secular culture takes it for granted, and this incenses evangelicals. Writes Richard John Neuhaus, "They feel that they were not
consulted by whoever decided that this is a secular society. And they
resent that; they resent it very much."[33]

Some evangelicals see humanism as a grand conspiracy. The *Humanist Manifestos* and the American Humanist Association are only
the tip of a gigantic iceberg, according to Tim LaHaye:

> Almost every major magazine, newspaper, TV network, secular
> book publisher, and movie producer is a committed humanist,
> surrounding himself with editors and newscasters who share his
> philosophy and seldom permit anything to be presented that con-
> tradicts humanism, unless forced to by community pressure.[34]

With humanism's stranglehold on public education, it is no wonder
that mass media and government, both local and national, have systematically excluded Bible-believing Christians from exposure and
decision-making. LaHaye claims there are about 275,000 humanists
today in the United States, including most politicians and media opin-
ion-shapers. Since World War II, he estimates, approximately 600
humanists in Congress, the State Department, and the presidential
cabinets have molded our country's policies along atheistic, materi-
alistic lines.

Many humanists, LaHaye maintains, are socialists at heart and hope
that the country will ultimately become part of "one-world" government. He questions their patriotism: "All committed humanists are
one-worlders first and Americans second."[35] And he contends that they

promote a bloated federal bureaucracy: "Humanists have a running romance with big government."[36]

LaHaye's solution begins at the ballot box. Evangelicals must go to the polls, with their ministers in the lead, to vote humanists out of public office and elect Bible-believers. He argues:

> No humanist is qualified to hold any governmental office in America—United States senator, congressman, cabinet member, State Department employee, or any other position that requires him to think in the best interest of America. . . . The major problems of our day—moral, educational, economical, and governmental—are primarily caused by the fact that over 50 percent of our legislators are either committed humanists or are severely influenced in their thinking by false theories of humanism.[37]

More sophisticated attacks on humanism do not attempt to estimate the number of humanists residing on the Potomac or to stress a conspiratorial mindset. But, like Tim LaHaye, many evangelicals have a profound sense that secular humanism—whether through the Supreme Court or other agencies—has managed to pervert the First Amendment, completely separating God from government, the schools, even medical decisions about who shall live and who shall die. The Founding Fathers, they believe, never intended the strict church-state separation we now have. Some, such as Thomas Jefferson, were deists; others, such as Benjamin Franklin, may have had scandalous private lives. But one thing they assuredly were not was humanist.

The danger of the humanist separation may be the state's totalitarian hand in our every affair, as John Whitehead argues. Or it may be "the naked public square," in which there is no consensus on the basis for civic morality. Warns Neuhaus, "When recognizable religion is excluded, the vacuum will be filled by ersatz religion, by religion bootlegged into public space under other names."[38] Demagoguery, fascism, cults—these are some of the unpleasant possibilities Neuhaus contemplates for our nation.

The cultural revolution that is unfolding in America is fueled by anger and fear. Conservative Christians are angry that a liberal, secular, humanist philosophy has made them a dispossessed people in their own country. Worse than being attacked by mainstream insti-

tutions, they have been ignored. And they are fearful of very real social problems for which the liberal powers-that-be don't seem to have any workable solutions.

That is why evangelicals responded when religion met up with the most powerful communications medium in history. That is why the marriage of evangelical Christianity and politics is not a passing fad, as some commentators would have us think. "What may well emerge in the years to come," says liberal radical Jeremy Rifkin, "is nothing short of a second Protestant reformation, one that may have as powerful an effect on the world as the first."[39]

5

The Other Americans

Millions of Americans have for a long time felt put upon.
Theirs is a powerful resentment against values that they
believe have been imposed upon them, and an equally
powerful sense of outrage at the suggestion that they are
the ones who pose a threat to undemocratically imposing
values upon others.

—Richard John Neuhaus,
The Naked Public Square

A quarter-century ago, Michael Harrington shocked the conscience of the nation with the revelation of vast poverty in the midst of the highest standard of living the world has ever known. His book *The Other America* contrasted the familiar Americans of suburbia and Madison Avenue with those he said formed an invisible but nonetheless massive segment of our population.[1] The America familiar to most of us was largely middle class, comfortable, and optimistic. The other America, about which Harrington wrote, was poor and consisted of very large proportions of minorities, unskilled and migrant workers, and the aging.

Harrington's book dramatically raised our consciousness about people shut out of the American dream and the post–World War II economic miracle. Some of them were tucked away in America's rural hinterland. Most of them, by the tens of millions, were in our midst, but just far enough out of sight to be easily ignored. They were largely uneducated. In the cities, a large proportion of them were black. They were invisible because they had drifted into older, deteriorating neighborhoods left behind by Americans enjoying their rising affluence in

the suburbs. Freeways, built over and around the deteriorating ghettoes, helped keep the Other Americans out of sight.

So moved were liberals, including Presidents Kennedy and Johnson, by the discovery of this other America that they declared a war on poverty. They quickly determined that the plight of these people was not of their own making. They were victims of generations of discrimination and impersonal economic forces. The nation passed laws to prohibit discrimination against the Other Americans, and created all kinds of agencies and bureaus to administer programs to help them.

Twenty-five years after Michael Harrington's epochal book, there is a gradual awakening to the inescapable reality of yet another America. This other America is not a place so much as it is a state of mind. The "new" Other Americans are right in our midst. But until recently, they have been too timid to reveal their identities.

Whereas the inhabitants of Harrington's other America were poor, the new Other Americans span the full economic spectrum. Nevertheless, they have much in common with Harrington's underclass. They, too, have been victimized for generations by being ignored and discriminated against. Their "peculiar" beliefs and lifestyles have made them objects of scorn and mockery. For most of this century they have experienced the gradual erosion of a way of life. Of late they have begun to protest their victimization, with the result that they are victimized all the more. They are being told that they are dangerous, that they are un-American when they try to create a social milieu in which they can practice their creeds.

Who are these Other Americans?

Thanks to the secular mass media and secular intellectuals, we know them only through distorted caricatures and stereotypes, according to which they are unsophisticated, reactionary, fatalistic, antimodern, inflexible, and doctrinaire; they are mostly small-town or rural, uneducated, and aging. In practically every respect imaginable, they are distinctly marginal to mainstream American culture.

Diverse though they may be, the modern secular world has lumped them all together and given them a highly derogatory label. In short, they are the *fundamentalists*.

According to the conventional wisdom of the mainstream of American culture, these Bible-thumping fundamentalist Christians retreated into the cultural hinterland after the Scopes "monkey" trial of

1925 revealed the truth of their backward antievolutionist know-nothingism. Presumably, the fundamentalist faith of this earlier generation of simple rural folk who could not adjust to a modern world lives on in the backwaters. Shamed and shunned, they are now a shrinking remnant of outcasts from American society.

Mass media usually portray the survivors of this pathetic and archaic belief system as defensive, rigid, and fanatic. They are depicted in a sour-grapes funk, proclaiming a pox simultaneously on modern industrial society, Christianity enlightened by biblical and historical scholarship, and all higher education.

Before there was any awareness that they might be interested in politics, their dogmatic militancy was a source of amusement and snide comment. Nostalgic, unreflective throwbacks, they were hardly to be taken seriously in our high-tech society. Said one commentator in *The New Republic*, "Many of the grassroots evangelicals come out of the tradition of 19th-century small-town Midwest Republicanism and Southern Democracy that has survived unexamined and unmodified into the late 20th century."[2]

The fundamentalists, say the media pundits, are now having delusions of grandeur and they are out of touch with reality. They have no long-range view of this country's needs or interests. They are still trying to reduce evolution from science to speculation, to have the Bible taught as science, and to reintroduce prayer in the schools. They have frighteningly dangerous beliefs about the military and world conflict. Their expectation of an imminent Armageddon freezes any hope of social reform beyond their narrow religious goals and even prompts them to anticipate a miraculous rescue from any future nuclear holocaust.

They are allegedly naive in a political and organizational sense, having sat out involvement in "the real world" for generations while they clung to concerns about sin and salvation, concepts no longer relevant to a secular age. Those who have sought public office, whether as president or state representatives, in order to promote their points of view, are labeled "regressive," not progressive.

In late 1986, when Pat Robertson suggested that the U.S. Supreme Court had accumulated policymaking power that the Founding Fathers had never intended it to have, and when he said that the Court was not necessarily the final authority on law in the United States,

the press as well as liberals reacted with a mixture of guffaws (at what they assumed was a colossal gaffe) and outrage. After all, the Supreme Court has been the fount of liberal social policy for the past thirty years. But Robertson turned liberal tradition on its head and spoke for many unhappy Other Americans when, in the tradition of Thoreau, he wrote on civil disobedience:

> Whenever the civil government forbids the practice of things that God has commanded us to do, or tells us to do things He has commanded us not to do, then we are on solid ground in disobeying the government and rebelling against it.[3]

Politicians unfamiliar with people who take their religion seriously come away amazed from their encounters and fall back on stereotypes. When Kay Danks, secretary of the Texas Republican party, was defeated in her bid to become the party's vice chair in 1986, she pointed to her failure to sign a nine-point "covenant" drawn up by a conservative Christian group called the Crossroads Coalition. "They have unwavering ideas," she claimed. "They won't accept you if you have one little doubt about anything."[4]

Robertson and the Other Americans believe in a universe of absolute values, not relative principles bound by time and place. And while that may make them look fanatic or quixotic or narrow-minded in the contemporary political arena, it also makes them highly motivated, with a genuine sense of righteous indignation and purpose.

Their religious beliefs tell them that Divine Intervention is passé only if men and women choose it to be so. Otherwise, the supernatural and the miraculous are all around us, ready to be assimilated into all human affairs, including politics. To harness the power of miracles, as Robertson wrote in *The Secret Kingdom*, "You have to be involved in a personal relationship with Him—a relationship that arises from a firm commitment on your part."[5]

Many people assume that any voting clout conservative Christians may have demonstrated in recent elections was exaggerated and will be short-lived. As a political force to be reckoned with, they have had their day. They don't have what it takes to stick it out in the long run. Their presumed demographics—disproportionately Southern, blue

collar, and lower middle class, lacking much formal schooling—have been devised to type them as unsophisticated hicks.

The stereotype may be comforting to uneasy liberals, but it is dead wrong. To lump together all sorts of conservative Christians and proceed without hesitation to paint them all with the same broad brush is to miss critically important differences.

But the sad truth is that most liberal commentators and lay persons cannot recognize the distinctions among fundamentalists, charismatics, Pentecostals, or evangelicals. Nor have they knowledge of premillennialism, postmillennialism, amillennialism, and the implications of all three for social action. Most cannot properly identify the theological orientations of the stars of the video vicarage. Yet these distinctions are crucial for understanding what the various groups believe about God and the world, as well as how they respond to other religious traditions.

In a word, if the new Other Americans are to be understood, they have to be understood on their own terms—what they believe and who they are in the vast and complex social and demographic structure of America.

To be sure, the different terms for these varieties of Christians can be bewildering. Thumb through the magazine rack in a Christian bookstore and you will come across at least the following designations: fundamentalist, evangelical, neo-evangelical, conservative, moderate, Pentecostal, neo-Pentecostal, charismatic, and holiness groups. Some of these labels, like Pentecostal, refer to institutionalized traditions. Others, like fundamentalist, refer to a posture toward Scripture *and* the modern world. Still others, like born-again, are not categories used to identify a discrete biblical tradition as such.

Furthermore, almost all of the groups are very touchy about attempts to characterize or distinguish their group from others, particularly if the one doing the characterizing is an outsider. And to muddy the waters, some notable leaders, such as Jerry Falwell, may shift from one category to another, depending on who is doing the labeling. Falwell proudly calls himself a fundamentalist. Bob Jones, another fundamentalist, considers Falwell's doctrines and practices to be heretical to this tradition and has labeled him "a liberal" and "the most dangerous man in America." We ourselves would characterize Falwell

as a "neo-fundamentalist," but that is a category that has not yet entered the already confusing array of labels used to differentiate among significant traditions.

For all the confusion, it is possible to map out some very rough guidelines. A full delineation of the complex and subtle differences in usage would require a lengthy essay. Some groups and individuals adamantly disagree with these distinctions, although they have become fairly conventional among scholars of American religion.

It is often assumed that fundamentalism is a very old biblical tradition. Actually, its roots were not clearly delineated until the second decade of this century. Fundamentalism originated as a separatist movement in rebellion against late-nineteenth-century liberalism (then called modernism), which was viewed as an encroachment upon and compromise of the biblical doctrine of inerrancy. In time, the fundamentalists would become what evangelical scholar Richard Quebedeaux refers to in *The Worldly Evangelicals* as "the evangelical far right."[6] But when the movement started, it counted among its membership some of the leading intellectual and academic theologians of the day. Only gradually did they gain notoriety as a noncompromising tradition of separatism from "worldly" society.

For fundamentalists, "right doctrine" is everything. And emphasis on doctrine has led to an incredibly complex maze of variations on fundamentalism, with scores of sectarian movements. With the exception of the Southern Baptist Convention, fundamentalism is not organized along denominational lines. Rather, it consists of hundreds of independent churches, some of whom are loosely aligned with other independent fundamentalist churches. In its most extreme form of separatism, fundamentalists deny they are even evangelicals.

In the early twentieth century, almost all Protestants in America considered themselves to be evangelicals. They (1) believed in the inerrancy of Holy Scripture; (2) accepted a creationist (rather than evolutionary) explanation for the origins of the universe, earth, and mankind; (3) put their faith in Christ's crucifixion, atonement, and resurrection for salvation; and (4) believed they had a mandate—the so-called Great Commission—to take the redeeming message of Christ to all the peoples of the world.

In broad terms, this is still a fairly accurate definition of what an

evangelical is today. In this sense, *evangelical* is an umbrella term, and there are lots of groups that subscribe to these tenets. But there is serious disagreement about how wide the umbrella extends.

The self-designation of evangelical was claimed by a significant number of groups who, in the 1940s, sought to differentiate themselves from fundamentalists. Their quarrel with fundamentalism stemmed not so much from doctrinal disagreement as from a weariness with the highly combative and negative posture of most fundamentalists. The term neo-fundamentalist probably would have been a more accurate designation of their theology, but sensing the negative cultural image of fundamentalism, they chose to call themselves evangelicals. Even today, these groups do not accept the legitimacy of labeling fundamentalists as evangelicals. Nor are they happy when some liberal Protestant groups, drawing upon the historical differentiation, insist that they too are evangelical.

The holiness movement began around the turn of the century as an attempt to chart personal rectitude in the chaos and laissez-faire morality of the nation's burgeoning urban centers. Holiness groups emphasize strict personal ethics, piety, and "perfection" in the sense of an evolving personal relationship with God.

The Pentecostal movement also began in early twentieth century urban centers. Pentecostals stress experiential faith and "life in the spirit." What such faith jargon means is that these Christians try to relive in this era the original spiritual "gifts of the Holy Spirit" that the first-century Christians experienced on the Feast of Pentecost, as described in the Book of Acts. These gifts include speaking in tongues (*glossolalia*), healing, prophecy, and miracles.

Charismatics are Christians who also believe in these gifts. Until the 1960s, there was not much evidence of charismatic behavior outside of Pentecostal churches. But from the late 1960s forward, rapid growth in charismatic behavior has been witnessed in the so-called mainline denominations, such as Episcopalians and Presbyterians, as well as among Roman Catholics.

To complicate matters further, some charismatics refer to themselves as neo-Pentecostals. Generally, although not exclusively, these are people from older Pentecostal traditions—e.g., Church of God—that had gradually come to deemphasize the "gifts of the Holy Spirit."

The designation *neo* is testimony to their recovery of the traditional gifts.

Neo-charismatic, on the other hand, is the designation chosen by some Christians in mainline Protestant and Roman Catholic traditions. They are not Pentecostal, and their religious traditions have not previously accepted the "gifts of the Holy Spirit" as legitimate doctrine. While still not officially acknowledged in these traditions, it is no longer uncommon to hear glossolalia in an Episcopal or Catholic service, or to see a healing service announced in the church bulletin. According to current estimates, almost 8 million Roman Catholics and more than 6 million Protestants claim to be charismatics.

For the most part, the charismatic movement has not penetrated fundamentalism, but there are important exceptions that further muddy the conceptual waters and spur doctrinal disputes. Pat Robertson, who was ordained by the Southern Baptist Convention, is now the most visible charismatic in America.

More recently, televangelist James Robison (the fiery Texas fundamentalist who was instrumental in organizing the National Affairs Briefing that brought candidate Ronald Reagan face-to-face with fundamentalists in Dallas) has received the "gifts of the Holy Spirit." This has not gone down well with his fellow Southern Baptist colleagues, but Robison's audience showed no decline when his program switched to a charismatic format. Either he attracted a whole new audience or he has brought his old audience along with him into this new spiritual venture.

To outsiders, all of these distinctions may seem like so much nitpicking. And the shifting limits of the categories *are* somewhat bewildering. But to the believers of these distinctive traditions, the differences are critically important. Fundamentalists, for example, go beyond dismissing the "gifts of the Holy Spirit" as improper behavior for modern times; to them, speaking in tongues is positive evidence of delusions (or, worse, Satanic influence). But to the charismatic, failure to have received the "gifts of the Holy Spirit" (also referred to as "the baptism of the Holy Spirit") is evidence of inadequate spiritual nourishment.

Beyond these groups, there is a whole coterie of conservative Christians who emphasize the adult conversion experience of being "born

again" but would prefer not to get bogged down in labels. That would include a lot of Southern Baptists.

Many people take the concept *evangelical* to include all conservative Christian traditions. Given the common origins just traced, this is technically correct, although it excludes the liberal Protestant tradition. In order to cut through some of the intramural quibbling, and out of respect for the parties in question, the authors have usually maintained the distinction between evangelicals and fundamentalists, referring to the broad spectrum of conservative Christianity as "fundamentalists *and* evangelicals." But because this is awkward, on occasion the authors use the word *evangelical* alone to refer to the wide spectrum of conservative Christianity. This should be evident in context. The solo use of *fundamentalist*, however, is employed only when the authors are referring to that rather more limited group.

If the stereotypes of evangelical theology are incredibly unsophisticated, the demographic stereotypes are sadly dated. Many conservative Christians—yes, even fundamentalists—have moved into the ranks of well-paid entertainers, athletes, beauty queens, and prominent national politicians. The whole movement has expanded far beyond the rural South and the lower economic levels of society.

Such an assertion can be supported by looking at the facts. For example, Stuart Rothenberg and Frank Newport, in a 1984 survey conducted for the Washington-based Institute for Government and Politics, found that under half (45 percent) of the evangelicals they sampled nationally lived in the South. Likewise, one-third of the evangelicals were working in white-collar/nonmanual occupations.[7] In another regional study of the burgeoning Dallas–Fort Worth Metroplex in the early 1980s, University of Texas sociologists Anson Shupe and William A. Stacey found that 60 percent of supporters of the Moral Majority, a group disproportionately evangelical/fundamentalist, worked in white-collar jobs.[8]

In the area of income, evangelicals fail to live up to their lower-class stereotype. Rothenberg and Newport concluded: "There is no reason to believe that there is a major income disparity between evangelicals and the country as a whole." Only 37 percent of the evangelicals they studied had a total income *under* $20,000, and fully one-third had family incomes of at least $30,000 per year. In the

Shupe-Stacey study, 60 percent of evangelical/fundamentalist respondents had incomes *over* $30,000 per year.

Perhaps some of the most dramatic evidence of the mainstreaming of evangelical Christians is the growing proportion who have achieved some level of higher education. For example, according to University of Massachusetts sociologist Wade Clark Roof, in 1960 only 7 percent of those from the various evangelical traditions had attended college, but by the mid-1970s the proportion grew to 23 percent. No other religious group approached this dramatic change in the level of higher education during this period.[9] Rothenberg and Newport found a slight majority (61 percent) in their sample who had at least some college or a college degree, while Shupe and Stacey in their Dallas–Fort Worth study discovered an even larger majority (79 percent) of evangelicals/fundamentalists with similar education levels.

As a result of this dramatic increase in educational achievement, as well as advances in occupational prestige levels, unprecedented numbers of fundamentalist and evangelical Protestants are entering the middle class. Says Wade Clark Roof:

> . . . in large numbers they began to taste affluence, becoming middle class, Republican, suburban, and well connected in business, social, and political circles. Increasingly represented in the lower-middle echelons of American life, conservative Protestants gained entrance into the mainstream during this period and came to enjoy greater respectability, social and economic standing, and a new self-esteem.[10]

So much for being culturally marginal.

What about age? The stereotype of the group is that of embittered old conservatives out of step with the modern age. Out of step perhaps, but certainly not an aging remnant. Evangelicals and fundamentalists—not the liberal mainline groups—have the highest proportion of young adults. In mainline denominations, the percentages of total membership over age fifty-five run as high as 41 percent in the United Methodists and 43 percent in the United Church of Christ.

Various studies shatter the age myth. A national study conducted in 1978–79 by the Princeton Religious Research Center for *Chris-*

tianity Today found more than half (54 percent) of the evangelicals queried were between the ages of eighteen and fifty.[11] Shupe and Stacey in Texas found 41 percent of their evangelicals were under the age of fifty-five, while Rothenberg and Newport reported that only 17 percent of their nationally sampled evangelicals were over sixty-five.

These young adults are having children—lots of them. The fertility rate among conservative Protestant women is higher than for women in liberal denominations—because they are younger and because they *believe* in large families.

Rigidness and narrow-mindedness? Another myth. Says sociologist Roof: "Contrary to popular understanding, fundamentalist belief systems are flexible and lend themselves to rich and varied interpretations, depending on the cultural context."[12] Indeed, both fundamentalists and evangelicals have been busy doing all sorts of things they were not "supposed" to do.

For instance, Reverend Jerry Falwell, an independent Baptist, has courted Mormon groups in Utah to block undesirable legislation and squelch issues such as the Equal Rights Amendment.[13]

Mormons and Baptists? Baptists believe that Mormons are a heretical faith. For years they have been antagonists—like snake and mongoose. Writes master cult-watcher Walter Martin, ". . . Joseph Smith's religion is a polytheistic nightmare of garbled doctrines draped with the garment of Christian terminology."[14] Yet, here at the fundamentalists' initiative, they are building coalitions.

Or consider Falwell's own flexibility. During the 1960s he preached against social activism for ministers, particularly in the civil rights movement. In the late 1970s he, along with millions of fellow conservatives, reassessed the situation. Even liberals are beginning to recognize Falwell's capacity to moderate his stances and accept compromise as he has turned to a "reformist" rather than a confrontational style. The world cannot be made over in a week, and he realizes it.

Sociologist James Hunter has suggested other ways in which fundamentalists and evangelicals have adapted to modern America.[15] For one thing, most of them have toned down their traditionally harsh condemnations of Christians who are unlike themselves. They have also grown comfortable with twentieth-century materialism. Following the initiative of televangelists such as Oral Roberts, Robert Schuller,

Pat Robertson, Kenneth Copeland, and a host of clones who preach a "Gospel of Prosperity," they believe that God wants Christians to enjoy the fruits of this life, both spiritual and physical. They have allowed their faith to be "codified" into step-by-step procedures and principles packaged in classic American marketing terms. Billy Graham promoted a self-help manual on *How to Be Born Again*, Bill Bright promotes "the four spiritual laws," Oral Roberts has *A Daily Guide to Miracles*, Robert Schuller can teach you to *Discover Your Possibilities*, Kenneth Copeland can clue you in on *The Laws of Prosperity*, and Pat Robertson's eight "Laws of the Kingdom" are designed to accumulate wealth and happiness in this life as well as in the next.

Underneath it all, there may be old-time religion, but, like capitalism's finest products, faith has been updated, refined, and repackaged to give consumers the very best product that money can buy.

One might question the theological appropriateness of these developments. Certainly a number of fundamentalist-evangelical communities have done so. The liberals are angry, too. One reason is that the conservative Christians have stolen much of their stuff, and not just from Norman Vincent Peale. And when they see evangelicals translating the Gospel of Prosperity into their language, it seems trite and superficial.

On the whole, the evangelical is much more appropriately characterized by a willingness to explore, enthusiasm for learning, and openness to change than the traditional stereotype of a closed-minded ideologue. This trend has given rise to an enormous growth industry of Christian sex manuals, Christian financial guides, Christian soap operas, and Christian bumper stickers; a gigantic market for popular Christian music; and even a Christian amusement park at PTL's Heritage Village, USA. Inflexible dogmatism is fading from the scene, and evangelicals and fundamentalists are increasingly open to new ideas.

Labels of antimodern and unsophisticated also fail to pass muster. One of the foremost qualities of the new fundamentalists and evangelicals is their astute mastery of electronic communications, the latest in organizational and political strategies (including lobbying, political action committees, and think tanks), and the psychology of fund-raising and mobilization of followers. Their leaders, in three-piece suits and elaborate coiffures, are as comfortable before the television cameras

as in air-conditioned churches with stereophonic sound systems. The electric church itself is testimony to the fact that fundamentalists and evangelicals are creatures of *this* era.

Nor are they nearly as extremist as portrayed. Various national and regional polls conducted during the early 1980s consistently found that only small percentages of the public had heard of Jerry Falwell's Moral Majority organization and supported it. Yet the statistics also showed that the majority of noncommitted or neutral respondents were in agreement on issues such as prayer in schools, pornography, drugs, homosexuality, and declining academic performance. When it comes down to the controversial issues, many Americans have more in common with Jerry Falwell than with Norman Lear and his People for the American Way. We'll see the evidence of this later.

Finally, the reality of the fundamentalists' and evangelicals' numerical strength and significance in modern American culture makes short work of the myth that they are a tiny but vocal remnant of a rear-guard movement eventually destined to wither away. This underestimation is perhaps the greatest mistake of liberal commentators.

Never mind that in 1976, when James Earl Carter, a born-again Christian, became president of the United States, both *Time* and *Newsweek* declared it the Year of the Evangelical;

Or that religious autobiographies, such as Charles Colson's *Born Again*, were best-sellers in the secular trade market;

Or that in 1980 Billy Graham's newspaper, *Decision*, topped 24 million in circulation;

Or that there are more than 1,370 religious radio stations; 221 religious television stations; three major religious television networks broadcasting seven days a week, twenty-four hours a day; and perhaps a dozen other television networks struggling to get a foothold in the marketplace;

Or that every month 16 million people watch Pat Robertson's "700 Club" and more than 35 million see one or more of the top ten syndicated religious programs;

Or that evangelical *Christianity Today*'s subscribers outnumber liberal *Christian Century*'s subscribers five to one;

Or that according to the Evangelical Christian Publishers Association the 37 million buyers of Christian books made up a huge, billion-

dollar consumer group—more than 20 percent of the entire book-buying public in one year;

Or that Hal Lindsey's 1970 prophecy book, *The Late Great Planet Earth*, selling over 30,000 copies a month for years, may be the non-fiction best-seller of all time—next to the Bible;

Or that the number of Americans who considered themselves born-again evangelicals exploded from 30 million in 1980 to 35 million in 1986, according to a Gallup poll that year;

Or that 16,000 private Christian academies, opening at a rate of one per day, have developed into a $2 billion-per-year industry in this country.[16]

Or that . . . the list goes on and on. The point is simple: The media took bemused note that populist President Jimmy Carter, a Southern Baptist, called himself an evangelical, but they treated it as an inconsequential fact.

The time for such misinterpretation is long past. The Other Americans know who they are, even if others do not. They rankle at distortions of their intentions and qualifications, but they are not put off. They have tasted organizational and even political success and they believe they can achieve more.

This is the crucial difference between *these* Other Americans and the deprived multitude about which Michael Harrington wrote. The banners for the War on Poverty during the 1960s were flown by liberals on behalf of the poor. The victims were not expected to fight the battles. And the critics may well be right that one reason the massive amounts of money poured into social programs did so little good was that it had to trickle down through such an immense bureaucracy that proportionately little of it reached the poor directly.

The "new" Other Americans, on the other hand, are ready to do their own fighting. This war is theirs, not one conceived for them by well-meaning third parties, its active support coming from bottom up, not top down. Unlike the War on Poverty, which was couched mainly in secular moral language, this new war, or cultural revolution, is understood in sacred terms. It is not distributive justice that is at stake but Divine Providence.

Part of this new Christian activism has been achieved by adopting a fresh interpretation of Scripture. For instance, Pat Robertson tells

readers of *Answers to 200 of Life's Most Probing Questions* that "Cae-
sar" means something different in American democracy than it did
during the days of the Roman Empire:

> In our society, Caesar is all the people. When we are told to
> render to Caesar what belongs to Caesar, that means we ourselves
> should be responsible for government. Therefore, we owe the
> obligation of serving in public office, of being informed citizens,
> of voting, and of being active in politics at all levels. That is part
> of the duty we render to Caesar. [17]

This activism is more than standard good citizenship; it is a moral
imperative. Robertson goes on:

> . . . in a country such as America, where there is waste of mam-
> moth proportions, and when money is being used for programs
> that are abhorrent to Christians, the Christian should do every-
> thing he can to bring about change and reform. He must help to
> curtail the excessive spending of government, the growth of gov-
> ernment, the profligate nature of government; and he must pro-
> test the improper use of his money. [18]

In 1975 renowned sociologist Robert Bellah published a book called
The Broken Covenant, [19] written especially to coincide with America's
bicentennial. It was not the kind of book expected to capture the
imagination of American sociologists, preoccupied as they are with
empirical measurement. It was an ethical-moral treatise on American
history, and, from the outset, highly controversial among sociologists,
who questioned that the book had anything at all to do with sociology.
Many were thus surprised when *The Broken Covenant* won the So-
rokin Award, the highest honor bestowed by the American Sociological
Association for scholarly achievement.

Bellah argued that America's concept of itself in relation to Divine
Providence has always been a core cultural ingredient, observing that
"Biblical imagery provided the basic framework for imaginative thought
in America up until recent time and, unconsciously, its control is still
formidable." [20] Americans, according to a "civil religion" shared by all
citizens in addition to their individual denominational loyalties, are a

chosen people, holding a special covenant with God. The terms of the covenant are simple but demanding: righteousness and faithfulness in return for God's blessing.

This sense of covenant and special mission began in North America before there was even a United States. It is commonly recognized by historians that the American Revolution, with its radical assumption that "all men are created equal" and "endowed . . . with certain unalienable rights," was a secular expression of religious values drawn from the early religious eighteenth-century transformation called the Great Awakening. Later, the struggle over the slavery question and the religious zeal both North and South brought to their causes had to be worked out on the bloody battlefields of the Civil War. Both ordeals demonstrated that the idea of covenant entailed periodic rebirth, a painful process resolved only by major conflagration and conflict.

Bellah's thesis was that Americans' sense of covenant had again been called into question, our lack of moorings in civil religion leaving the nation confused and disheartened. The broken covenant would have to be reworked carefully to avoid the civil strife that characterized the first two revisions.

Bellah's picture of American society was grim. "Today," he wrote, "the American civil religion is an empty and broken shell." Society has drifted dangerously toward the "edge of the abyss. . . . We certainly need a new 'Great Awakening.' " Wrote Bellah:

> The inward reform of conversion, the renewal of an inward covenant among the remnant that remains faithful to the hope for rebirth, is more necessary than it has ever been in America. The great experiment may fail utterly, and such failure will have dark consequences not only for Americans but for all the world.[21]

Harvard-educated Bellah sensed that America was passing from the hands of the liberal establishment, and he feared chaos was the alternative. His solution was for liberals not to abandon their critical humanist tradition but, rather, to recover it with a sense of renewed idealism:

No one has changed a great nation without appealing to its soul, without stimulating a national idealism, as even those who call themselves materialists have discovered. Culture is the key to revolution; religion is the key to culture.[22]

Bellah became an enormously popular speaker among liberal Protestants, who found his vision of recovering our religious heritage and forging new concepts of liberty and freedom quite compatible.

Yet, writing from the vantage point of disillusioned academic liberalism in the mid-1970s (post–Vietnam, post–War on Poverty, post–Watergate), Bellah did not see the profound cultural transformation stirring among the religious "outs" of his day, i.e., the fundamentalists, the charismatics, the Pentecostals, and the evangelicals who composed the Other Americans. He ignored the rich religious ferment that had gone on elsewhere for the previous fifty years.

Bellah lamented the collapse of the *liberal* version of covenant, mistaking it for the version held by all Americans. Contrast Bellah's sense of a "broken covenant" with the ebullient, optimistic rhetoric of Pat Robertson, Jerry Falwell, and Bill Bright. Whose sense of covenant is an "empty shell"? Not theirs!

In fact, for many Americans, God's covenant with the nation was (and is) not only alive and well but strengthened during the two Reagan administrations and the ascendancy of the New Christian Right. True, it is a reworked understanding of covenant. Modern interpreters have had to adjust it in order to address issues such as abortion, which never existed for the first generation of Americans. But the covenant is resilient. It lives!

Just how aware Bellah may have been of the emergence of a New Christian Right while he was writing *The Broken Covenant* is not clear. He did warn "critical Americans" not to leave idealism in the hands of the chauvinists, but one must resort to conjecture as to what he meant.

A decade later, Bellah published another major work, entitled *Habits of the Heart*[23], which he considers his most important to date. In collaboration with four junior colleagues, Bellah searches for a core of commitment to community and finds only "cancerous" individualism. America has lost her way, Bellah concludes. Her people still believe in God, but their liberal faith impels no public duty.

Bellah's analysis of the origins of the nation's covenant may be right on target. But he seems to miss what was already beginning to unfold in earnest by the bicentennial.

A new covenant was being forged, but liberals were not the architects of the new vision.

In the fall of 1986, shortly after Pat Robertson announced that he would seek the Republican nomination for the presidency if he received the signatures of 3 million people pledging their support for his candidacy, the Thomas Nelson publishing company released a new book by Robertson entitled *America's Dates With Destiny*.

In important ways, *America's Dates With Destiny* can be viewed as a conservative answer to Bellah's *Broken Covenant*. Robertson takes his reader on a journey through American history, focusing on critical dates and incidents that served first to solidify and then to break the covenant with God.

Like Bellah, Robertson sees a nation in conflict and poses tough questions regarding our ability to endure the troubled times ahead. "America stands at the crossroads," he writes:

> . . . either we will return to the moral integrity and original dreams of the founders of this nation . . . or we will give ourselves over more and more to hedonism, to all forms of destructive anti-social behavior, to political apathy, and ultimately to the forces of anarchy and disintegration that have throughout history gripped great empires and nations in their tragic and declining years.[24]

But in Robertson's vision, America is beginning to find her way again. *America's Dates With Destiny* is upbeat and optimistic. A postscript is addressed to his fellow evangelical Christians:

> As has been the case throughout the nation's political history, a tiny minority working faithfully in each precinct usually determines the nation's political platforms and party candidates. That tiny minority could be reshaped by evangelical Christian volunteers and our allies, with lasting positive results for the nation.[25]

Robertson and others seem to perceive an emerging unity among conservative Christians. Assuming, for the moment, that this is so,

what explains the "new ecumenism" among conservative Christians? What lowered the onetime barriers among them that caused infighting more venomous than any railings directed against non-Christians? What has united them as allies?

Some argue that just as evangelicals and other conservatives have recently rediscovered the sense of social and political responsibility that was part of their religious heritage, so have they rediscovered their cooperative ecumenical spirit of 150 years ago. During the first half of the nineteenth century, enthusiasm over evangelism and social reform produced a variety of interdenominational missionary and Bible tract societies. The different churches were perceived as separate variations on a basic agreed-upon core of biblical beliefs. Evangelical Christians saw (or thought they saw) a religious canopy above them that transcended sectarian differences.

Historians tell us that this notion was necessary to prevent quarreling sectarian groups from fracturing the young American Republic. Some understood it in Calvinist, others in dispensationalist, terms; but all had to accept plurality in order to preserve the fragile union of states.

As Protestantism in the early twentieth century splintered into various groups, liberal denominations were left at the helm of America's cultural mainstream. In 1908, liberal Protestants established the Federal Council of Churches. While the fundamentalists sought to stake out a rear-guard position and then proceeded to quibble over just who was doctrinally fit to be included in the fold, liberals relaxed their boundaries and proceeded with such crusades as the reform-centered Social Gospel and accommodation to modern society.

In most cases, however, the ecumenism of liberals in the twentieth century was due to a de-emphasis on theological dogma. Specifically traditional beliefs, in other words—whether the literal virginity of Jesus's mother, Mary, or the historical reality of Christ's miracles— no longer seemed worth a quarrel.

At the same time, evangelical Protestants were moving toward their own brand of ecumenism. While they also had to accept a certain relaxation of doctrinaire dogma, they never approached the theological laissez-faire of liberals.

These two "ecumenisms"—liberal and evangelical—can best be

understood as having quite different aims. Sociologist James Hunter has astutely observed that the ecumenism of liberal mainline denominations has sought church unity—that is, actual merger of separate organizations into conglomerates such as the United Methodist Church in 1968, the United Church of Christ in 1961, and fusions of Presbyterian and Lutheran bodies. Alternatively, evangelical ecumenism does not pursue any unity of organizations or bureaucracies. Instead, their ecumenism is project-oriented.[26]

Hunter also notes that it is not technically a "new" movement. The "projects" of evangelicals are vast and span many decades: publishing, missionary activities, broadcasting, charities, education at every level (primary, secondary, and higher education), and campus ministries, to name just a few.

In recent years they have come together to form special-interest groups primarily aimed at redressing what they perceive as declining morals in America. It is this development that has led them to agree, at least for the time being, to ignore their doctrinal differences and unite as allies seeking a common purpose: the realignment of the moral character of American public policy as well as the piety of individuals.

Their truce may be temporary, allowing them, in Jerry Falwell's words, to work together now so that they can fight among themselves later. But there has been a growing realization among most conservative Christians that if they do not close ranks and pull together to resist the encroachment of secular humanism, they will as individuals and as a sector of society be overrun and rendered powerless.

Theirs is a struggle for the survival of an endangered way of life even as it is a search for a new vision, a new way of coming to grips with problems that confront all of America.

Why has this consciousness of common interests arisen only in the past few decades? Why did it not develop sixty years ago when the threat of *modernism*, with all the secular and irreligious implications of that term, confronted them?

One answer is that the evangelical ecumenical movement *did* begin earlier. Youth for Christ, for example, was founded in the 1940s. The Billy Graham Evangelistic Association, the founding and expansion of evangelical colleges, and the National Association of Evangelicals—all

are important manifestations of ecumenical cooperation dating back
nearly a half-century.

But the other answer, the answer that accounts for the tremendous
surge of evangelical consciousness into the public arena of modern
American culture, is to be found in the power of televangelism and
the electric parachurches. All of the broadcasters have developed projects and made public appearances that have brought together peoples
previously separated by sectarian differences and have contributed to
the perception that those differences are not as important as many
once believed. Religious broadcasting has served as the crucible in
which grievances and common causes have crystallized.

Perhaps even more important, the National Religious Broadcasters
organization has provided a forum for dialogue and cooperation among
the broadcasters. They understand that NRB was instrumental in their
struggle against the liberal denominations for access to the airwaves.
They know that together presidents and senators and congressmen
and Federal Communications commissioners will come and talk with
them, while as individuals they would be lost in the crowd of lobbyists
in Washington.

Pat Robertson appreciates the wide range of differences among evangelicals and fundamentalists, yet he also knows they can be mobilized
effectively so that their actions have a combined impact. In the postscript to *America's Dates With Destiny*, Robertson describes them:

> Their biblical translations vary. They celebrate the Lord's Supper
> in dozens of different ways. They are scattered across the nation
> in great cities and tiny villages. They represent an amazing cross
> section of the total American culture and experience. And al-
> though these evangelicals love each other as their Lord com-
> manded, they remain independent from each other in a thousand
> different ways. Evangelicals are not one uniform, homogenized
> group as their critics fear. . . . But in recent months evangelicals
> are finding themselves more and more united in their concern
> for the nation's spiritual and political renewal. . . . They have
> rediscovered the central significance and ultimate necessity of
> spiritual renewal to this nation's strength, and they are committed
> to a speedy and wholehearted return by America to her Judeo-
> Christian heritage.[27]

And in a section addressed especially *to* evangelicals, Robertson added:

I have addressed your conventions, your rallies, and your citywide meetings. I am excited about your new commitment to the nation's spiritual and political renewal. You are coming to life as a political force, and already you are making a difference.[28]

6

Legitimizing the Movement

The New Englanders are a People of God Settled in those which were once the Devil's Territories, and it may easily be supposed that the Devil was exceedingly disturbed when he perceived such a People here accomplishing the Promise of old made unto our Blessed Jesus, That He should have the Utmost parts of the Earth for his possession.

—Cotton Mather (1692)

The "big picture" of evangelicals-and-fundamentalists-turned-political cannot start with the Washington for Jesus rally in 1980 or the Moral Majority in 1979. Most journalists and commentators make that mistake. They stop short of looking beyond the immediate scene to answer the question: Where did all this activism come from?

The fact is that the roots of the cultural revolution now underway, including televangelism, are sunk deep in the history of belief, specifically the belief that America is a special nation holding a covenant with God, with dominion as the payoff for faithfully honoring it.

The American quest for dominion actually began in another land across the ocean, in the hands of the English Puritans. The Puritan "Awakening" during the early 1600s was a movement aimed at "purifying" and reforming the Church of England.

But, as often happens in history, within a generation the Puritans had become more revolutionaries than reformers within their own society. They held the heretical view that the Bible alone was absolutely authoritative, an assumption that potentially undermined im-

portant customs and traditions of the Anglican Church. What they found in the Bible was even more heretical still. They believed that an individual could communicate directly with God and that the power of the Almighty could transform the hearts of individuals.

This doctrine "privatized" religion, making it a personal matter between the individual and God. The authority of any religious leader or church lost ground because, in the final analysis, only the individual could say what claims God made on his or her behavior. The impact of this was not sudden but, over the long haul, it has been the most radical doctrinal transformation in the history of Christendom. Indeed, the effects of the privatization of faith are still unfolding.

The Puritans also believed in the possibility of radical social transformation and the creation of God's Kingdom on Earth.[1] They were stern Calvinists, believing that some among them were "saints" exclusively predestined by God for salvation. Worldly success accrued to those who enjoyed the blessed status of being foreordained for the Kingdom of God. They viewed thrift, diligence, and hard work as virtues; by practicing them, they frequently *did* prosper.

These budding capitalists were mavericks in a society yet to emerge fully from an older economic and spiritual order of things. The English Crown was politically unstable and increasingly intolerant of this growing, influential set of misfits. So, fleeing persecution or the threat of persecution, the Puritans found their way to North America in great numbers.

By 1640, approximately 60,000 Puritans had settled in the colonies, principally in New England but also southward along the Eastern Seaboard. Such a large influx had a profound influence on these fragile societies. By virtue of sheer numbers as well as aggressive beliefs, the Puritans overran other religious perspectives and made millennial Calvinism the dominant theology in the colonies for nearly a century. They gave the new land its core culture, with the idea of a special covenant with God at its heart.[2] They also contributed a value that would have enduring importance for later generations of Americans: freedom of conscience and the separation of church and state.

In tracing the story of God's covenant with America, the concept of awakening is critical. For awakenings are signposts of Americans' repeated attempts to rework their understanding of the covenant—to make it "fit" their circumstances—and the terms under which they

must live up to it. Revivals merely reach the already converted, re-committing individual souls but breaking little new ground outside a narrow spiritual community. Awakenings, on the other hand, reshape whole civilizations and alter history. They touch great numbers, chang-ing their most fundamental understanding of culture and their visions of where society is, or should be, headed. Revivals last a specified length of time; awakenings may take a generation or more to work themselves out.

In the mid-1700s the colonies experienced what historians call the First Great Awakening, a phenomenon that not only revised the entire notion of covenant that the Puritans had transplanted here, but also created the necessary cultural foundation for the American Revolution a generation later.

By the early 1700s the colonies had lost much of their religious vitality. This was an era when church membership was definitely a matter of social class, when wealthier families owned private pews toward the front of the church while their poorer brethren sat or had to stand in the back. These churches conducted a staid, reserved, formal style of worship, fine for the refined but inappropriate for the common man and those who lived farther inland on the expanding frontier.

Most urban dwellers did *not* belong to these upper-class congre-gations. In fact, historians estimate only about 4 percent of the colonial population was churchgoing. Many living on farms simply had no church within reachable distance. In short, a very significant propor-tion of the population, regardless of their tastes or perceived religious needs, went unchurched.

What precipitated the awakening was the arrival in 1739 of dynamic British evangelist George Whitefield. An Anglican-turned-Methodist, Whitefield captivated audiences with his charismatic, energetic preach-ing style. More important than his style, however, was his message. Whitefield preached Arminianism, the belief in human reason and free will to choose the grace of redemption offered by Christ, rather than predestination.

Other notable clergymen, among them Jonathan Edwards, quickly adopted the idea that no one was either irrevocably damned to hell or guaranteed salvation. Many older Puritan and Congregational

churches regarded the emotional, "evangelical" preachers with contempt and horror, but their influence spread like wildfire nonetheless.
From New England to Georgia, thousands converted to this "new
light" on the Gospel message.

There were good reasons for its popularity. In many ways the "new
light" was a message whose time had come. It had gradually become
apparent to many that predestination simply was not compatible with
the vast opportunities of the frontier. Glum Calvinist fatalism rang a
hollow note in the middle of the burgeoning, energetic environment
of the prospering colonies.

Part of the problem with the doctrine of predestination was its
pessimistic *premillennialism.*

Millennialism generally refers to the expectation that Christ will
return (soon or at some future time) to battle the forces of Satan at
Armageddon, rule the world for a thousand years, and hold a final
judgment of all souls. Premillennialists believe that this world is hope-
lessly corrupt and depraved beyond redemption, so that only Christ's
imminent return can rescue it from Satan's clutches. Postmillennialists, alternatively, believe that Christians must create a foundation or
early transformation *before* Christ can return to rule for the millennium.

Arminianism, on the other hand, was quite comfortable with its
secular counterpart of opportunity and achievement. Dominion and
empire-building struck many as closely tied to individualism and egalitarianism. The Puritans may have first kindled the thought that the
Kingdom of God could actually be built on the North American continent, but they had no monopoly on it.

The First Great Awakening reshaped religious values and ideas not
simply because its dynamic preachers appealed to less-educated colonists. More important, this cultural transformation democratized the
Puritans' old exclusionary covenant, and in so doing it wiped away
assumptions about predestination. Dominion became the promise for
all who would enter into a righteous covenant with God, not just for
some members of some sects.

The awakening had dimensions beyond religion. It created the conditions for nation-building and political revolution in two ways. First,
the awakening offered the colonies a new set of values and hopes that

rose above any local boundaries or religious groups. George White-field's ecumenical message would give the young Republic an important source of cultural unity to transcend regional differences.[3]

Second, the personal conversion experience had important political spillover. Historian R. C. Gordon-McCutchan calls this "the irony of evangelical history," that men and women trying to cope with personal or spiritual problems by turning to an "inner" religion of personal transformation can be led to engage in social upheaval and revolution. The "rebirth" of conversion loosens their ties to the older order; indeed, new spirituality may even alienate them from it. Intense religious experiences often prime people for other changes as well.[4]

In fact, the optimism and sense of empowerment that the First Great Awakening brought to many individuals eventually created a sense of postmillennial destiny, a feeling that improvement was possible, not just of individuals but even of society. It was heady stuff. Suddenly the tables turned. The covenant now rested on the efforts of Americans and no longer on a passive, predestined elect.

Man's obligations to the Deity, in covenant terms, were rethought. Now they called him to reach out into the world—to build a better society, to resist evil, to overthrow tyranny. This theological idea—that men and women were the masters of their own fates—is probably the most important and yet underappreciated idea in American history.

Thus, the secular consequence of the First Great Awakening was the creation of a new political philosophy that became the basis for legitimizing the young Republic. But make no mistake: While these values were ecumenical and nondenominational, they were never secular. They emerged in an overtly biblical context. In the Arminian scheme of things, God's Providence may have included all Americans, but it was still His. Even with the First Amendment's formal neutrality in not "establishing" any particular religion, there was a popular consensus that the Republic rested on a divinely based, Old Testament–style covenant. Despite its growing tolerance of diverse religious faiths, writes historian Paul Johnson, America embraced religious freedom "in the spirit not of secularism but of piety."[5]

The terms of the covenant, newly refashioned by the generation that fought the Revolution, promised dominion for all in return for honoring the fatherhood and authority of God. Americans emerged

from the Revolution with strengthened confidence, having beaten the mightiest empire in the world. As they began their conquest of a continent, their new understanding of covenant was both a powerful motivator and a justifier. Providence and democracy proved a powerful mixture. Together they spelled Manifest Destiny.

In the early nineteenth century, the young American nation embarked on a literal dominion quest. It had, of course, powerful economic interests pushing its boundaries ever westward. The Louisiana Purchase in 1803 opened up a vast area for exploration and settlement. Later, the Minnesota Territory offered rich farmlands and orefields. In the years to come, improved transportation and communications—particularly the transcontinental railroad and the telegraph—made economic opportunities mushroom. The continent seemed to have an unlimited capacity to absorb pioneers, homesteaders, and entrepreneurs.

And through it all, dominion served as the conscious rationale, for both the government and the public, for pacifying and settling the expanding frontier regions. Dominion excused a great many wrongs. For example, Indian resistance to being forced off tribal lands was answered by the Indian Removal Bill of 1830, a quasi-official military policy of extermination, and the vigilante activities of white pioneers. The "savages" were "in the way" of America's white, Christian destiny.

Politicians were quick to voice the Deity's support for this empire-building. Echoing Puritan clergyman Cotton Mather's sentiments from well over a century before, Senator Thomas Hart Benton claimed that it was "according to the intentions of the CREATOR" that whites had exclusive use of the land. Governor William Henry Harrison, for his part, rejected the idea that America was meant to be "the haunt of a few wretched savages, when it seems destined by the Creator to give support to a larger population."[6]

However transparently self-serving such statements seem to our modern ears, there was a powerful religious belief behind them, for in the early 1800s, and lasting until midcentury, a Second Great Awakening occurred. And this awakening was every bit as sweeping and revolutionary as its predecessor.

The Second Great Awakening came at a time when the young Republic was experiencing great strains on the fragile loyalties of its member states. There were obvious divisions of geography and eco-

nomics, such as between the industrial-mercantile North and the largely agricultural South. The two-party political system was emerging, in part from the conflict between those who wanted to preserve tax-supported state churches and those who were trying to disestablish them. There was also interreligious conflict. Despite the First Amendment's pragmatic attempt to contain such frictions, numerous sectarian groups still vied for converts and ran up against more established churches.

The Second Great Awakening began as a series of evangelical revivals in the Appalachian frontier region. Its style and message in many ways resembled those of the First Great Awakening: emotional, pietistic, millennial. And, like its predecessor, this awakening did more than simply save souls. It helped forge a sense of national direction and unity through its emphasis on covenant.

Preachers and evangelists helped bring the order and discipline of Christian ethics to a violent, often lawless frontier. But just as the conversions and camp meetings took hold because they met the needs of many unchurched rural folk, the same movement returned to the cities, where it addressed a different malaise: the sins of disorganization and national confusion about the nation's destiny. There, for example, New England preachers such as Timothy Dwight, Lyman Beecher, and Nathaniel W. Taylor delivered sermons reminding Christians of the terms of the covenant and calling for national repentance as the price for regaining dominion. Young lawyer Charles Grandison Finney underwent a dramatic conversion experience and went on to preach to enormous crowds in the major cities of his day, including Boston, New York, and Philadelphia.

In sheer numbers, the extent of the Second Great Awakening was colossal. One estimate has it that while in 1800 only one in fifteen Americans was a church member, by 1850 one in seven belonged to a church.[7] But a more telling sign of its impact is in the resulting influence of the concept of dominion.

Preachers raised the quest for dominion to a near idolatrous level and created the creed of providential "Americanism" that still characterizes the New Christian Right. God's grace in the New World was seen as having a specific purpose: to reform and establish a Christian nation, then to evangelize the world. Americans believed themselves to be uniquely raised up for this task.

The Second Great Awakening merged a growing sense of national identity with postmillennial evangelical Christianity. The results were explosive in two ways. First, the dominion quest was carried directly from the pulpits into the streets. Those caught up in this awakening invested enormous energy in social reform as the fulfillment and extension of the Christian message. Evangelicals plunged themselves into attacking the growing problems of urban society, such as poverty and slum conditions, prostitution, family desertion and orphans, alcoholism, brutal prisons, and women's rights.

Abolition in particular became *the* crusade of many evangelical reformists. Evangelicals and evangelical institutions such as Oberlin College became leaders in the "underground railroad."

Second, the goals of dominion shifted for the first time from simply building a Christian nation on the North American continent to carrying the quest around the world. Nationalism and Christ's Great Commission to carry his message "unto all the nations of the earth" became fused. America had a mission beyond itself.

A host of benevolent societies, often interdenominational, sprang up to evangelize the world: the Home and Foreign Mission Society, founded in 1812; the American Bible Society in 1816; the African Colonization Society in 1817; and the American Tract Society in 1825. When American Indians proved less than receptive to missionaries, the latter redirected their sights and aimed for more exotic locales in Africa and the Far East.

Thus, the generation of the Second Great Awakening reworked the covenant theme once again. God's grace was still free for the choosing, but America was to be the vessel for carrying it to the world. Christians were to have dominion, and Christian America was to spread Christianity. The political and economic motives for pushing back the frontier took on a sacred meaning, variously called Manifest Destiny, Providence, or Divine Mandate. It was at once a crusade, a mission, a quest. Dominion was to be Americans' heritage as long as they observed the new terms of covenant.

It is paradoxical that the idea of covenant/dominion has been both the anchor of continuity in American culture and the agent of substantial change. The two Great Awakenings reworked Americans' understanding of their covenant with God, each time altering it to conform better to their own historical circumstances. Yet whatever the

twists and fluctuations, the core idea of covenant was always there.

Since the First Great Awakening, dominion had been closely in-
terwoven with postmillennialism. Around the beginning of the twentieth century, however, something significant happened. There appeared
a rent in the fabric of the covenant message, splitting it into two
competing visions—a liberal or modernist quasi-postmillennial version
and a conservative premillennial version.

The first version of covenant hearkened to the reformist optimism
of the nineteenth century as well as the liberal tradition of the eighteenth-century Enlightenment in Europe. The second version was the
product of several factors, especially a growing pessimism about the
future and the inability of literalist Bible believers to make this world
conform to their faith.

Evangelicals were split into these two broad camps for years to
come. In the process there was a critical, though not fatal, dampening
of enthusiasm about the covenant and dominion.

A number of factors contributed to the decline in popularity of
postmillennial evangelical theology and the rise of premillennialism.
Among them were inescapable sociological forces, such as the immense
influx of non-Protestant/non-Christian/non-Anglo-Saxon immigrants and
the accompanying labor unrest, which became blurred for some with
fears of anarchists and Bolsheviks. The sheer scale of industrialization
and urbanization, with the problems of substandard housing, pollu-
tion, poverty, unemployment, and crime "overwhelmed the capabilities" of the previous era's call for private philanthropy through the
churches.[8] The social reform "naturally" flowing from personal salvation and reformation, which Charles Finney's generation had called
for, seemed discouragingly remote to many evangelicals.

Theological factors also undermined postmillennial confidence in
dominion. Science had become a prestigious, unstoppable machine
rolling over every form of superstition or resistant tradition, and many
evangelicals struggled unsuccessfully (or unconvincingly) to reconcile
scientific discoveries with a literal biblical faith. Darwin's theory of
evolution was the prime culprit. But there were also the naturalistic
sciences of psychology and psychiatry, sociology, and anthropology,
which explained the human condition quite handily without any reference to biblical Christianity, even asserting the relativity of such
religious beliefs. A new science of biblical scholarship—the so-called

"higher criticism"—that drew heavily on linguistics, archaeology, and history began to disseminate from Europe. This new school of interpretation argued against a naive, verbatim acceptance of English translations of the Bible, redefining (or even excluding) certain traditionally accepted authorships of its various books and putting miracles into symbolic and historical contexts rather than accepting them at face value.

These were some of the forces that collectively came to be termed "modernism" and that turned many evangelicals toward premillennialism.

One other significant event is critical to understanding the decline of postmillennialism among evangelicals. World War I politicized evangelicals. Some realized that not to support the war branded them as unpatriotic or even sympathetic to the enemy and gradually became its staunchest supporters. Billy Sunday was a highly visible example. Initially skeptical about America's entry into the war, he later became a complete chauvinist. Germany had fallen into decadence and barbarism because "higher criticism" of the Bible and evolutionary theory had undermined that nation's religion and culture, according to his logic. Premillennial pessimism, which had kept many of his contemporaries at arm's length from worldly affairs, was now being overshadowed by the pressing need to preserve America as a Christian bastion against the corrosion of modernism. "If you turn hell upside down," Sunday once cried, "you will find 'Made in Germany' stamped on the bottom!"[9]

"The war to end all wars" produced slaughter and destruction beyond any in human history. For some evangelicals, it made the dominion dream seem permanently out of reach. They turned instead to cryptic biblical prophecy, often within the dispensationalist scheme of John Nelson Darby, who implied that earthly reform was impossible. Only Christ's imminent return would set in motion a cleansing force of sufficient magnitude to vanquish wickedness and restore virtue to the populations of the earth. While these evangelists still paid lip service to the notion that there remained some chance Americans would repent and rededicate themselves to the principles of a "Christian nation," they held out little hope that the increasingly urbanized, diversified populace would do so any time soon.

Of course, not all evangelicals exchanged their postmillennial ex-

pectations for premillennialist pessimism and spent their remaining days decrying modernism. Instead, some embraced it, faithfully persisting in the prophetic quest for social reform that was the mandate of the Second Great Awakening—too faithfully, as they were to be accused when many of them began to believe that man, through personal effort and good works, can achieve his own salvation. These were the liberal evangelicals who followed the path known as the Social Gospel.

Social Gospel clergy and laity alike understood their role to be anti–status quo in many ways. They became champions of women, children, workers, and the underprivileged. Some Social Gospelers, notably Walter Rauschenbusch, Jesse H. Jones, and William D. P. Bliss, became so radical as to embrace socialism, claiming that Jesus and his twelve disciples were history's original Socialists. They responded to criticism by charging that some Protestant evangelicals had become narrowly preoccupied with simple soul-winning revivalism.

Many in the movement embraced the new discipline of sociology. As one scholar has observed, "Prominent among the students of the first [American] sociologists were clergy and other religionists filled with a sense of mission to reshape the social structure along the ethical lines sketched by Jesus." Not only were Social Gospelers leading authors and journal editors in the field, but at seminaries and divinity schools the Social Gospel movement was sometimes referred to as "Christian Sociology."[10]

Yet, as the premillennialists suspected, many of the Social Gospel's fellow travelers, whatever their reformist goals, were hardly committed to Christian evangelism. A study of academics conducted by psychologist James Leuba in 1914 found that only 29 percent of the sociologists in his sample even believed in God, and among the discipline's leaders only 19 percent were believers.[11]

Premillennial evangelicals identified the Social Gospelers with modernism, theological liberalism, and sometimes even anticapitalist collectivism. Social Gospelers also stood for ecumenicism at a time when many evangelicals pursued separation from, rather than accommodation to, the urban, secular society. Thus, in 1908 they founded the Federal Council of Churches of Christ in America, the precursor of the modern National Council of Churches. The Social Gospelers put as much or more stock in the liberal arts/humanistic tradition than in

the ability to recite thousands of Bible verses by memory, and they refused to trace every social ill to some problem of personal sin.

The sins they did address—such as greed, political corruption, and the myopia of smug personal piety in an age of real deprivation and suffering—were not always the same as those for which more conservative evangelicals, with their legacy of frontier vices such as card-playing and dancing, felt concern.

In fact, American evangelical Christianity had arrived at a crossroads at the beginning of the twentieth century. Conservative evangelists such as Dwight Moody and Billy Sunday had, in some sense, "sold out" to big business interests. Their premillennialist tendencies were useful for quashing reformist sentiment among the masses, but basically these evangelicals were uncomfortable with the modern world. It was filled with too many forces they feared and did not understand.

The liberal Social Gospelers, on the other hand, successfully accommodated, both theologically and socially, and their denominations went on to become the mainline groups that within another decade or so lost most of their evangelical fervor. In the process, ironically, they also abandoned much of the quest for dominion, since dominion involved more than simply building a good and just society; it entailed a special spiritual covenant with a biblical deity. Although they never completely gave up dominion, as a driving force it became dormant and largely untapped.

Thus it was solely the conservative premillennialist evangelicals who clung to the dominion theme and who, while it lay suspended, preserved the lifestyle, commitment, and spiritual fervor that would relaunch it in the years following World War II.

As the proportion of Americans who were evangelicals began to shrink, those who still identified with the tradition had to choose between one of two options: to join the Social Gospel (and eventually lose many of their evangelical characteristics), or to fall back with the noncompromising wing that rejected the demon of modernism. This second option became a social movement generally referred to as *fundamentalism*, a loose alliance of antimodernist evangelicals.

The movement took its name from a series of ninety articles, published in twelve volumes beginning in 1910, called *The Fundamentals*. Financed by two businessmen-brothers, Lyman and Milton Stewart,

the articles were written by leading conservative evangelicals to defend
biblical inerrancy and attack "higher criticism." Defensive and strident
in tone, the essays were sharply critical of modernists, Roman Catholics, and various other Christian sects (e.g., Mormons). More than 3
million copies of these booklets were ultimately distributed free to
pastors, evangelists, and theology students in America.

Although academics and ministers in mainline denominations largely
ignored the series, it clearly expressed a need felt by conservative
evangelicals to close ranks and reassert the boundaries of orthodoxy.
This in itself was an open admission that evangelicals could no longer
assume the general acceptance of their beliefs.

Fundamentalism became identified with a particular narrow worldview that was militantly separatist in rejecting modernism. Among its
specific traits were anti-intellectualism and biblical literalism; emphasis on individual piety; superpatriotism; conservative (rural) lifestyle
practices that were often raised to the level of biblical commandments.

Many of the authors of *The Fundamentals* were evangelicals who
had battled modernism in their universities and seminaries, then left
to form or join parallel conservative institutions. J. Gresham Machen,
who left Princeton Theological Seminary to found Westminister Theological Seminary in 1929, was one. Charles Hodge, who also taught
conservative Christianity at Princeton, once even boasted, "I am not
afraid to say that a new idea never originated in this seminary."[12]

In *Discovering an Evangelical Heritage*, historian Donald Dayton
observed that the evangelicals' suspicion of higher education had grown
as the nineteenth century progressed. Before the Civil War, revivalists
founded liberal arts colleges; after it, they established Bible schools,
many of which remained unaccredited. Some institutions changed
their identities. Colleges that would later be regarded as bastions of
fundamentalism, such as Wheaton College at Wheaton, Illinois, were
founded in a different day by postmillennialists who heard a spiritual
call to social reform.[13]

This unabashed anti-intellectualism among even fundamentalist
writers had its populist counterpart in Billy Sunday's coarse preaching
style. It became the earmark of the entire movement in the public
mind, particularly after the press coverage of the Scopes trial. If ever
there was a knock-down-drag-out fight between fundamentalist Christians and the forces of secularism, second only to the battle of Ar-

mageddon prophesied in Revelation, it occurred a little more than sixty years ago in that Dayton, Tennessee, courtroom.

The issues in the case were crystal clear. John T. Scopes, a substitute high school biology teacher, had taught from a text that featured an evolutionary perspective, thus violating a Tennessee law that forbade teaching "any theory that denies the story of the Divine creation of man." As a result, Scopes was put on trial in 1925 and achieved instant immortality in the history of American church-state relations.

Tennessee's pro-creationist law was a product of concerns from many directions. Many state legislators no doubt had been hard put to make sense of rapid scientific and social changes challenging the small-town rural values they cherished. Others, such as Georgia state legislator Hal Wimberly, acted out of the sort of smug know-nothingism for which fundamentalists were rapidly becoming notorious. Arguing that same year against a bill to allow counties, school districts, and municipalities in Georgia to maintain public libraries either through taxes or donations, Wimberly said,

> Read the Bible. It teaches you how to act. Read the hymnbook.
> It contains the finest poetry ever written. Read the almanac. It
> shows you how to figure out what the weather will be. There isn't
> another book that is necessary for anyone to read and therefore
> I am opposed to all libraries.[14]

The public library bill in Georgia failed that year.

In the state of Tennessee, at fundamentalists' urgings, William Jennings Bryan, three times the unsuccessful Democratic candidate for president and a popular evangelical orator, was enlisted to lead the prosecution's attack. The defense chose Clarence Darrow, an agnostic and one of the most famous trial lawyers in American history.

For eleven sweltering July days, spectators and the press were treated to a classic confrontation. Dayton swarmed with sympathetic religionists holding camp meetings and prayer fests, hard-drinking and cynical journalists (including the master iconoclast, H. L. Mencken), and expert witnesses from the country's most prestigious universities. The trial ostensibly was about one young teacher's alleged violation of law. It proved to be a watershed event in American history.

Far from reviewing Scopes's actions (which, incidentally, were not

contested by anyone), the entire subculture of fundamentalism was placed on trial, along with William Jennings Bryan, who took the witness stand at Darrow's request. Darrow goaded Bryan as a self-styled expert on the Bible, demanding that he reconcile a literalist interpretation of Scripture with apparent contradictions and ambiguities. By probing for explanations of miraculous biblical events in scientific and rationalist terms, Darrow entangled Bryan in a web of implausibility and illogic.

In the end, Scopes was found guilty of violating the pro-creationist law, but, in what turned out to be one of the great ironies of American history, the trial was a debacle for fundamentalism. Fundamentalists were ridiculed by the liberal press, which delighted in portraying them as backwater fools comically battling the inexorable forces of modernity. The trial signaled the end of an era. Premillennialist, inerrantist, biblical literalists no longer had any significant clout or credibility.

Modernism versus fundamentalism was the driving tension in American religion during the first three decades of this century. It split seminaries and churches and created new denominations. Not all Christians who identified with the fundamentalists retreated into sectarian groups, however. Many remained within the mainline liberal denominations as a sort of Fifth Column, organizing their own newsletters, committees, and lay organizations and supporting outside "parachurch" evangelistic/mission societies representing their personal viewpoints.[15] But they fellowshipped in a distinctly sub-rosa fashion. They knew they had become outsiders.

The more aggressive, frustrated fundamentalists withdrew rather like a defeated army, rejecting modern society and awaiting the "last days" in grim but fervent premillennialist style.

Historians refer to many of the turn-of-the-century events as The Great Reversal. But it was more than evangelicalism's decline from being the most popular form of Christianity in America. The Great Reversal also saw the notions of covenant and dominion—with their motivating sentiments of Christian nation and personal repentance— go into exile. Patriotism kept the covenant theme alive, barely, but the liberals had lost the spiritual aspects of their reformist zeal, while the pessimism of premillennialists kept it fairly well subdued.

With the dormancy of the covenant/dominion themes, the evan-

gelicals-turned-fundamentalists essentially reversed their view of social reform, abandoning it to the Social Gospelers and other evangelicals-turned-liberals. Thus, the evangelical phenomenon had come full circle since the earliest days of the First Great Awakening and the glory days of the Second.

Liberals had won the modernist battle. Moreover, they controlled the media, the major educational institutions (public and private), and the Protestant denominations that fit comfortably with each.

When liberals did acknowledge the persistence of the covenant theme, they treated it like some atavistic beast, lumping it together with the largely aberrant doctrines of ultra-right-wingers, "Jewish conspiracy" advocates, Nazi sympathizers, and jingoist fanatics. Figures in the 1930s and 1940s such as William Dudley Pelley, Gerald B. Winrod, and Gerald L. K. Smith, who made up the "Old Christian Right," mixed crank politics with fundamentalism. They wallowed in sensationalist publicity and outraged liberals. Their association with fundamentalism added to the derision heaped on it and thereby helped distract the critics from seeing what was really happening.

Fundamentalism may have been hurt by the mainstream backlash after the Scopes disaster, but its wounds were not fatal. True, many leaders and followers became disillusioned and lost interest in further locking horns with modernists. Some coalitions of fundamentalists fell apart. Separatist factions became even more world-rejecting, while those who remained within the major denominations felt ever more marginal.

That liberals consistently ignored or discounted the movement's diverse activities after the 1920s was evidence of a colossal case of wishful thinking and selective perception. They knew only of the separatist fundamentalists who became ever more rigid, hostile, and uncompromisingly culture-denying. But many fundamentalists were still torn between resisting modern culture and feeling driven to convert that culture and its people to Christ. Rather than rejecting the modern world or hiding out in some quiet corner of a mainline denomination, many followers of the movement felt they had a third choice.

They could redirect their support to a wide assortment of parachurch activities that had always been the "core" of fundamentalism outside the established denominations, churches, and seminaries. These were

the older networks of Bible schools, missions, conferences, and publications (such as newsletters and magazines). Fundamentalists also created new interdenominational groups that would proselytize with only the conservative message they wanted.

These parachurch organizations generally were run by moderates who did not espouse the strict negativism of the separatists. They were willing to stay in this world, with all its flaws, and use its own tools for evangelism. Ironically, these fundamentalist groups prospered in terms of membership and financial support during the 1930s and 1940s at the same time that the mainline denominations began gradually to decline.

Historian Joel Carpenter, in an important series of articles, has explored this little-known history.[16] He notes that *The Sunday School Times* (a fundamentalist magazine) listed more than fifty Bible colleges and schools, mostly in major U.S. cities, in 1930. Another thirty-five schools were started up in the next ten years, and in the following decade (1940–50), sixty additional schools were begun.

The Moody Bible Institute, the "great-granddaddy" of them all, became the model: It trained pastors, evangelists, and Sunday school superintendents, and published a wide assortment of literature (from magazines and books to tracts). Subscriptions to its flagship publication, *The Moody Monthly*, increased by 13,000 during the 1930s to more than 40,000 in 1940. By its fortieth anniversary in 1934, the Moody Press had published more than 57 million items.

The institute had its own radio station and taped programs for other stations. The Moody Bible Institute Extension Department held weekend Bible conferences in 500 nearby churches during 1936. The institute had over 15,000 contributors in 1937 and an equal number enrolled in its correspondence school.

Soon conservative Christians had a wide variety of regular publications tailored just for them. Various Bible schools and institutes published their own magazines, such as the Philadelphia School of the Bible's *Serving and Waiting*, the Denver Bible Institute's *Grace and Truth*, and the Northwestern (Minneapolis) Bible and Missionary Training School's *The Pilot*.

In general, evangelical colleges and Bible institutes prospered enormously during the 1930s. For example, Wheaton College saw its enrollment climb from 400 students in 1926 to 1,100 students in 1940.

A host of summer Bible conferences held at lakes, resorts, and camps mixed the rustic camp-meeting atmosphere with Chautauqua-style lectures and preaching for youth, businessmen, ministers, housewives, and Sunday school teachers. *The Moody Monthly* published lists of upcoming conferences. In reviewing back issues, Carpenter found that the lists grew from twenty-seven different sites and eighty-eight conference sessions in 1930 to more than 200 sessions at fifty sites in 1941.

The fundamentalists could also stage huge rallies, and not in remote cornfields. Evangelists could fill stadiums and large auditoriums in urban centers. In 1935, evangelist Elwin Wright held a "Bible Demonstration Day" rally in Boston Garden, and 16,000 enthusiastic believers attended. In 1936 the Moody Bible Institute celebrated its fiftieth anniversary with "Moody Day," an event attended by members of more than 500 churches. Representatives of more than 800 congregations showed up during 1937 for the centenary of Dwight L. Moody's birth, with more than 400,000 attending courses in Bible teaching and evangelism. The institute decided to stage a second "Moody Day" that year, pulling in 2,300 participating churches and winding up festivities with a crowd of 15,000 at a Chicago Coliseum rally.

Fundamentalists were repeatedly encouraged by their ability to produce impressive audiences at public rallies and revivals. Charles E. Fuller, the radio evangelist of the Mutual Network's "The Old-Fashioned Revival Hour" (Jerry Falwell named his own television program "The Old Time Gospel Hour," he claimed, because he was converted by listening to one of Fuller's broadcasts), regularly drew crowds in tens of thousands throughout the late 1930s. For example, in 1938 at Chicago's Soldier Field, 40,000 believers showed up for Fuller's Easter service. In 1939 he completely filled New York City's Carnegie Hall.

Fundamentalists used the newest medium, radio, with great success. More than 400 religious programs on eighty radio stations in 1932 were endorsed by *The Sunday School Times* as "sound and scriptural." Charles Fuller's weekly program was broadcast on 152 stations in 1939 but on 456 by 1942, making it the largest radio broadcast in the nation.

Such exposure had tremendous importance, not just for demonstrating that conservative Christianity had not withered up and blown

away, but also for giving legitimacy to the evangelistic "style." Putting it on radio and sending it into people's homes made the message part of mainstream culture. Says Joel Carpenter, "It appears that no other religious movement went to the airwaves as extensively nor was able to fully integrate radio broadcasting into its institutional framework as did fundamentalism."[17]

There were numerous other areas, such as missionary work, in which Bible schools cooperated with independent agencies and simply bypassed the larger denominations. And, as Richard G. Hutcheson has documented in his book *Mainline Churches and the Evangelicals*, many fundamentalists remained within these denominations, sometimes in an uneasy state of détente, but redirected their support to missions that preached a more acceptable message. The Fundamentalist Fellowship of the [mainline] Northern Baptist Convention was one such example of "loyal opposition." As a group-within-a-group, it arranged for full autonomy in supporting its own missions, preferring to work with more conservative agencies.[18]

Other looser coalitions of independent fundamentalist congregations formed, such as the American Conference of Undenominational Churches and the Eastern Conference of Fundamentalists and Undenominational Churches. These worked closely with Bible schools in recruiting pastors, supporting missions, and obtaining instructional materials.

So the post–Scopes 1930s was not entirely an era of stagnation, retreat, or decline.

To be sure, the separatists were still bitter and outspoken. Many were appalled at the evangelism outreach, the radio ministers, and the mass rallies. It was as if a "sour grapes" anger consumed their sermons and writings, poisoning their capacity for cooperation, fellowship, or even civility in respect to any person or group that did not uphold their negativism.

They were quick to point fingers and throw out labels of "sellout" and "accommodationist." They were the world-rejecting fundamentalists whom liberal critics mistook for all conservative Christians. They were an embarrassment to those more interested in getting on with evangelizing the world. In their own culture-denying way, however, they inspired others to rediscover and resurrect the covenant theme.

Encouraged by the growth of parachurch activities and by their

successes in turning out large crowds for rallies and conferences, some fundamentalist leaders began to sense the opportunity for a large-scale revival in America. During the war years of the 1940s, in particular, a sense of mission and solidarity spread throughout the nation. The urgency of the crisis served as a powerful stimulant to the reawakening of the nationalistic and patriotic aspects of covenant and dominion.

Men such as Carl F. H. Henry and Harold J. Ockenga felt that conservative Christianity—what they deliberately called *evangelicalism* to distance it from fundamentalism—could deal with modern biblical scholarship and criticism, but only if it jettisoned the primitive know-nothingism of the separatists. Regretfully, wrote Carl Henry in 1947, "Modern prejudice, justly or unjustly, has come to identify Fundamentalism largely in terms of an anti-ecumenical spirit of independent isolationism. . . ."[19]

These evangelicals also sought cooperation, not division, among conservative groups, for the sake of the hoped-for revival. In 1942, J. Elwin Wright, Robert T. Davis, Torrey Johnson, Carl Henry, Harold Ockenga, and others brought together all shades of fundamentalism, Pentecostalism, holiness groups, and charismatics, including representatives of some mainline denominations in the Federal Council of Churches, for a National Conference for United Action among Evangelicals. Out of that fateful meeting sprang the National Association of Evangelicals (NAE).

The separatists declined to join. Carl McIntire, who regarded many of these "moderates" as apostate—forever barring common fellowship—founded his own American Council of Christian Churches in September 1941. McIntire was a thorn in the NAE's side, but to these new "postfundamentalist" evangelicals, the enmity of fundamentalists like him was a price worth paying.

The NAE succeeded as a conservative ecumenical effort. At the end of its first four years, its membership included twenty-two denominations and hundreds of single congregations, twenty-two regional offices, numerous regional and local chapters, and approximately a million souls. The NAE also spun off the National Religious Broadcasters, the National Sunday School Association, the Evangelical Foreign Missions Association (with forty-three missionary boards), the Commission for War Relief, and the Commission for Army and Navy Chaplaincies.

Meanwhile, evangelicals and some moderate fundamentalists labored on other parachurch fronts. The year 1944 saw Christ for America rallies held in several major cities, as well as the founding of Youth for Christ (YFC). In 1945, 70,000 evangelicals gathered at Soldier Field for a memorial/rededication service sponsored by YFC. By 1946, an estimated one million young people were YFC members. By 1948, YFC had spread to forty-six countries and held its first postwar evangelistic missions conference in Beatenberg, Switzerland.

Evangelicals underwent a transformation of self-image. They no longer considered themselves outsiders, a new reaction reinforced by the comments of various national leaders. Joel Carpenter recounts in a *Christianity Today* retrospective:

> The day after he heard Winston Churchill's "Iron Curtain" speech in 1946, President Truman told a group of churchmen that without "a moral and spiritual awakening," America would be lost. Gen. Dwight D. Eisenhower echoed him, suggesting that there was no hope of avoiding disaster "except through moral regeneration." Likewise Gen. Douglas MacArthur, invoking the theme of Americans' divinely ordained duty, invited Youth for Christ and other missionaries to Japan to "provide the surest foundation for the firm establishment of democracy."[20]

The end of World War II brought the covenant/dominion theme full circle. With a reawakened sense of national mission couched in distinctly spiritual terms, with a Billy Graham to assume the mantle of the greatest movement leaders of the past, with new and larger parachurch organizations, and with faith in themselves, the evangelicals were on a roll.

It should now be obvious that if the mass media, academics, or other observers thought the evangelicals came out of nowhere during the late 1970s, they had prevailing liberal "group think" to thank. The fundamentalist stereotypes held by mainline America were glaringly misleading. This branch of Christianity regained the momentum it had lost shortly after World War I and was merely returning to "normal."

The turbulent decade of the 1960s helped obscure matters, particularly in the area of evangelicals' social concerns. Mass media paraded

a constant stream of protest, or countercultural, images: antiwar, women's liberation, civil rights, gay pride, environmentalists, even exotic religious cults and gurus of every conceivable stripe. Even the "Jesus movement"—which involved the start-up or expansion of evangelical ministries to ex-hippies and former drug culture "freaks" as well as college and high school youth—was lumped indiscriminately into the pot. Liberals ignored the fact that evangelicals had been calling for increased social action since the 1940s.

In 1947, for example, Carl Henry's *The Uneasy Conscience of Modern Fundamentalism* laid out an activist manifesto: "A Christianity without a passion to turn the world upside down is not reflective or apostolic Christianity."[21] Henry's call was answered in the ferment of the 1960s, as young evangelicals such as Jim Wallis of the People's Christian Coalition in Washington, D.C., Fred and John F. Alexander, founder-editors of Philadelphia's *The Other Side*, and the various countercultural-style members of the Berkeley Christian Coalition, took on the contradictions and injustices of American capitalism ignored by an earlier generation of fundamentalists. Richard Quebedeaux called them "the worldly evangelicals":

. . . a new generation of evangelical Christians who repudiate and disown the social and political conservatism and culture rejection of traditional evangelicalism without giving up the basic tenets and faith of Christian orthodoxy.[22]

Most important, evangelicals may have been fairly low-key during the 1960s (they rarely burned draft cards or American flags), but they learned a critical lesson. The righteous crusades of that era, in sociologist Robert C. Liebman's words, "blurred the distinction between private morality and public institutions." Liebman argues that the trauma of Watergate and its regular media exposure altered conservative Christians' thinking about supposedly impersonal events. As both Watergate and the abortion controversy were driven home to many previously apolitical evangelicals, "morality came increasingly to be viewed as a public issue, rather than a matter of private concern."[23]

Thus, despite the presumed dispersion of fundamentalists and evangelicals to America's cultural hinterlands, they never left its heartland.

Their history from the Scopes trial to the present reveals a remarkable continuity of energy and only a relatively brief interruption from addressing social concerns. One evangelical writer concluded, "In the two decades between 1930 and 1950, evangelicals laid the foundations for the renovation of the gospel witness that caught national attention in the 1970s."[24]

Likewise, the sudden attention paid to the New Christian Right is more a product of selective perception by liberals than it is an accurate reading of religious change in this country. The fact is that years of grass-roots networking, settling in-house squabbles, and accumulating political savvy is finally paying off. The evangelicals are returning to cultural center stage.

7

In My Father's House . . .

The overall media ministry of Christ in America has not been as open and as accountable as we should be. We are getting our hands smacked and we deserve it. . . . [W]e have had a little sense of arrogance out there in the church that it is none of your business or anybody else's what we do or how we do it . . . [but] that sense of arrogance is over. . . .[W]e are coming to the painful conclusion that if we are public figures leading Christian ministries, using public monies, contributions, then we are publicly responsible.
—Jerry Falwell,
Press Conference, April 28, 1987

Revivalism never disappeared from American culture, but after the glory days of Billy Sunday and the disaster of the Scopes trial, it subsided temporarily. Billy Graham was well on his way to creating an effective evangelistic organization when he received an unexpected boost in 1949 from newspaper magnate William Randolph Hearst. Hearst's celebrated two-word editorial directive, "puff Graham," triggered a flurry of media attention that hoisted the young evangelist into the national limelight.

The following year, Billy Graham decided to do a weekly radio program, "Hour of Decision," a move that firmly linked nineteenth-century urban revivalism to modern religious broadcasting. Indeed, Graham's decision to go on radio was even more momentous to his career and the future of religious broadcasting than the great boost he got from Hearst's patronage. Almost immediately, he was preaching to the largest audience ever to hear a religious program. Within five

years, his program aired on a thousand stations with an estimated audience of 15 million.[1]

In 1951, Graham made another decision of paramount importance. The Billy Graham Evangelistic Association began packaging his crusades for the powerful new medium of television. This gave Graham even greater visibility and success and transformed evangelical religion into a mainstream phenomenon.

Like Dwight Moody and Billy Sunday before him, Graham relished rubbing shoulders with the rich and powerful. He particularly liked U.S. presidents (until he became soiled by the carnage of Watergate). His role as the "preacher of presidents" lent legitimacy to the political status quo, whatever its sins, and he eventually came to realize it.

Graham's sermons have always had a ring of patriotism, although never the bellicose "100 percent Americanism" of Billy Sunday in his later days. Still, while Graham eventually would repudiate his own involvement in politics, he set the stage for others to become even more deeply involved. Indeed, Pat Robertson has gone Graham's presidential hobnobbing one better in becoming a candidate himself. But it was not until much later that the latent and overt political messages of modern urban revivalists were to become a significant feature of religious broadcasting.

At about the same time that Billy Graham decided to go on television, two itinerant evangelists from Oklahoma and Arkansas also recognized the medium's potential for saving souls. Oral Roberts brought television cameras into his Pentecostal revival tent. Rex Humbard sold his tent and built a cathedral especially equipped for broadcasting. A new era was born.

These three men played roles in the development of the electric church that parallel those of Finney, Moody, and Sunday in the development of urban evangelism. Building on the organizational principles that resulted in the institutionalization of urban revivalism, Graham, Roberts, and Humbard created yet another institution—the electric church.

The pastors of this electric parachurch found that their predecessors' legacy—the publicity, the organization, the fanfare of urban revivalism—was important not only in attracting souls to the Lord. It also brought in funds, enabling them to raise the millions of dollars needed to purchase and operate the new electric technology.

Essentially, technology circled back on strategy. Soon these preachers and those who followed them found that their enormous broadcasting costs dictated that they run continuous fund-raising campaigns. The "saved" and "born again" had to be continually offered new incentives to give to these ministries. Using computers, word processors, and toll-free telephone numbers, the electric ministers developed sophisticated ways of creating a sense of personal relationship between viewer and evangelist, between donor and parachurch. But, as we shall see, the medium began to affect the message.

The Billy Graham Evangelistic Association modeled its crusades after the techniques of Finney, Moody, and Sunday: the engagement of local pastors and churches before the decision to conduct a crusade, advance-planning activities to arouse interest, topflight entertainment (albeit in a much more subdued form than Sunday's vaudeville antics), celebrity guest appearances, appeals to the emotions, emphasis on the urgency of making a Decision for Christ, and follow-up contacts. The Hearst boost gave Graham a competitive edge in access to evening prime-time television. Roberts and Humbard were never able to overcome that momentum, nor the reluctance of network executives to open their doors and airwaves to evangelical preachers. As a result, they were forced to become innovators in the structure of programming and in the development of feedback with their audiences.

In spite of his reputation as the biggest and the grandest, Billy Graham has never been particularly innovative. His worldwide crusades are taped, and then edited for television. Whereas Roberts has been through five major format overhauls, Graham's programs have changed very little in thirty-five years. Because Graham has always drawn large audiences, the Billy Graham Evangelistic Association has never gone through the agonies of the boom-and-bust cycles experienced by all the other television ministries.

Of the other two evangelists, Oral Roberts has been the more innovative. He hired topflight secular entertainers to appear on his programs as a way of hooking audiences. He gauged audience size and aggressively bought the best time slots. He learned early that people get more excited about brick-and-mortar projects than they do about paying the bills for airtime. Special projects can elicit donations far in excess of what is needed; the surplus can pay the bills for airtime

and general operations. With this knowledge, he built a university. Then he built a medical center.

And Oral Roberts couched the expansion of his parachurch conglomerate in terms of visions, not corporate ledgers or cost-effectiveness. In May 1980, he wrote supporters to say that he had spoken with a 900-foot vision of Jesus Christ, who assured him that Roberts's City of Faith medical complex would be completed. Later, he reinforced that sort of spectacular revelation with a second message from God that his medical facilities eventually would find a cure for cancer.

That Oral Roberts eventually overextended himself with his medical center has not detracted from the principle that he established and almost every successful televangelist has copied: Major projects excite audience response.

Of the three electric-church pioneers, Rex Humbard was the most successful in mastering the art of parapersonal communication. He included his whole family in the act—wife, children, and grandchildren. They sang, read the Bible, and listened attentively to Rex's stories and sermonettes. A whole generation grew up with the Humbards and, for many of them, the Humbard family was a part of their own—or they a part of the Humbard family. Humbard developed an audience that was intensely loyal. They stuck with him for a very long while.

The Cathedral of Tomorrow Humbard built in Akron, Ohio, served as the base for a local congregation and his television ministry until the early 1980s, when he moved his television studio to Callaway Gardens in Georgia. Especially constructed for television production, the Cathedral of Tomorrow was a spectacular achievement. It boasted a 220-foot domed roof without interior support and a huge cross suspended from the ceiling with 4,700 red, white, and blue lights.

In the early 1970s, it appeared that Humbard was way ahead of his televangelist peers in developing a ministry that mixed preaching with spectacular brick-and-mortar projects. In 1971, he broke ground on the construction of what was to have been the tallest building in Ohio. Atop the 750-foot structure would be a revolving restaurant and a television transmitting tower. At about the same time, Humbard purchased property on Mackinac Island, Michigan, with plans to open a college.

Challenges by neighbors to the construction of the tower, by the

Ohio Commerce Department to his sale of securities to finance his projects, and by the Internal Revenue Service regarding the tax status of a girdle factory owned by the ministry in New York, among other financial headaches, left Humbard with little stomach for the high-rolling, high-pressure lifestyle that would later consume some of his colleagues.

Humbard turned away from that road and stuck to preaching the Gospel. After his flurry of activity in the early 1970s, Rex Humbard never took on another building project. This fact, perhaps more than any other, accounted for Humbard's being the first to fold his Big Gospel Tent of the airwaves in 1986. Humbard himself seemed to understand this. In a television interview granted only weeks before he closed shop, he sadly laid bare the truth: "People will not give a dollar to win a soul or bring a person to a saving knowledge of Jesus Christ. They give their dollars to build giant cathedrals, projects, schools."[2]

In 1985, the cost of airtime exceeded the revenues coming in from his shrinking audience. When it became evident that he couldn't pay, television stations all over America canceled his program. Almost without notice, Rex Humbard's long and illustrious television career passed from the scene.

An army of competitors—as the economics of Arbitron and Nielsen ratings and syndication costs would inevitably make all televangelists—arrived in the 1970s and 1980s, spurred by the catalyst of cable television. Some were clones of the better-known personalities; some were originals. Liberals could look on in bemusement at the likes of Lester Sumrall, with his lackluster camera presence and constant struggle with diction; stoop-shouldered, toupeed Ernest Angley healing the hard-of-hearing by smacking them between the eyes with the heel of his palm; or Dr. Gene Scott, the white-haired Ph.D. with his cigar and funny hats, berating his audiences and refusing to preach if they didn't telephone in their gifts immediately.

But there were others, bigger and more recognizable, who created the public image of televangelism.

Based on average quarter-hour audience ratings, Jimmy Lee Swaggart is the biggest. In 1983, *Newsweek* proclaimed him "King of Honky-Tonk Heaven." Swaggart hails from the backwaters of Louisiana, and his greatest appeal is among his own kind—people who have been

left behind by the whirlwinds of change. His populist appeal reminds one of Huey Long, and his aroused preaching style comes about as close to Billy Sunday's as that of anyone on the scene today.

Swaggart is an unabashed Assemblies of God Pentecostal who has no use for Coors beer, *Penthouse* and *Playboy*, the "Solid Gold" program's scantily clad dancers, Roman Catholicism, and contemporary country music—and frequently tells his audiences so. It was Swaggart who blew the whistle on fellow Assemblies of God televangelist Jim Bakker. Bakker, in turn, accused Swaggart of attempting a hostile takeover, but as the unholy wars of televangelism unfolded in the spring of 1987, it became evident that Swaggart didn't want to run the PTL ministry. He just wanted his wayward brother out of the pulpit and out of the business of deceiving the faithful.

An accomplished pianist and singer, Swaggart's gospel albums sold more than 12 million copies while he was building a $30 million World Ministry Center in Baton Rouge, Louisiana, and accumulating more than a half-dozen radio stations. Swaggart's southern drawl, loud exhortations about sin, and three-piece suits have made him the archetypal televangelist.

Robert Schuller is Swaggart's antimatter counterpart. He is cool, rational, and optimistic where Swaggart is sweaty, emotional, and premillennially pessimistic. Schuller preaches "Possibility Thinking," which is an unapologetic play on Norman Vincent Peale's "Positive Thinking." Swaggart preaches hellfire and brimstone and is trying to save all the souls he can before the battle of Armageddon.

Schuller is the only television minister who is a member of a mainline Protestant denomination. Ordained in the Reformed Church in America, Schuller arrived in Southern California's Orange County just as that part of the country was beginning to boom. When he began his "missionary" ministry, the only place he could find to hold church services was a drive-in movie theatre. The novelty of a drive-in church attracted media attention and folks who were curious to know what it was like to go to worship in their automobiles.

Schuller's Calvinist work ethic and charisma did the rest. He soon moved his congregation across the freeway and gradually built one of America's great superchurches. In 1979 he launched the construction of the Crystal Cathedral, one of architect Philip Johnson's crowning achievements and one of the great religious edifices of this century.

From here his "Hour of Power" is transmitted to more than 150 stations.

Schuller is the closest thing to an intellectual and a liberal in televangelism. In a profession that has more honorary doctorates than any other, Schuller's doctorate is earned. He doesn't appreciate being lumped in with the rest of the televangelist crowd.

"God's angry young man," as *Texas Monthly* once described him, is James Robison of Hurst, Texas. A Southern Baptist with a Pentecostal's pulpit-pounding style, Robison has been a loose cannon on the decks of the video vicarage. In 1979 he outraged homosexuals in Texas by attacking local Dallas–Fort Worth Metroplex gay-rights organizations. They in turn forced WFAA-TV to provide them with equal response time under the Personal Attack and Controversial Public Issues provisions of the Federal Communications Commission's Fairness Doctrine. Tired of his tirades directed at specific groups (the station had already been forced to provide equal time to the Mormons, Christian Scientists, and Garner Ted Armstrong's Worldwide Church of God after similar attacks), WFAA-TV canceled Robison's weekly program, though later they reinstated it.

Then, in 1980, Robison took to politics. He fell in with Jerry Falwell, and for a while served as vice president and media sage of Religious Roundtable, a group with aims and goals similar to those of the Moral Majority. "I'm a preacher, but I'm no longer just going to be talking about going to heaven," he told everyone who would listen. Then, after a brief period of high visibility, he renounced politics just as emphatically as he had seized the political pulpit. He had come under the influence of charismatics and took up their ways

One of Robison's most celebrated converts was millionaire industrialist Cullen Davis. The conversion took place while Davis was on trial for the attempted murder of his wife and a judge in Robison's divorce trial. Together, Robison and Davis gained more notoriety when they claimed to have smashed $1 million worth of rare Oriental art objects and dumped them in Lake Worth because they were pagan "religious idols."

In spring 1983, Robison added demonology and exorcism to his repertoire after meeting Milton Green, a Baptist layman from Tennessee whose followers were dubbed "Greenies." In the furor that followed, Robison left the Euless, Texas, church where he was a mem-

ber and took his ministry, now Pentecostal in all but name, deep into the charismatic land of tongue-speaking, healing, and prophecy.

An evangelist with a much lower profile but a growing following is Kenneth Copeland, another Texan. Once Oral Roberts's personal pilot, he is a former pop singer and now a successful recorder of gospel albums. Copeland's sermons are Pentecostal, with a heavy dose of fitness and health advice (he is a vegetarian) and a wide range of humorous, satirical characterizations that he uses to drive points home. Copeland has recently moved onto the list of the top ten televangelists in the country.

Then, of course, there were the cherub-faced Jim Bakker and his wife, Tammy Faye. Even in exile, Jim and Tammy remain the couple that liberal watchers of the electric church love to scorn. Remarkably, their antics did not succeed in disillusioning many among their army of loyal viewers. Even as the excruciatingly bizarre details of their unheavenly deeds unfolded in the mass media, loyalists formed a group called the PTL Partners Association. Their goal: to oust Jerry Falwell, the man hand-picked by the wounded Bakker to save the ministry. From the beginning, the chances of salvaging the PTL Network and Heritage USA were exceedingly dim. The guerrilla tactics of Bakker and his loyalists make the mission virtually impossible.

Once employed by Pat Robertson, the Bakkers left CBN to join Paul and Jan Crouch in creating Trinity Broadcasting Network in Southern California. After a quick falling-out between the Crouches and the Bakkers, Jim and Tammy Faye returned to the East, where they founded the PTL Network. To Bakker's critics, PTL has always stood for Pass The Loot. After Bakker was revealed to have paid hush money to a church secretary with whom he had a sexual encounter, PTL stood for Pay The Lady. Other uncomplimentary meanings of PTL are best left unstated.

The Bakkers' most ambitious project was Heritage Village, USA, a hybrid of a spiritual Disneyland, an old-fashioned Pentecostal camp meeting grounds, and a late-twentieth-century resort. Whatever else it may be, or have been envisioned to become, Heritage USA was meant as a "total Christian living center" where people could escape from the evils and annoyances of the secular world.

From ground-breaking ceremonies in 1978 until the Bakkers' hasty departure on March 19, 1987, Heritage USA grew to include the 504-

room Heritage Grand Hotel (with a 513-room tower addition under construction), a shopping mall, a village church with a 5,000-seat auditorium, television studios, a replication of the Upper Room (site of the Last Supper), a recreational village, a farm, a residence for disabled children, a child-care and adoption agency, a prison outreach program, a drug rehabilitation center, time-share units, retirement housing, condominiums, a dinner theatre, and more.

Megan Rosenfeld, feature writer for the *Washington Post*, described Heritage USA as "a place somewhere between the Land of Oz and a straitlaced Club Med." She notes further that Heritage USA is:

> . . . a trash-free, profanity-free, sin-free zone . . . bathed in a glow of conspicuous friendliness, a reassuring and comfortable atmosphere that comes from crowds of people secure in the knowledge that on most issues they think alike.[3]

"What is Heritage USA/PTL?" the promotional material asks. The answer: "A unique 21st century Christian retreat and campground, and so much more."

It was the "so much more" that got the Bakkers in trouble. The Bakkers and their closest associates enjoyed an opulent lifestyle beyond the reach of all but a few of the world's jet-setting "beautiful people." It is doubtful that anyone will ever know how much money they spent on themselves. Rolls-Royces, Mercedeses, Jaguars, vacation homes in Florida, California, and Tennessee, and especially bonuses. Notes Jerry Nims, the chief executive officer under the Falwell administration of PTL, "There were birthday bonuses, Christmas bonuses, Valentine's Day bonuses, Saturday morning bonuses . . . unscheduled bonuses."[4]

Along with their penchant for the spectacular, the Bakkers cultivated the impression that they were developing and contributing large sums of ministry money to social-service projects. In reality, these projects often had low priority, and initial enthusiasm quickly waned. For example, in 1983 Ronald Reagan singled out an emergency social-service project called People That Love Centers as a sterling example of volunteerism. The exact amount of money allocated to PTL Centers is not known, but within three years Jim Bakker had lost interest in the project and cut off support for the centers.

In 1986, only 2.9 percent of PTL's $129 million budget was earmarked for social-service and charitable programs. The Bakkers' own passion for high living took precedence over even the glitzy, high-visibility projects at Heritage. In the end, they were quite literally robbing the corporate treasury.

And all of this was financed with $10 and $15 and $25 contributions from a grateful and unsuspecting crowd of loyal parachurch followers. It was also financed with Life Partnerships, in effect a time-share condominium scheme. Heritage USA sold, at $1,000 a clip, more than 120,000 Life Partnerships that were supposed to entitle holders to three free nights each year at the Heritage Grand Hotel or the Heritage Grand Tower.

It was the most successful of many fund-raising schemes created over the years, but it was a scam and a fraud. A little simple arithmetic will show that there was no way they could ever have honored those commitments. In fact, they didn't try. Only fifty rooms were set aside to service the Life Partners' demands for free rooms. At one point, when there was a rash of complaints, Bakker said they had miscalculated the demand for rooms during peak season. To quiet the criticism, he offered a refund to anyone who wanted one.

The monies raised exceeded the combined cost of the two hotels, but when Jerry Falwell took over PTL management, the corporation owed vendors more than $14 million and the tower was incomplete. There was no cash in the treasury, so construction had to be halted.

Bakker is the closest thing to a manic-depressive in the electric church. In front of live audiences, he can be cheery and ebullient one moment and then plunge into deep depression the next. Near the top of the list of what can plunge him into near-despair are cash-flow shortfalls and criticism of his lifestyle. His insatiable desire to make PTL and Heritage USA bigger and better virtually assured frequent cash shortfalls.

Bakker handled criticism of how he spent viewer donations the way water runs off a duck's back. His on-air talks to the camera bemoaned the imminent bankruptcy of the PTL Club. Pleas of insolvency usually were mixed with self-pity and paranoia, particularly when the *Charlotte Observer* and its investigations of Bakker's ministry were mentioned.

"I think we ought to want the best for our pastors. I believe a pastor

should live at least, *at least,* as good as the wealthiest member of the congregation. When you bless the man in the pulpit, you will be blessed," he explained.[5]

Many people seem to agree with this assessment, for they have stood with Jim and Tammy Faye through thick and thin. Some of the couple's appeal is no doubt a vicarious pleasure in a lifestyle most supporters cannot afford. But the Bakkers also elicit a lot of empathy; they are real people who let it all hang out.

Jim's personal struggle with ambition, his sometimes-ecstatic-some-times-whiny approach, Tammy Faye's incredibly open on-air discussions of their marital difficulties, and her unforgettable singing have always been right there for viewers to see. Sometimes the Bakkers' problems were so overwhelming that one or both of them had to get away for a few days. And when they did, there often was no attempt to hide their emotional and spiritual exhaustion. All of these are elements of real people opening their lives to public examination in ways that we see in soap operas, but rarely in real life. It is possible that the Bakkers' greatest weaknesses are also an important source of their strength.

All of the televangelism ministries have at least two features in common. First, they are oligarchies, organizations governed by a very few. The Greek origin of the word implied the notion that the few were superior to the masses. They understand better than the masses what is best. And they are accountable to no one. Although the electric churches have boards, the charters and bylaws of the organizations are written to give the founder/leader the power of appointment and dismissal. Thus, the leader of the oligarchy often borders on being a despot. A benevolent despot perhaps, but a despot nevertheless.

Given this organizational form, the scandals of PTL are not so surprising. All the money, all the building projects, all the "yes men" are doing the bidding of leaders accountable to no one but "God." In retrospect, it seems almost inevitable that someday, someone would stumble badly and that the fallout would cast a dark shadow across the whole of religious broadcasting.

The Bakker tragedy could not have happened if the empires of televangelism were not oligarchies, allowing individual entrepreneurs a great deal of freedom to follow their instincts. From this fact stems

both irony and paradox. Without such a system, the electric church would not have grown and developed into the important force it has become in America in the late twentieth century.

The second feature common to all these ministries—and one that has revolutionized religious broadcasting—is a unique relationship to the audiences. They have perfected parapersonal communication in a way undreamed-of by commercial television. Whereas commercial broadcasting sells advertising to support programming, the electric church sells Jesus, itself, and usually some wonderful project.

When Johnny Carson breaks for a commercial, even if Ed McMahon is hawking the product, there is a psychological distance between the "real" program and the selling of a sponsor's product. For religious broadcasters, the tasks of preaching, entertaining, and selling are all intertwined. A devoted listener feels good about Jesus, the minister, himself or herself, and the project that is being promoted. The concept of "partner" has a very powerful meaning. People get involved. They are indeed partners in the venture. Together with the televangelist and his staff, they are cofunders and coproducers—not just of a television program, but of the much broader ministry.

Televangelists solicit support from their audiences for their projects, offering premiums in exchange for donations. While some electric churches utilize professional fund-raising organizations, others have developed a sophistication that exceeds the capabilities of many such organizations. And many critics would relish the opportunity to employ the skills of the electric church to raise money.

With increased competition, airtime has become very expensive. And with costs increasing faster than audiences, there is an ever-present prospect that the whole process could crumble. Broadcasting seems to have become an instrument to pay off bills incurred in the pursuit of other projects rather than an end in itself. Billy Graham's biographer, Marshall Frady, found the same inverted process at work with the Graham crusades, which originally existed for the purpose of saving souls. Then, over time, they came to exist "for the sake of their own self-propagation." But with the passage of still more time, they "existed for their televised reproductions." Hence, "the television event . . . existed to produce more television events."[6]

The reason is clear: Theology does not exist in a vacuum. It exists in a medium, a context. And the values and pressure of the context

help shape the theology. The medium is not neutral to the message.

The fund-raising tactics of the televangelists—of Pat Robertson no less than his colleagues—are a prime example of this truism. These tactics undoubtedly have been the most controversial aspect of the electric church. Indeed, fund-raising has become an integral part of prime-time religion's theology.

There are numerous variations on the theme, but most televangelists end up at a common point: the Gospel of Prosperity. God *wants* you to be financially prosperous and content. Poverty and illness do not stem from God's Providence; they come from problems in a person's Christian attitude and understanding. Sacrifice and suffering have little to do with the contemporary Christian message.

Many televangelists say the keys to financial success are actually embedded in the New Testament. By supporting their particular ministries with donations, they assure viewers, anyone can learn what these keys are.

Pat Robertson calls these rules "Kingdom Principles," taught by Jesus Christ and "as valid for our lives as the laws of thermodynamics or the law of gravity." They are in the Bible, but you need the Virginia Beach televangelist as a guide for discerning them. Then the Good Book becomes a potpourri of information that can be applied to all sorts of secular situations. Says Robertson, "The Bible, quite bluntly, is a workable guidebook for politics, government, business, families, and all the affairs of mankind."[7]

In particular, God works on a principle of reciprocity. The more money you send to Him (presumably, in Robertson's case, through "The 700 Club"), the more God will return materially on your investment. In *The Secret Kingdom*, Robertson writes:

If we want to release the superabundance of the kingdom of heaven, we first give. . . . I am as certain of this as of anything in my life. If you are in financial trouble, the smartest thing you can do is to start giving money away. . . . Your return, poured into your lap, will be great, pressed down and running over.[8]

Oral Roberts refers to his twist on the same theme as "seed-faith." Contributions to his ministry have the potential to return mighty dividends, spiritual and material, within this lifetime. (He once wrote

an article in his *Abundant Life* magazine entitled "You Sow It, Then God Will Grow It.") While the concept can be applied to various aspects of life, it gives viewers a special justification for contributing to Roberts, since he claims to have uncovered the dynamics of how God apportions miracles.

In *Miracle of Seed-Faith* (1974—the twenty-fourth printing), Roberts discusses Three Key Principles of seed-faith and how to make "blessing-pact covenants" with God. There is, for example, the Law of Sowing and Reaping ("Remember, only what you give can God multiply back") and his frank admonishment: "If you want God to supply your financial needs, then give SEED-MONEY for Him to reproduce and multiply."[9]

On the other hand, Kenneth Copeland, Roberts's pupil, preaches "Prosperity Theology" based on biblical laws. He has written a string of best-selling books on the subject, including *The Laws of Prosperity*. His wife, Gloria, recently wrote one entitled *God's Will is Prosperity*.

In the weeks immediately following the Roberts and Bakker scandals, a half-dozen national polls made it abundantly clear that televangelists are not a very popular lot among the general public. As we read these polls, it is fund-raising more than anything else—including the sex scandals and the mixing of religion and politics—that has given religious broadcasters a black eye.

Oral Roberts's "donate or God will call me home" gimmick was but the latest in a long series of fund-raising scams he has perpetrated upon his viewers. Unfortunately, it is not just Roberts who has utilized fund-raising tactics that are, to say the least, of questionable integrity.

The scandals may have hastened an eventual, perhaps inevitable, backlash against their very strategies for success. Before the scandals broke, even Billy Graham criticized televangelists' endless projects, money-raising campaigns, and tearful warnings of bankruptcy.

Sociologist Razelle Frankl studied video telecasts of Oral Roberts, Robert Schuller, Jim Bakker, Rex Humbard, Jimmy Swaggart, Jerry Falwell, James Robison, and Pat Robertson in 1981 and found that no preacher used less than 10 percent of broadcast time for *direct* fund-raising appeals. Two-thirds of the televangelists' appeals for money were targeted at the personal needs of viewers.

"In addition," she discovered, "television preachers made funding appeals that were integrated into the program content and were not

as easily distinguished as commercial appeals." The result was what Frankl termed a "hybrid" of traditional revivalism and television. "The ministries are combining religious norms and broadcasting norms."[10]

Thus have the financial exigencies of the televangelists become part of the Great Commission. Their theology is closely intertwined with the budgets of their electronic empires. Electric Christianity is not simply traditional Christianity broadcast across cable channels and beamed around the globe by satellites. It is a transformed message, befitting the needs of those who purport merely to serve it.

The subtleties of theology do not carry well over television. The medium is fundamentally visual, not cerebral. It is not an easy medium to master. Perhaps that is why many liberal critics are so quick to mistakenly dismiss what they see as raw hucksterism.

Whatever one may think about the televangelists, it is helpful to understand the unique free-market position they occupy in the world of broadcasting.

Commercial television is paid for by advertising. Public television, on the other hand, is funded by a combination of government grants, philanthropic gifts from corporations and foundations, and private contributions or subscriptions from individuals.

Religious television occupies a position in between these two models. It is commercial in the sense that televangelism is selling a product— Jesus Christ. The funds don't come from commercial sponsors but, rather, directly from viewers. But the viewers have to be coaxed into giving. And, as mentioned earlier, people are more willing to give to specific projects than they are to pay for airtime. Hence, projects become the means to raise money to support the television ministries. Unfortunately, fund-raising has virtually become the tail that wags the dog, even to the point of dominating, in some instances, the theologies of some of the televangelists.

The downfall of Oral Roberts's ministry comes from the fact that his projects have exceeded the capability of his audience to give. The root of his demise goes back to the late 1970s, when he undertook his most ambitious building project. Falling behind on the revenues needed to keep on schedule, Roberts stepped up the amount of time devoted to appealing for funds. It finally reached a point where he did nothing but beg for money during the entire program.

And for this he paid a heavy price. People turned off their television

sets or tuned in to a program that would afford them some spiritual uplift. Throughout the period of the medical complex construction, Roberts's ratings slipped. And they continued to slip. From 1980 through 1986, Roberts lost 59 percent of his audience. He obviously could not use any more heavily mortgaged brick-and-mortar projects to dun his shrinking pool of supporters for funds. So he portrayed God as an extortionist (never mind his pious protestations to the contrary).

The "ceiling" or upper boundary of funding for religious broadcasting is still unknown, but Oral Roberts's troubles strongly suggest there are limits. It needs to be said, on the other hand, that there are dangers in failing to build. Rex Humbard's experience confirms that.

If we step back and look at the process, without normative sentiments, it is evident that it conforms remarkably to the American free-enterprise system. There are still lots of new syndicated programs going on the air and trying to plug into the success formula. While some are failing, others are on the ascent.

Viewed as a market activity, the sham and scam of the Roberts and Bakker ministries reveal a system that is working. When American automobile makers produced an inferior product and the top executives raked off huge bonuses, the American people began buying foreign cars. And, similarly, when raw ambition and greed turned preachers of the Gospel into hucksters, their motives were discovered and their clients sought another product.

Of course, a lot of people have been deceived by a televangelist. They gave funds believing in the purity of the motives of those who asked for them. But people get burned in a lot of ways. Some who can't afford it put down hard-earned money on lottery tickets that have a minuscule chance of winning. The telephone rings daily with dozens of get-rich-quick schemes that are pure-and-simple telefraud. Good friends encourage involvement in substance abuse that can kill. And many charitable organizations and social causes use fund-raising techniques that are not much different from those used by televangelists. It all boils down to a matter of perspective.

No one has to like any of the hundreds of ways people separate other people from their money. But the huckstering of some televangelists takes on a somewhat different complexion in the context of lots of other hucksterism in society. And what may appear as huckstering

by a televangelist may not be so construed if we are approached by a charity we approve of.

Clearly, American televangelism is a unique organizational hybrid. Its unique oligarchic form has provided a structure for its growth and development within a free market. As a religious institution, it is protected by the First Amendment and, hence, has been relatively unmolested by critics who would rather see the entire enterprise dismantled.

If the electric church were not meeting important needs of those who watch and contribute, it would have gone out of business long ago. And if televangelists do not move quickly to regulate themselves and their peers, it is unlikely that public opinion will permit them to continue without some kind of government regulation. But it seems unlikely that this step will be necessary. Those who have placed their trust in individual television ministries, regardless of which one, felt a little more cautious about their support in 1987 than they did in 1986. A condition of their continued trust and support will be public accountability of how money is spent.

Time will be the test of how committed Jerry Falwell and his fellow televangelists are to a new openness. The authors think he does appear serious and his colleagues, whether or not they like it, will probably be caught up in a new mode of public accountability.

This new accountability, assuming it is forthcoming, will substantially check initiatives for government oversight of religious broadcasters. For the foreseeable future, televangelists will continue to go about the business of building their empires—perhaps a little less oligarchic than in the past, yet essentially the products of highly motivated and talented individuals. And the organizations they are creating seem destined to have a significant impact on the future of American society.

A closer examination of two of the most significant television ministries will reveal that there are different routes to success. Comparing and contrasting the parachurches and the organization-building strategies of the two best-known televangelists—Jerry Falwell and Pat Robertson—reveals how growth can be accomplished in different ways.

Reverend Jerry Falwell, an independent Baptist and a graduate of

Baptist Bible College in Springfield, Missouri, founded the Thomas Road Baptist Church in Lynchburg, Virginia, in 1956. From an initial membership of thirty-five members who met for services in a former Donald Duck soft-drink bottling plant, Falwell built Thomas Road into one of the nation's largest congregations.

Soon after he began Thomas Road Baptist Church, Falwell initiated a radio ministry, and then one in television. His ministry prospered and expanded: Within five years the organization included a Christian academy, a bus ministry for children, and an expanded 3,000-seat sanctuary. He created Liberty Baptist College in 1971 and Liberty Baptist Seminary in 1973.

Liberty Baptist College has mushroomed—from a few students meeting at the Thomas Road Baptist Church into Liberty University with an enrollment of approximately 6,500 students. Falwell's twenty-five-year plan projects an enrollment of 50,000 men and women in both undergraduate programs as well as in professional schools of law and medicine. The campus already has thirty-three buildings valued at $30 million, with another $10 million of construction underway. Although tuition, room, and board cost about $6,000 per year, the average per-student subsidy is $2,000. All these funds are covered by the $72 million-plus that Falwell's broadcasting and direct-mail appeals bring in from sympathetic viewers and supporters.

This growth undoubtedly has been stimulated and abetted by the "Old Time Gospel Hour," Falwell's weekly telecast of church services from Thomas Road. The creation of the controversial Moral Majority in 1979 gave Falwell's emerging empire further visibility.

The "Old Time Gospel Hour" is a critical cotter pin in Falwell's parachurch empire, but it is not the *raison d'être* of the ministry. Likewise the Moral Majority. Both are means to other ends. Falwell was several years into his ministry before he clearly understood what he was doing. But he understands perfectly now. He has unabashedly proclaimed, "It is our goal to be the Harvard of academics, the Notre Dame of athletics, and the Brigham Young of religious schools to evangelical and fundamentalist boys and girls."[11]

There are not very many people who would quarrel with the proposition that these are ambitious, if not grandiose, goals beyond any reasonable expectation of achievement. But Falwell doesn't think so.

The Liberty University complex is the key to understanding Jerry

awell's plan for expanding his parachurch empire and his influence
on American history. Already the Liberty University complex is emerging
as more than just another conservative educational institution on the
order of Bob Jones University or Oral Roberts University, where
accepted features of campus life are curfews and student pledges never
to smoke, drink alcohol, or listen to rock music.

In 1980 Falwell claimed that his former students had already founded
200 new churches; his goal for the decade is to establish 5,000. Toward
this goal, Falwell in 1981 organized the Liberty Baptist Fellowship
for Church Planting, whose purpose is to provide "a degree of monthly
support for pastors who start local autonomous, fundamentalist Baptist
churches." Such financial aid would eliminate the need for pastors of
small, struggling churches to take a second job in order to support
their families. The extra money would free them to concentrate their
energies on church growth.

In order to be eligible to receive between $100 and $600 a month
for up to six months of the start-up phase, the pastors must agree with
Liberty's evangelistic mission to "capture their towns for Christ." By
late 1985, the fellowship provided financial assistance (the bulk of
which came from donations by Liberty alumni and their churches) to
fifty-four new pastors, most of them graduates of Liberty Baptist Col-
lege/University.[12]

A total of 688 graduates took part in the May 1985 commencement
exercises of Liberty University. By now thousands have matriculated
and gone on to establish careers and families. Thousands more will
follow in the next decade.

Female alumni cannot pursue the goal of becoming a fundamentalist
minister (though to be the supportive wife of such a pioneering man
is explicitly encouraged). And many male students are preparing for
various careers other than the clergy. Yet a persistent minority of
every class of Liberty graduates, loyal to the "base" institution as they
go about setting up new congregations, is all it takes.

Falwell's estimate of 5,000 churches by 1990, or even by the end
of this century, probably is wishful thinking. But a parachurch based
on a core of loyal ministers and their churches' support, as well as
individual television viewers, is not.

Liberty University is more than simply a training ground for young
missionaries, and Jerry Falwell knows exactly what he is doing. He

understands that his university will send out literally thousands
graduates who have been trained to think about the world in a manne
highly consistent with his own religious beliefs and socioeconomic
philosophy. His graduates will enter every walk of life. Hundreds,
perhaps thousands, will establish "independent" Baptist churches. A
fair proportion of those churches are likely to be called Liberty Baptist
Church. But neither are these churches an end in themselves. They
are a means to the goal of changing America. Jerry Falwell thinks big
and believes in long-term projects and goals.

Whereas Jerry Falwell's religious conglomerate began with a church
and gradually shifted its epicenter to an institution of higher learning,
Marion G. "Pat" Robertson's strategy for developing a world-trans-
forming base has, from the beginning, depended heavily on communications technology. His move into broadcasting may well have
been influenced by his involvement after law school in an electronic
components business.

Based in Virginia Beach, Virginia, the Christian Broadcasting Network has not always possessed state-of-the-art technology. In 1961,
Robertson felt "called" to purchase a defunct television station in
Virginia Beach with a minimal down payment and only the meagerest
of assets.[13] From that modest start, Pat Robertson has built CBN into
one of the most sophisticated communications networks in the world.

The $230 million CBN empire has become the nation's third largest
cable television network (behind Ted Turner's Cable News Network
and ESPN sports), and it may eventually become, as Robertson once
prophesied, the fourth national network.

"The 700 Club" program, for which Robertson is best known and
which helped launch his network, took its name from a 1963 fund-
raising telethon—still one of Robertson's favorite tactics for obtaining
viewers' donations. Robertson asked for 700 viewers to each pledge
$10 a month to meet the operating budget of his station. He got the
money, and the response inspired the program's title.

"The 700 Club" has evolved in some important ways since its ini-
tiation in the fall of 1963, when it copied the format of Johnny Carson's
"Tonight Show." In 1980, the program was radically restructured, from
a "talk show" to a "magazine" format. The new structure included a
combination of entertainment segments, most closely modeled after
"PM Magazine," along with in-depth investigative reporting along the

lines of "60 Minutes." Also included, to varying degrees, has been a news summary. In 1986, Robertson's commentaries on the news were formally packaged in a segment called "Pat Robertson's Perspective on the News."

Whereas the program once was exclusively live, approximately three-quarters of it is now pretaped. This innovation proved to be particularly valuable as Robertson stepped up his public appearances across the country in a preliminary exploration of a presidential candidacy. With two co-hosts, the program could be spliced together so that Robertson's physical absence from CBN studios in Virginia Beach was hardly discernible.

Robertson's parachurch conglomerate includes several television stations, a satellite earth station, and modern television studios in Virginia Beach. Other facilities include a newly established university—with a law school and a library—of more than 940 students, a conference center and hotel, and the World Outreach Center, which houses Robertson's computers, printing and mailing facilities, offices, and space for counseling. CBN's 1,500 full-time and part-time employees manage production of "The 700 Club" (broadcast five days a week to forty-three countries in various languages), handle his fund-raising/counseling telephones, and process donations.

Robertson is interested in pushing his electronic enterprise beyond merely state-of-the-art communications into more innovative technologies and strategies. To this end, his university's graduate school aims to produce a special elite generation of Christian communicators.

Like their secular colleagues, they will be technically sophisticated. Unlike the secularists, however, they will possess both the skills and the perspective to fit news into a distinctly Christian context. They will not have to dilute their reporting on religious subjects because they don't understand it, nor avoid the Christian inferences to be drawn from the news stories they report and present. In that sense, they portend an acceleration of the crystallization of Christian sentiments that the electric church has already set in motion. Their news, packaged in a Christian context, will have maximum impact on mobilizing evangelicals for future social and political activism.

More so than Falwell, however, Robertson depends heavily on the telephone. Indeed, the telephone is one of the linchpins in Robertson's parachurch growth; he has created a massive telephone prayer and

counseling network throughout the United States. The toll-free counseling hotline receives an estimated 4.4 million calls annually.

People call for a variety of reasons, although usually they request prayer and advice for personal problems such as unemployment, alcohol and drug addiction, marriage/romance difficulties, and poor health. Counseling centers for "The 700 Club" have been established in forty-four metropolitan areas. Typically, these are small, unobtrusive offices whose local telephone numbers flash at the bottom of the television screen during the program, particularly during Robertson's telethons. Most important for Robertson's parachurch empire is the fact that these counseling centers also serve as referral agencies to direct "unchurched" callers to local congregations. CBN has a church referral list of more than 15,000 churches in all denominations.

CBN offers a powerful means for producing a motivated parachurch following. After all, viewers seek out Robertson's counselors, not vice versa. To put it another way: What salesman wouldn't like to have a list of 4 million or more prospects who have already volunteered that they are interested in his product?

Still, ambitious ministers building electronic parachurch empires have to be careful. They are faced with the delicate matter of being accused of siphoning monies, if not members, from existing denominations. They might even be charged with creating new denominations themselves, something both Falwell and Robertson have vigorously denied.

It is conceivable that Falwell and Robertson are not consciously aware of how easily a parachurch grounded in electronics could slip over the line and emerge the next moment as a denomination. In any case, televangelists such as Robertson have been insistent that their only purpose is to evangelize and support local churches' outreach. They stress that they have no wish to compete with local congregations for members' loyalties or donations. They have strong reasons to deny publicly (and even to themselves) that denomination-building is a goal or might ever result unintentionally from their ministries. Many audience members would be shocked or outraged to discover that they were contributing to an emerging new denomination, and support might recede.

Televangelists, through broad grass-roots support of their parachurches, speak for a constituency of Americans interested in a con-

servatively directed cultural revolution. It is unlikely that this revolution will meet the fate of the youthful protest movements of the "Woodstock" generation, coopted as they were, or commercialized into insignificance. As Jeremy Rifkin points out in *The Emerging Order*, change-oriented evangelicalism now has "its own communications structure . . . formidable enough to withstand a frontal assault."[14]

If a television ministry could build colleges, cathedrals, hospitals, and spiritual Disneylands, it seemed likely that it could also be used to pursue projects that are not necessarily direct offspring of religious broadcasting. Jerry Falwell's decision to create the Moral Majority was the first bold attempt to test this proposition. While Falwell made a great deal of separating his role as leader of the Moral Majority from his role as preacher on the "Old Time Gospel Hour" and pastor of the Thomas Road Baptist Church, there is no question that his multiple roles of preacher and politician reinforce one another.

Pat Robertson, too, used his religious television role to demonstrate his political acumen to the world, and his local Freedom Council chapters (disbanded in 1986) to build a following for his political views. Whatever his fate as a politician, there is no question that Robertson's blending of religion, politics, and economic analysis on "The 700 Club" has elevated his personal status as a respected conservative spokesperson. His potential to capitalize upon this status is considerable.

Other televangelists, such as Jimmy Swaggart and D. James Kennedy, are also positioned to channel their audiences toward explicit political projects. As long as the Federal Communications Commission, the Congress, and the courts do not change broadcasting rules, religious broadcasting has strong potential as a base for social and political movements. Indeed, for the evangelicals who are discovering their activist heritage and feeling "mad as hell," it may prove irresistible.

8

Is Anybody Listening?
The Great Audience-size Debate

*Starting in the predawn hours of each Sunday morning,
the largest religious gathering in America takes place,
drawing almost 130 million people to their radio and
television sets. What happens is both exciting and miraculous. It involves a new approach to the problem as
old as the Bible: how to introduce struggling, helpless
individuals to a loving God who wants them to meet Him
and be born again.*

*This amazing event takes place every week, all week,
from early Sunday morning through the final midnight
stroke on Saturday night. Making this possible is the
awesome technology of broadcasting, which many consider to be one of the major miracles of modern times;
and making it meaningful is the overwhelming love of a
God who cares passionately about each one of the world's
four billion people. I believe that God has raised up this
powerful technology expressly to reach every man, woman,
boy, and girl on earth with the even more powerful
message of the gospel.*

—Ben Armstrong, Executive Director,
National Religious Broadcasters

T he ageless riddle of whether a tree
falling in the forest makes a crashing sound if no one is present to
hear it has an analogue in the world of broadcasting. Has a broadcaster
communicated anything if there is no one out there picking up his
transmitted signals?

The sociopolitical meaning of the televangelists pivots on the ques-

tion "Is anybody listening?" Obviously, people are listening. But how many? A great deal hinges on the answer.

A small but steadily growing audience might suggest that the potential social and political influence of the televangelists is on the ascent. And, similarly, a declining audience would suggest that the potential for the video vicars to shape American politics is waning.

On the surface, nothing would seem to be simpler. Two major organizations, the A. C. Nielsen Company and the Arbitron Company, monitor America's radio and television listening and viewing habits. Theoretically, Arbitron and Nielsen have the technological capability to measure all radio and television audiences in the nation on a continuous basis. But for the large majority of programs, they don't do so; the cost does not warrant the value of the information.

Three times a year—February, May, and November—Nielsen and Arbitron study the entire country in what is called the "sweeps," assembling great quantities of data about audiences to serve the needs of stations, networks, producers, advertisers, and other interested parties. This information is published in a separate volume for each of the 200 "base" markets in the country. In addition, both Nielsen and Arbitron publish summary volumes for all syndicated programs. In recent years, both companies have commenced publishing separate volumes on syndicated religious programs.

So why not just ask Arbitron or Nielsen how many people are watching religious television? Or, better yet, why not borrow their studies from a local library and study the data?

The seemingly simple question of the audience size of religious programs is actually complex—to the point of defying an answer. It is, nevertheless, a question that must be addressed in order to assess the potential of religious television as an instrument for mobilizing conservative Christians to social action.

Television audiences have to be estimated based on sampling, a science that is reasonably sophisticated. The difficulties in measurement arise from variations in human behavior that no sampling technique can monitor adequately.

First, since people may be watching one moment and doing something else the next, reliable measurement requires more-or-less-continuous sampling, which can be done with meters hooked up to a carefully selected sample of television sets. The meters automatically

read whether a set is on or off, as well as the channel to which it is tuned. But the meter cannot tell you who is watching, if anyone.

To measure who is watching, Arbitron and Nielsen ask a sample of Americans to complete a diary (log) of their viewing habits. While diaries can provide an approximation of the demographic character-istics of viewers, this method is notoriously flawed. Most people do not keep an ongoing log, and when they do sit down to record their viewing from the previous hours or days, they tend toward systematic inclusion or exclusion of certain types of programs. Further, cable television has significantly increased the number of available channels, and this, in turn, has increased the possibilities for error.

The methods used to measure audiences has been called "a mix of science and voodoo." It is, nevertheless, a "quirky but agreed-upon ratings system" that has been altered very little in commercial tele-vision over the last thirty-seven years.[1]

In the fall of 1987, Nielsen introduced an innovation in audience measurement that created a storm in the industry. Called a "people meter," the new method combines a meter and a diary. It monitors the set, as with the old meter system, while providing a hand-held device individual household members can use to electronically log in or log out when they watch television.

In theory, the new method should produce more accurate and re-liable data than the old tried-and-true methods. But William Rubens, vice president for research at NBC, thinks the people meters will produce "chaos." We may never know for certain whether the people meters produce better or merely different statistics.

What has upset network officials is that preliminary tests of the new technique produced smaller audience numbers. CBS's "Dallas," for example, had 11 percent fewer viewers with the people-meter method than with the old system. And NBC's "Cosby Show" lost two rating points, which translates roughly into 1.7 million households.

Lower ratings made a tempest inevitable because ratings determine how much broadcasters can charge for advertising. Network advertis-ing rates range from $80,000 to $400,000—more for such extravaganzas as the Super Bowl—for thirty seconds. Take away advertising and you take away the major reason for audience ratings.

Gathering audience data is very expensive. While very limited sum-

mary data are published weekly in the entertainment sections of major newspapers, the details of the data-gathering process are carefully guarded industry secrets. Arbitron and Nielsen sell the results of their studies to the networks, to advertisers, and to syndicated programmers for a very handsome price. Their data books are not found in libraries because that would make the results public information.

Prior to 1980, there was little interest in the audience ratings for syndicated religious programs. Since there is no commercial advertising during these broadcasts, the information on audience size seemed to have limited intrinsic worth. Only a few of the producers of religious programs subscribed to either the Arbitron or the Nielsen service. Many were even unaware that a service existed.

The general public's lack of interest in the audience size for religious broadcasters changed sharply during the summer of 1980, when candidate Ronald Reagan made appearances at the National Affairs Briefing in Dallas and the eastern regional meeting of the National Religious Broadcasters in Lynchburg. The latter took place on the campus of Jerry Falwell's Liberty University. Reagan's appearances greatly spurred the media's discovery of the potentially large voting bloc religious broadcasters were attempting to mobilize. It was a matter of straightforward political arithmetic: the larger their audiences, the greater the potential political influence of televangelists.

At the time this "need" to know how many people were listening arose, it would not have been easy to predict the storm of controversy that would later ensue. The great audience-size debate continues, although the broad parameters are better understood today than they were in 1980.

The first round in the audience-size controversy was a direct outgrowth of the recognition that TV preachers might exercise political clout from their airwave pulpits. In the beginning, many prominent print and broadcast media, including the *New York Times*, cited Ben Armstrong's estimate of a weekly audience of 130 million for religious broadcasting without raising an eyebrow.[2]

Armstrong, executive director of the National Religious Broadcasters, based this figure on an extrapolation of a study conducted by a sociologist. It was an unrealistic figure, and Armstrong knew that. But it was a powerful attention-getter for the opening paragraph of

his book, *The Electric Church*. Later in the book he cited as more
reasonable an A. C. Nielsen estimate of 14 million weekly television
viewers.[3]

Armstrong, who initially expressed serious reservations about the
movement of religious broadcasters into the political arena, inadver-
tently contributed to that process with his audience-size hyperbole.
So did Jerry Falwell, the most visible of the televangelists who were
speaking out from their video pulpits on political and social issues.
His public-relations promotion packet claimed an audience of 17 million for the "Old Time Gospel Hour," and on numerous occasions he
claimed even larger audiences.

Then, in July 1980, at the Republican National Convention in Detroit, Falwell told at least two reporters that the "Old Time Gospel
Hour" really had an audience of 50 million viewers! It was as if R2D2,
who was starring in *The Empire Strikes Back* that summer, had fixed
the hyperdrive on his Old Time Gospel Ship so it could travel at
astronomical speed to spread the Good News.

Armstrong and Falwell, of course, were not the only ones with a
tendency to get carried away when talking about their audiences.
There were many others. One televangelist (who realistically could
barely claim an audience of six figures) frequently boasted that while
he didn't know the size of his audience, he was sure that it measured
"in the millions." It may be an occupational carryover from the days
of urban revivalism, when preachers were known to exaggerate the
number of souls they saved. Jerry Falwell is now more cautious about
throwing around grossly exaggerated audience figures. When he does
use unsubstantiated figures, he often quips, "ministerially speaking,"
as if to say, "Preachers don't lie, but sometimes they remember big."

After a while, reporters became skeptical of the audience claims
made by television ministries, but the doubters seemed content to
deal with their misgivings by simply writing, "So and so *claims* X
million viewers," rather than digging around to see if any bonafide
statistics were available.

In the months following the 1980 election, there were literally scores
of articles and broadcast reports attempting to assess the role of the
New Christian Right in the outcome. Audience size of the television
ministries was intensely debated. Meanwhile, no one seemed aware

of the fact that Arbitron and A. C. Nielsen had been routinely collecting "hard data" on audience size for many years.

The second round of the audience-size controversy commenced in mid-1981, when Arbitron and Nielsen data were made public for the first time. In June, Jeffrey K. Hadden and Charles Swann presented Arbitron data in their book *Prime Time Preachers*,[4] while sociologist William Martin reported Nielsen data in an article entitled "The Birth of a Media Myth" in *The Atlantic*.[5]

The two data sets were not entirely comparable, but the rankings and audience-size estimates agreed remarkably. Similar conclusions coming from independent sources lent credibility to the craftsmanship of both organizations.

The most important conclusion to be drawn from these two independent surveys was that the audience size for the syndicated religious broadcasters was much smaller than the claims that had been made by many of the ministries. Martin reported an audience of 13.8 million for the top ten programs in the Nielsen ratings for November 1980.[6] Hadden and Swann reported a total of 20.5 million for Arbitron's sixty-six syndicated programs, with a total of 14.9 million for the top ten programs—a discrepancy of a mere 8 percent for data gathered nine months apart.[7]

The infusion of hard (or at least harder) facts into the controversy did not settle the debate about audience size and trends. If anything, it added fuel to the flames. The reason: Lots of people have vested interests in how many people are watching and how the numbers are interpreted.

Enter the political factor.

It should not have come as a surprise that religious broadcasters themselves were not happy with these numbers—particularly those who had publicly claimed vastly larger audiences than the Arbitron and Nielsen analyses showed.

Ironically, some of the electric church's strongest adversaries also challenged these smaller audience estimates. Their reason for doing so was understandable. *If* the number of persons watching Jerry Falwell and other politically minded televangelists was much smaller than they claimed, then the rationale for the liberal People for the American Way organization, for example, was diminished. In short, the greater

the audience size of the right-wing televangelists, the greater the threat and, hence, the greater the urgency to support countermovement organizations such as "People For," which had been formed to do battle with the New Christian Right.

Meanwhile, another group of adversaries argued that the Arbitron and Nielsen figures *overestimated* the "real" audience size of the televangelists.[8] These figures, they argued, do not take into account the duplication of audience when the same person watches more than one religious program. The point is well taken, but the data regularly reported by Arbitron and Nielsen provide no basis for determining what proportion of the measured audience involves duplication. Thus, any attempt to adjust the Arbitron or Nielsen data downward to account for duplicated audience involves unverifiable assumptions. In short, it's back in the guessing game.

One of us, having been a party to the controversy, felt no particular need to defend either the Arbitron or the Nielsen figures if a more satisfactory method of measuring audience size came along. So he listened to the arguments of broadcasters who claimed larger audiences and the critics who claimed audiences were smaller.

Although both sides raised interesting and possibly legitimate arguments in behalf of their case, there was no compelling reason to conclude that the factors that would produce a larger audience number were more significant than the overestimation that resulted from duplication. Hence, in the absence of clearly superior data, a reasonable conclusion seemed to be that the Nielsen and Arbitron figures were not too far off the mark. Furthermore, they had the merit of being standardized measures that could reveal trends over time. Comparing data from the two companies would call attention to any great discrepancies. In a word, the Arbitron and Nielsen data seemed much preferable to nonempirical "guesstimates."

Debate about how many people are watching religious programming was one factor leading to the creation of an ad hoc committee to investigate the effects of religious television, which grew out of the Consultation on the Electronic Church sponsored by the National Council of Churches in February 1980. From the beginning, the project was conceived as bipartisan, and the committee consisted of a coalition of evangelical religious broadcasters and the mainline church traditions. It was co-chaired by William Fore, director of the National

Council of Churches Communication Commission, and Ben Armstrong.[9]

The ad hoc committee raised more than $150,000 and commissioned the Annenberg School of Communications and the Gallup Organization to conduct the research. Even before research had commenced, the Religion and Television Research Project was heralded as "the definitive" investigation of religious broadcasting.

Throughout the study, the two investigative teams worked independently. George Gerbner, dean of the Annenberg School, was responsible for coordinating and integrating a final report. In the spring of 1984, the long-awaited report appeared.[10]

As it turned out, there was little integration of the two investigations. De facto, they became two studies, with the Gallup study appearing as an appendix to the Annenberg study.[11] The findings of the two studies were at odds on several critical points—including the important question of how many people are watching.

The two research teams used different methods to measure audience size, and, with hindsight, it is not particularly surprising that they came up with radically different conclusions. Piggybacking on Arbitron "sweeps" data, the Annenberg team came up with a figure of 24.7 million viewers. Then, turning to viewing diaries kept by a sample of Arbitron respondents, they concluded that the nonduplicated audience was 13.3 million. In contrast, the Gallup survey asked people if they had watched a religious television program during the previous month. Thirty-two percent, which would represent approximately 70 million viewers, claimed that they had.

The Annenberg measure was for one *week*, the Gallup measure for one *month*. Certainly, if there was duplication during a week, the amount of duplication would increase over the course of a month. Thus, the discrepancy of more than 500 percent—13.3 million versus approximately 70 million—was even greater than it appears.

Regrettably, the Annenberg team took an imperialistic view, assuming the superiority of their method and ignoring the Gallup data in the Executive Summary. So also did the news release, which was prepared by the National Council of Churches.

Furthermore, the text of the study was treated as a quasi-secret document. Only the Executive Summary was made available to the press. Naturally, the audience figures were disputed by the religious

broadcasters. So the great audience-size debate was back to ground zero.

But not quite. There remained the puzzle of why some adversaries of the electric church, who had earlier accepted the myth of huge audiences, abruptly changed their minds and became adamant in pressing the case for even smaller audiences than those measured by Arbitron and Nielsen.

Most vociferous in this group of liberal churchmen was William Fore, the chief spokesperson of the National Council of Churches. In a July 1980 *TV Guide* article, Fore wrote, "Some 47 percent of Americans see at least one religious program a week on TV."[12] Later, when the Annenberg team reported the weekly "unduplicated" viewing audience for religious programs at 13.3 million, Fore whittled the number down to a mere 7.2 million. Precisely how he did this calculation was not clear.[13]

Why the great reversal? The most plausible explanation is that the mainline Protestant communities now see their chances of tapping into free airtime if they can "prove" that the current syndicated broadcasters are not reaching nearly as many people as they claim. Given the confusing nature of the data, and the absurdity of the claims made by some, why not claim that the electric pews are empty—or nearly so? If hardly anyone is watching the current offerings, so this logic goes, then stations and networks should give the liberal churches free time so they can produce programs that are more in keeping with the tastes of "mainline Protestants" and thus will attract much larger audiences.

Pursuing this strategy, the liberal church leaders have created another myth, which is just as misleading as the myth of exaggerated audience size debunked in 1981.

This new fabrication might be dubbed "the myth of the tiny and insignificant remnant." It seeks to create a self-fulfilling prophecy. If nobody believes that anybody is watching, then perhaps nobody else will tune in. And if nobody is watching, how can stations justify selling airtime to the televangelist charlatans, who are, supposedly, getting that money by ripping off poor little ole ladies?

If this is indeed a conscious strategy for returning mainliners to a significant place in religious broadcasting, it is doomed from the beginning, less a strategy than a futile, head-in-the-sand response. The

liberal church tradition in America has lost every major battle for access to the airwaves in the past three decades. Its leaders are bankrupt of ideas for getting back into the competition. Furthermore, they have duped their liberal church constituencies into half-believing that the airwaves are inherently evil and that they shouldn't be there. Unless, of course, they get a chance to do so—in which case they will do better than evangelicals and commercial broadcasters. In this way the mainline leadership exhibits a schizophrenia that staggers the imagination, reminding one of Humpty Dumpty's proclamation that words mean just exactly what he chooses them to mean.

Part—though certainly not all—of the debate about the audiences of religious television results from using different measures. Comparing the Gallup and the Annenberg statistics is rather like comparing apples and oranges. The figures don't lend themselves to comparison. It is impossible to obtain a comparable figure by multiplying the Annenberg figure by four (the number of weeks in a month) because part of the audience is duplicated—i.e., individuals who watched more than once. But neither does dividing the Gallup figure by four produce a comparable figure. Whereas the Gallup figure is a cumulative one (the total number of people who watched), the Annenberg figure represents an average quarter-hour.

How do we get out of this quagmire? We begin by recognizing that measuring a television audience is not as simple and direct as counting how many people go through a turnstile at a football game or attend church services in a local congregation, where people are either present or not present. Most people do not watch television the way they attend a church service or an athletic contest. They tune in late and depart early; they switch channels and then leave the room. In front of a television set, people generally feel at greater liberty to talk with one another than they do in church. They may also do lots of other things—take a phone call, prepare breakfast, eat, do dishes, get ready to go out, and so on.

No one would contend that the only legitimate audience count for the electric church covers those who arrive on time, listen attentively in a fixed location, and stay until the program is over. Even if someone did want to apply the standard of attentiveness, it simply is not possible. Thus, all measures are inexact and arbitrary.

The question is, what counts? Abstractly, the answer is that there

are many ways to count, and no single way of counting is necessarily better than another. All ways involve some degree of arbitrariness and some degree of error. Furthermore, what constitutes a reasonable or fair way of counting an audience for one purpose may not be a fair measure for some other purpose.

On the practical level, it is helpful to understand how the professionals count. Pollsters, such as the Gallup Organization, ask people to recall whether they watched television. The questioner may specify a time period—such as last night, last week, or last month. And the interviewer may further inquire as to whether the viewer watched a specific program, some category of programming, or just any program. Nielsen and Arbitron use combinations of diaries and meters. And both Nielsen and Arbitron supplement their national surveys with individual market surveys. As with the case of nationwide estimates, local market surveys are used to set advertising rates. Larger markets have larger surveys because there are higher advertising revenues at stake. Smaller samples are drawn in smaller communities, producing a greater error ratio in the findings.

The most frequently cited Nielsen and Arbitron statistics are quarter-hour averages, a statistic they use for at least two very good reasons. First, the quarter-hour unit is the basic building block and common denominator for accumulating all statistics. Second, the quarter-hour average has commonsense utility for marketing airtime. For the potential advertiser it answers the question, "If I buy advertising time on this program, what size audience am I going to be reaching?"

Many different types of information are gathered beyond quarter-hour averages. Household data are the most easily accessible and the most reliable. But there are also important reasons for obtaining detailed demographic information about individuals, such as sex and age characteristics. Advertising is geared to demographics. To cite an obvious example, it makes no sense to advertise a product for children in the late evening when most children have already gone to bed.

There are also important reasons for comparing one program with another. One way of doing this is by examining audience share—what proportion of the television sets that are turned on are tuned to a particular program? Audience rating, on the other hand, indicates what proportion of all the households in the survey are tuned to a particular program.

For all of these statistics, the industry builds upon the average quarter-hour data. But there is no intrinsic reason why other statistics should not be used. It all boils down to what a statistic is used for. Statistics may be valuable in making economic decisions (e.g., setting advertising rates), or in creating public-relations images, or in establishing that a certain program has the potential to communicate to a particular audience.

The average quarter-hour rating may not be a particularly useful figure for assessing the audience of an event lasting several hours. A professional football game, for example, will have fluctuations in its audience size depending on the ebb and flow of the contest. If the score of the game is close, the audience may build toward the end, whereas a lopsided score may result in a thinning-out of the audience.

Another reason the average quarter-hour audience may not be useful is the simple fact that programs are not all the same length. "Oral Roberts and You," for example, is a thirty-minute program, while "The 700 Club" airs ninety minutes a day, five days a week, with reruns on Saturday and Sunday in some markets. In terms of average quarter-hour audiences, Oral Roberts has a much larger audience than "The 700 Club," but his cumulative audience is much smaller, because "The 700 Club" has fifteen times more airtime per week. Comparing the simple quarter-hour averages, then, distorts the market significance of daily broadcasters.

And this brings us back to the politicized nature of statistics on the religious television audience. In 1980 it was the perceived potential of mobilizing viewers for political purposes that made us all conscious of audience size. Now audience size has taken on a political significance of its own. As noted earlier, religious programming is governed by free-enterprise market principles even though advertising does not figure in the scheme of their programming. As more programs have entered the market, competition for airtime and audiences has increased.

Every producer has a stake in presenting his or her program to its audience and other interested parties in the most favorable light. What now exists is the creative use of statistics to achieve this goal. One religious television program after another claims to be Number One. And there is a fair chance that they are all telling the truth. Everything depends on the statistic being cited. Clearly this is a case where the

phrase *caveat emptor* applies. Viewers need to develop judgment and consumer sense in listening to the competing claims.

Whereas the audience statistics have become politicized as a matter of market competition, Pat Robertson's candidacy for the presidency has renewed interest in religious television audiences as a potential political bloc. Who is listening? Do evangelical Christians represent an important new force in the political process in America?

Pat Robertson, far more than any other religious broadcaster in America, has utilized market research to understand his audience. Thus, it was not surprising to learn in 1985 that he had commissioned the A. C. Nielsen Company to conduct special research to better assess the size of his audience.

A cumulative study of "The 700 Club" audience should inevitably produce much larger numbers than the average quarter-hour figures. Thus, CBN's Nielsen project seemed self-serving at first glance. But CBN was interested in a number of vexing issues about audience size as well. For several years, CBN marketing personnel had been convinced that the average quarter-hour ratings were themselves an underestimation. Their analysis of volume of audience response showed a higher proportional response from households receiving "The 700 Club" on cable than from regular syndicated broadcasts, suggesting that cable households were underenumerated.

A third issue of interest was the matter of audience duplication. In order to measure cumulative audience, to check out their suspicions regarding underenumeration of cable audiences, and to examine the extent of audience duplication, CBN had Nielsen do special tabulations, utilizing their national meter sample, during the period of the February 1985 sweeps. Data were to be collected for the other top ten syndicated religious programs in addition to "The 700 Club."

Having followed the technical issues in the religious-television-audience debate for several years, the authors immediately recognized that this study would provide unprecedented data and insight. When the study was initiated, Hadden was president of the Society for the Scientific Study of Religion, an international organization of scholars from thirty-five nations, and Shupe was program chair for the organization's annual meeting.

The authors asked David Clark, CBN's vice president for marketing,

to share the findings with the international community of social scientists that would be gathering for the annual meetings of SSSR in Savannah, Georgia, in October 1985. The authors specified only that Nielsen send a representative to the meetings to certify that the data had been gathered in a manner consistent with the organization's high standards of scientific data collection and to answer questions from scholars regarding the research methodology. Both CBN and Nielsen agreed to participate.[14]

Before summarizing the findings, the authors should note that a few critics have claimed the statistics are inflated and that they were produced purely for political purposes. The authors do not agree with this conclusion, nor have we seen evidence that would give it plausibility.

Since one of us had been an early skeptic of the audience claims of televangelists, we approached these new results with great caution. We examined the data carefully before concluding that the statistics are accurate within the parameters of error normally expected with sample survey methods.

The highlights of the CBN/Nielsen study follow the three broad areas of concern described above.

1. The cumulative audience sizes were significantly larger for the ten programs studied than were the average quarter-hour audiences.

• The average quarter-hour audience size for "The 700 Club," using Nielsen's conventional measure, was 424,500 households. The cumulative ninety-minute daily audience was 2,547,000 households, the weekly total was 7,216,500, and the monthly grand total of viewers came to 16,300,000. Thus, the daily cumulative audience is six times larger than the average quarter-hour, the weekly audience thirty-eight times larger.

• The top ten television programs had a combined average quarter-hour audience of just under 8 million. The cumulative figure for a week came to 27 million and for the month 68 million.

2. The national meter sample, which included households receiving the broadcasting via cable, revealed significantly higher average quarter-

hour audiences than had been measured by the conventional method of averaging the diaries from 200 separate markets.

- Utilizing the meter sample, including cable households, increased the average quarter-hour audience of "The 700 Club" from 424,000 to 1,443,300—an amazing 340 percent increase. This confirms CBN's suspicion that cable reception was being significantly undercounted.
- The data reveal that all quarter-hour estimates obtained by the conventional method are undercounted. Falwell's quarter-hour estimate increased from 594,300 to 1,358,400 and Jimmy Swaggart's from 1,443,300 to 2,631,999. For the top ten programs, the meter method produced an average quarter-hour audience 82 percent higher than the conventional method.

3. A significant proportion of the audience estimates, regardless of the method of measurement, consists of duplication, that is, counting the same viewer more than once. Still, the total cumulative audience of religious television is far from insignificant.

The cumulated monthly audience—cume, in the trade—for the top ten religious programs was 67.7 million households; the unduplicated cume, 34.1 million households. On a monthly basis, then, the duplicated cume is inflated by 98 percent. Since Nielsen estimates a total of 85.9 million TV households in America,[15] the unduplicated figure indicates that, on average, 40 percent of all American households watch at least one segment of religious television each month. The unduplicated figure for an average week is 21 percent.

The credibility of these figures is supported by a Gallup survey, conducted in April 1987, in which 39 percent of the American public reported viewing a religious program within the previous thirty days and 25 percent said they had watched during the previous seven days.[16] That weekly figure of 25 percent is up sharply from the 18 percent reported in 1983.

Furthermore, televangelism is a regular part of the religious diet of evangelical Christians. In the Gallup survey, 79 percent of all evangelicals reported watching religious broadcasting; 46 percent reported viewing in the week preceding their interview.

CBN has continued to have Nielsen monitor its own "700 Club"

audience with the more sophisticated cumulative audience surveys. Regrettably, there are no data for other religious programs, so there will not be an opportunity to study trends.

The cabling of television in America has increased the complexity of measuring audience trends. Each year sees expanded cable penetration. From October 1983 through February 1987, the number of households in the United States receiving television via cable grew from approximately 31 million to 42 million, representing an increase in cable penetration from 38 percent to 48 percent.[17]

With cable television has come a decline in the networks' share of television viewing. From 1981 through early 1987, the networks experienced a decline from 83 percent to 76 percent of the audience share during prime-time viewing.[18] During this same period, religious broadcasters moved increasingly into cable. The syndicated program analysis books published by Arbitron and Nielsen largely miss the cable audience, to the point where the utility of the syndicated reports is dubious.

Consider the following: From 1980 through 1985, Arbitron figures show an increase in audience size from 20.5 million to 23.9 million, for a net growth of 16 percent.[19] Averaging just a little over 3 percent annually, this is not a torrid pace of growth, but still an upward trend. Then, in 1986, the combined Arbitron figures show a sharp drop to 19.2 million, a decline of almost 20 percent.

Nothing in the collective experience of syndicated religious broadcasters would confirm a calamity of this magnitude. But data prepared by Nielsen for CBN suggest the decline may be substantially attributable to the crossover to cable broadcasting. The CBN data do show a dramatic decline of 17 percent in the average quarter-hour audience for their syndicated broadcasts of "The 700 Club."[20] But the daily cumulative audience for syndicated and cable programming combined shows a slight decline of 2 percent, while the total cumulative monthly figures show an increase of 2 percent.

If caution is the best advice in dealing with any data on religious broadcasting, it is evidently difficult to communicate that advice. Reporters hungry for statistics, and critics anxious to make a point, continue to pick up whatever they can find, or whatever makes a point that supports their case.

The feature stories that appeared in the days following the Bakkers'

resignation from PTL communicated lots of misinformation regarding audience size. Perhaps none was more confusing than the "Guide to Sunday Morning Services" published by *People* magazine.[21] Capsule summaries of six leading religious broadcasts indiscriminately mixed together average quarter-hour figures with cumulative weekly figures with household access via cable, terribly distorting any attempt to make an intelligent comparison.

The sharp declines in the average quarter-hour figures are certain to be picked up and heralded as evidence that the electric church is collapsing. Further, someone is likely to conclude that the evidence of a collapsing audience before the Bakker scandals lends credibility to the claim that Jimmy Swaggart or Jerry Falwell or someone was attempting a hostile takeover to buoy his own sagging audience size and revenues.

In the final analysis, the answer to the simple question, "How many people are watching?" is simply that we don't know. Furthermore, the inherent flaws in the data are likely to cloud rather than clarify the issue in the years ahead.

But the answer to the question, "Is anybody listening?" is an unequivocal YES. The audiences are not as huge as some of the televangelists and their supporters were maintaining prior to the addition of Nielsen and Arbitron data to the debate. But, just as certainly, the audiences are not as small as some of their adversaries would like the American public to believe.

The best assessment of the data would indicate that the general trend in audience size has been upward. But evidence of this growth is obscured by the inadequate measure of cable viewing, an ever-increasing proportion of all religious viewing.

As the 1988 presidential primary process unfolds, there can be no mistaking the fact that the audience watching religious broadcasting is very large indeed. And the show Pat Robertson started, as measured by cumulative audience size, is the top drawing card. The Nielsen data indicate "The 700 Club" is daily reaching approximately 2.5 million viewers, and, on a monthly basis, more than 16 million tune in. That is a very substantial base on which to build a grass-roots political organization. But the major question remains—do television audiences translate into voter constituencies?

The powerful medium of television—aided by space satellites and

cable networks—has provided the vehicle for the consolidation of conservative Christian feeling and opinion. Television, in a word, can mobilize that most crucial resource for a social movement in American democracy: committed voters.

Slowly but surely, the electric church appears to be transforming its audiences. The process is far from finished, but it is underway.

9

Politics As the Instrument of a New Ecumenical Movement

I'm frankly sick and tired of the political preachers across the country telling me as a citizen that if I want to be a moral person, I must believe in "A," "B," "C," and "D." . . . And I am even more angry as a legislator who must endure the threats of every religious group who thinks it has some God-granted right to control my vote on every roll call in the Senate.
> —Former U.S. Senator Barry Goldwater

Evangelicals face a tough assignment. Secular minds virtually dismiss biblical values as a legitimate basis for public policy. Some are openly hostile, gratuitously tolerating religious beliefs as innocuous enough when confined to the purely personal, but off limits in the "real world."
> —Robert P. Dugan, Jr.,
> National Association of Evangelicals

Are we bigots? Are we trying to force everyone into our narrow molds? Or are we, as Christians, merely trying to act in self-defense?
> —Vern McLellan,
> Christians in the Political Arena

Long before the New Christian Right had a name or its constituency had a self-conscious identity, there were tens of thousands of evangelical Christians who had become fed up with a number of trends in American society. The issues that

concerned them were not new. Education, abortion, and pornography—to identify three of their concerns—were issues that had been troubling them for a long time, but each issue took on renewed significance and urgency during the 1960s and 1970s.

Evangelical Christians were not alone in their concern for the quality of public education. Books such as *Crisis in the Classroom* and *Why Johnny Can't Read* were national best-sellers during the 1960s. For evangelical Christians, the crisis went beyond the failure of public schools to produce students competent in basic skills. The public schools, they believed, had become institutions for the indoctrination of students with values antithetical to their fundamental beliefs.

They believed this strongly enough that, at considerable cost and sacrifice, they created private Christian schools, a movement that today remains a rapidly growing alternative to public education.

Parents' continued commitment to this expensive proposition required reinforcement of the values that persuaded them to take the step in the first place. Hence, Christian schools served as consciousness-raising institutions for the parents. The principals and preachers who ran them made certain that the parents remembered why they had sacrificed to pay for their children's alternative education.

The public explosion of hedonism, teenage pregnancies, public flaunting of alternative sexual preferences, pornography, and drug use further reinforced the conviction that they were doing the right thing by enrolling their children in a school system that repudiated the legitimacy of these things as individual options.

By the time various government agencies, including the IRS, began poking around in the affairs of the Christian schools, threatening their tax-exempt status, lots of evangelical parents were ready to fight.

The Supreme Court's *Roe* vs. *Wade* decision in 1973, which effectively legalized abortion, readied other evangelical Christians to do battle. The number who joined the National Right-to-Life Committee and other organizations opposed to abortion was not initially large, but the movement was growing slowly, and its members were beginning to make their presence felt nationally.

Phyllis Schlafly, whose Eagle Forum was one of the larger right-to-life groups, led the battle to defeat the proposed Equal Rights Amendment—an objective the New Christian Right achieved though receiving little public notice for it.

The explicitness of pornography in magazines and film, as well as its easy accessibility, was another issue of mounting concern to conservative Christians. *The Report of the President's Commission on Obscenity and Pornography* failed to condemn sexually explicit material. On the contrary, it concluded that pornography had no proven deleterious effects; it might, in fact, have some beneficial qualities. Even though President Richard Nixon refused to acknowledge or receive the report, its very existence reinforced evangelical Christians' belief that the government had become a partner in promoting harmful trends in society.

The Vietnam War took its toll on conservative Christians' trust in government, as did the Watergate scandal.

Disturbed by the direction of government, conservative Christians significantly contributed to the election of Jimmy Carter, a self-professed "born-again" Christian. But four years later, they had come to see Carter as indecisive, too willing to compromise Christian principles, and ineffective in rebuilding either America's military or its self-confidence. So in 1980 they dumped Carter in favor of Ronald Reagan, a man who spoke their rhetoric more explicitly, and also claimed to be "born again."

Even in early 1980 there was not yet a conscious sense among evangelical and fundamentalist Christians that they were participating in a significant social movement. Yes, the Washington for Jesus rally in April of that year had certain unmistakably political elements. But for a large proportion of the participants, their involvement was motivated by a feeling of angst. They prayed fervently that God would deliver America from the malaise in which she had become engulfed.

There was still no recognized leader of an emerging New Christian Right.

Both Jerry Falwell and Pat Robertson underwent long and difficult personal struggles over the decision to become publicly involved in the political process. Back in 1965, Falwell had said that he could not imagine ever turning his attention from preaching the "pure saving gospel . . . [which] . . . does not clean up the outside but regenerates the inside."[1]

After months of moving toward political engagement, Robertson withdrew after the Washington for Jesus rally. If he were destined to become a political leader, he felt, his time had not yet come.

By the time of the rally, Jerry Falwell had already created the Moral Majority, although it had yet to receive any significant national publicity. Falwell did not participate in the rally, claiming that it was not quite a political rally nor a real prayer meeting.

Falwell's interest in the political arena as an instrument for changing America began several years before the 1979 creation of the Moral Majority. By the middle of the decade, Falwell's sermons on "The Old Time Gospel Hour" were laced with practical suggestions for addressing the social ills of America. And in conjunction with the nation's bicentennial celebration, Falwell held I Love America rallies on the steps of state capitols all over the nation.

Falwell gradually inched himself into the role of reformer until he seemed like a nineteenth-century postmillennial urban revivalist. Although he is a premillennialist, he became passionately committed to addressing and changing the ills of this world. He called for reform. He called for prayer. He called for national repentance.

By the time Falwell formed the Moral Majority, he seemed to have no lingering doubts about his responsibility to help change this world as well as prepare people for the next. While he once viewed his role as limited to preaching the gospel of individual salvation, Falwell's ministerial agenda also came to incorporate the well-being of the nation. In his 1980 book called Listen, America!, he wrote:

> I vowed that I would never turn my back on the firm decision and sacred commitment I had made to myself and to God that I would preach and work and pray to stop the moral decay in America that is destroying our freedoms.[2]

He called the 1980s a Decade of Destiny. In his television sermons and in hundreds of speeches around the country, he summoned Americans "back to basics, back to values, back to biblical morality, back to sensibility, and back to patriotism."[3] And he was hopeful:

> If America will face the truth, our nation can be turned around and can be saved from the evils and the destruction that have fallen upon every other nation that has turned its back on God.[4]

Falwell was turning back to the old dominion creation myth, with its recurring cycles of sin, repentance, and redemption. Interestingly,

so does liberal sociologist Robert Bellah. The first lines of his prize-winning book, *The Broken Covenant*, read as follows:

> Once in each of the last three centuries America has faced a time of trial, a time of testing so severe that not only the form but even the existence of our nation have been called into question.[5]

Utopian socialist Bellah's understanding of why the covenant had been broken and what redressing needed to be done was clearly at odds with that of fundamentalist Falwell. The striking thing is that two men so different in their intellectual orientation were able to agree that America was broken and needed fixing.

It is important, further, to recognize that many others from various ideological perspectives also felt this sense of brokenness. Harvard theologian Harvey Cox's call for the return of the sacred to the secular city is a liberal church vision of repentance and redemption.[6] Neo-conservative Richard John Neuhaus would return God to "the naked public square" as a first step toward restoring the covenant,[7] and even Catholic-turned-atheist Michael Harrington agonized about "the politics of God's funeral" and pleaded for national re-creation of something like the creation myth.[8]

The American liberal tradition is not in a strong position to direct us out of this perceived cultural malaise. We stand too close in time to too many liberal programs that were supposed to solve the very problems so disturbing today.

While Ronald Reagan's popularity slipped badly as the Iran-*contra* scandal began to unfold in late 1986, his policies and philosophies have taken the mood of Americans even farther from the liberal solutions that dominated the 1960s. Political moods run in cycles that are not particularly synchronized with electoral cycles. Neo-conservative Irving Kristol is quite likely right when he notes:

> No Democratic successor is going to be able to "turn the clock back." Liberal Democrats who indulge in such a fantasy are comparable to conservative Republicans who, for some three decades, dreamed of a repudiation of Franklin D. Roosevelt and his "abominable" New Deal.[9]

The New Christian Right is not responsible for the resurgence of conservatism in America. The roots of conservative economic philosophy—of which Ronald Reagan is the first adherent to ascend to the presidency—were sown in the 1950s. Conservative Christians participated only nominally in that movement. Most significant for them during the same period was the creation of the Christian Economic Foundation, an organization financed in large measure by the late Sun Oil patriarch J. Howard Pew, who turned to it after failing in his efforts to put the new National Council of Churches on a more conservative course than its predecessor, the Federal Council of Churches. In the 1960s, the wide distribution to clergy of its free publication, *Christian Economics*, may have helped create an intellectual readiness for the political movement that would emerge in the late 1970s.

Liberal culture-watchers largely missed the development of the new conservatism. In the secular political arena, they tended to lump together everyone who was out of step with the dominant liberal mood as fellow travelers with Communist witch-hunters the likes of Joseph McCarthy and John Birch. And on the religious side, Carl McIntire and Billy James Hargis, two noisy, politically minded fundamentalists, were seen as successors to religious demagogues such as Father Charles Coughlin and Gerald L. K. Smith.

When Jerry Falwell and his Moral Majority first began to gain some visibility in 1980, it was assumed that he and his televangelist associates were genealogical blood brothers to the fascistic radical right of the 1950s. The emphasis here is on the word *assumed*. There does not exist, even today, a single scholarly work that genealogically links the New Christian Right with the "Old Christian Right."

The assumption was possible, perhaps inevitable, because of the legacy of American social scientists of the 1950s and early 1960s who developed a theory of political extremism equating conservatism with authoritarianism and paranoia. There were many articulations of this theory, but Richard Hofstadter's *Paranoid Style of American Politics*, published in 1964, was probably the single most important scholarly work.

Liberals saw themselves as politically "centrist." Those who did not agree with them were extremists, hapless victims of the clinical maladies of paranoia and "authoritarian personality." This "medicalization" of the motives of conservatives has provided three generations of lib-

eral Americans with a sanctimonious self-perception as guardians of democracy against extremism of every shape.

It is worth recalling here the wisdom of Kenneth Burke, perhaps the greatest linguist of this century. In his celebrated book *Permanence and Change*, written some fifty years ago, Burke proposed the profound adage that words are not neutral. "The names for things and operations," noted Burke, "smuggle in connotations of good and bad—a noun tends to carry with it a kind of invisible adjective, a verb an invisible adverb."[10]

The power of the Left to camouflage ideology in the neutral-sounding language of social science absolutely overwhelmed Senator Barry Goldwater in his 1964 bid for the presidency. He was successfully labeled a member of the paranoid and authoritarian Radical Right. In later years, America learned that Barry Goldwater was not the maleficent creature slick Madison Avenue advertising had portrayed him to be. But in 1964 he was seen, purely and simply, as a "nuclear madman," an extremist destined to lead America into oblivion.

The power of the Left to overwhelm its opposition with word-kill has considerably abated since the mid-1960s. When Ronald Reagan ran for president, he was given the same treatment, but the labels didn't stick.

The TV evangelists have not been so fortunate. From the beginning of their voyage into the political arena, the televangelists have been portrayed, with considerable success, as perpetrators of "holy terror."

Writing about the cleverness with which liberals interwove social science and medical concepts with self-serving ideological principles, Leo Ribuffo summarizes how extremists could be shunted from political participation without seemingly violating commitment to pluralism in a democratic society:

> If extremists differed tactically, psychologically, and perhaps "anthropolitically" from "rational men," then, without apparent contradiction, liberals could bar them from the "open marketplace of ideas."[11]

We ought never lose sight of the indiscriminate manner in which McCarthyists sought to label all liberals as Communists or Communist-

sympathizers. But by the same token, it is time to recognize that the Left uses very similar tactics in attempting to disqualify conservative Christians, and TV preachers in particular, from participating in the political process.

In the 1970s *Snapping*, by Flo Conway and Jim Siegelman, warned America of a new breed of religious gurus who were able to take control of the minds of young people, transforming their personalities to the point of servitude to their religious masters. So great was the power of these gurus, wrote Conway and Siegelman and many other anticultists, that normal principles of religious liberty could not be sustained.

None of the leaders of the scores of new religious movements that emerged in the late 1960s and 1970s possessed such awesome powers, as British sociologist Eileen Barker brilliantly documents in her award-winning book *The Making of a Moonie* (1984). Still, the anticult movement left a legacy of hostility toward sects and cults. During the 1970s, many states introduced legislation that would have denied fundamental liberties to individuals whose parents objected to their involvement in a new religious group. Under the proposed legislation, parents (even of adult children) would have had the right to get a "conservatorship" order, placing their child in their custody for the expressed purpose of "deprogramming."

The mentality that would severely restrict the religious and civil liberties of individuals who join sects and cults is extended in Conway and Siegelman's *Holy Terror* to members of "fundamentalist" groups. *Holy Terror* is an ideological tract that endeavors to terrorize readers into believing that the fundamentalists are poised and ready to take over America. The book warns of a new, more sophisticated fundamentalism waging war on America's freedoms in religion, politics, and private lives:

> Improving on the extremism of the cranky old right, which most of the nation saw through, the upstart fundamentalist right has wrapped its central issues in religious swaddling. In this way, it has put the old right's rejected social and political agenda back on the map: renamed, reborn, and crisply recorded in terms that are vague and misleading—and irrefutable.[12]

The major perpetrators of this threat, not surprisingly, are the televangelists. Although more sophisticated in their exploitation of modern propaganda techniques, these mental terrorists are not very different from the Shiite Muslims led by Iran's Ayatollah Khomeini. From their "electronic mosques" they threaten to tear down the wall of separation between church and state. "Precedent," argue Conway and Siegelman, "would seem to compel the disestablishment of the electronic church."[13] "At the very least," they continue:

> . . . the tax-exempt status of competitive religious broadcast enterprises should be rescinded. A more constructive course, in our view, would be to end the business of paid religious broadcasting altogether.[14]

From a pair who present themselves as civil libertarians defending human freedom, these are remarkable statements. In the name of defending liberty, they would deny basic constitutionally guaranteed freedoms, including First Amendment rights of free speech and freedom of belief and exercise of religious faith. Conway and Siegelman are alarmed by their own assessment that:

> Most branches of our government, including Congress, the military and many executive agencies, are now staffed with individuals who say they have *surrendered control of their lives to a living, supernatural being* [emphasis added].[15]

Right-thinking Americans, they argue, "must face squarely the magnitude of this picture."[16] "Surrender to the supernatural" and belief in a proselytizing faith are equated with rejection of "reason and science, caring and compassion, and the basic principles of human freedom on which this country was founded."[17]

Holy Terror aims hate propaganda at all conservative Christians who believe in their faith fervently enough that they want to share it with others and apply the principles of their beliefs to their daily lives and to the institutions that govern them. "In the world of the eighties," ask Conway and Siegelman rhetorically, "how can any missionary group, church or faith defend the principle of global conversion?"[18]

Without admitting it, Conway and Siegelman have argued that these

times require the suspension of the free-exercise-of-religion component of the First Amendment for groups judged to be dangerous.

And who decides who is dangerous? Conway and Siegelman obviously consider themselves up to the task. And they seem to have many left-wing confederates who are ready to help.

Jerry Falwell and his colleagues in the New Christian Right say they believe in pluralism. He argues, further, that they do not seek to deny basic freedoms to anyone else. They are only trying to protect their own rights from leftist assaults. Being religious, they contend, does not disenfranchise them from participation in the political arena.

Not everyone who has felt threatened by the emergence of the New Christian Right is equally zealous and quick to advocate suspension of First Amendment rights in the name of protecting America. And it is clear that some of the soldiers in the army of the New Christian Right are just as zealous as the likes of Conway and Siegelman. If this were not the case, the verbal wars long ago would have escalated into violent confrontation.

Sociologically speaking, excessive rhetoric is one of the tools all social movements use to denigrate adversaries and label them illegitimate, thereby indirectly legitimizing their own cause.

From the moment that Jerry Falwell and his Moral Majority burst onto the political scene in 1980, liberals sensed that something had gone terribly wrong in the American political process. Ronald Reagan's corralling of 1600 Pennsylvania Avenue, and the electorate's repudiation of the greatest number of liberal senators and congressmen since Franklin Delano Roosevelt led the Democrats to victory in 1932, was a shocking blow to liberals. Falwell wasted no time and showed no hesitation in taking considerable credit for the Reagan landslide, and in the early years of the Reagan administration, Jerry Falwell seemed to have replaced Billy Graham as the unofficial White House chaplain. Periodic telephone calls from the president to discuss international issues and such delicate matters as the nomination of Sandra Day O'Connor to the U.S. Supreme Court served to bolster Falwell's claim to being a Very Important Preacher in Washington.

THE FUNDAMENTALISTS ARE COMING! THE FUNDAMENTALISTS ARE COMING! warned the print and broadcast media across the land. And writers and publishers rushed to print with such titles as *God's Bullies*, *Religious Pied Pipers*, and *Holy Terror*. Television documentaries and

dramas such as "Give Me That Big-Time Religion," "Portrait of an American Zealot," "In the Name of God," and "Pray TV" warned of the impending danger.

During 1981 and 1982 the threat from the New Christian Right seemed to grow ever grimmer. But then, almost as suddenly as the New Christian Right story had exploded on the American scene, it was declared nonexistent. National Public Radio reporter Tina Rosenberg, writing in *Washington Monthly*, broke the news. She called the Falwell/Moral Majority story a gigantic hoax and said it was time to move on to another story and another game. Explained Rosenberg:

> Falwell wants attention, liberals want an ogre, the press wants a good story. Whenever all parties want the same thing, they tend to get it whether they deserve it or not.[19]

Beneath this cynical observation are some important truths about the development of social-movement organizations. Utilizing his own television program and his role as a leader among independent fundamentalists, Falwell had promoted a religious worldview that was preparing conservative Christians for a social movement. Even before he conceived of the Moral Majority, Falwell was preparing a constituency ideologically and emotionally for its political agenda.

While Falwell could and did preach about the ills of society and encouraged people to get involved, Federal Communications Commission regulations limited his ability to use his video pulpit as a platform for organizing the Moral Majority.

To build any kind of national organization effectively, Falwell needed a platform that was bigger than his television program. He seized that opportunity at the Republican National Convention in Detroit in the summer of 1980. With Ronald Reagan's nomination a foregone conclusion, there were hundreds of reporters looking for an interesting angle. Falwell's presence proved to be one of the more interesting "sidebar" stories at the convention. On the day after his nomination, when he was trying to select a vice presidential running mate, Ronald Reagan spent more than an hour with Falwell. And that meeting escalated interest in the noisy Baptist.

A month later, Falwell was on the platform when candidate Reagan

addressed the National Affairs Briefing in Dallas. And in weeks following, he was on the cover of several leading newsmagazines.

The attention Falwell received during the 1980 presidential campaign permitted him to communicate to a far larger audience than the few million who tuned in to his "Old Time Gospel Hour." Almost overnight, the conservative Christian social movement that had been burgeoning for a number of years had a national leader.

The Reverend Donald E. Wildmon, the nation's leading crusader against pornography, recently wrote that the most frustrating part of his ministry is getting the Christian community to listen.[20] The publicity Falwell received helped get the attention of conservative Christians. From thousands of pulpits across America, evangelical and fundamentalist preachers echoed Falwell's message that the ills of secular society were not inevitable. A battle was being waged against the evils of secular culture, and preachers were inviting their congregations to become soldiers in that struggle.

The negative press Falwell received helped make him the ogre liberals needed for advancing their case against the conservative Reagan administration. The relationship between movement and countermovement is reciprocal. By warning of the conservative danger, liberal organizations were helping to rally support for the New Christian Right, because the visible pressure of the Left helped confirm their presence as a sinister force.

A fundamental sociological principle regarding intergroup conflict is that external threat breeds internal solidarity. The principle works both ways. Falwell's high profile aroused liberals. Their saber-rattling, in turn, served to reinforce a deepening awareness among conservative Christians of the problems with secular society.

The hoax of it all, which Tina Rosenberg suspected but failed to document, was that Falwell's mighty Moral Majority was a lot more thunder and lightning than a bonafide grass-roots organization.

Despite skepticism on the part of the media, and a great many polls showing that Falwell had grossly exaggerated his support, he clung to the limelight, failing to fade like a morning glory in the noonday sun. Wherever he went, whatever he did, Falwell commanded attention with perhaps as much skill as anyone in America—with the exception of the principal resident of the White House.

Falwell crisscrossed the country, delivering hundreds of speeches

and sermons that aroused the excitement of the Other Americans.
And he drew the ire of the press and liberals the likes of Norman
Lear, Ted Kennedy, Walter Mondale, and Phil Donahue. Falwell
debated and challenged them with his unflappable countenance, his
Cheshire-cat grin, and his conciliatory tone of voice, which infuriated
them all the more.

Falwell thus drew attention to the political agenda of the New
Christian Right. He became the champion of many of the Other Americans. For others, he was an insistent thorn in the side of their indifference and inaction.

In January of 1986, without advance warning, Falwell boldly announced the creation of a new political arm to be named the Liberty
Federation. This new organization would continue the activities of the
Moral Majority, while also pursuing a broader agenda. "We want to
continue to be the standard bearer for traditional American values.
But it's time to broaden our horizons as well," Falwell said in a press
announcement.[21]

This dramatic move to disband the Moral Majority bore some re-
semblance to killing the goose that laid the golden egg. For more than
six years, the name of the Moral Majority—as much as the brilliantly
combative persona of Jerry Falwell—had served as both a cannon and
a lightning rod. The name was also a battle cry, encouraging conservative Christians to become involved in the political process. And
it sent tremors of fear and indignation into the hearts of millions of
liberals.

Why would Jerry Falwell decide to kill such an important symbol
and communications instrument? From the beginning of their high
visibility, both Falwell and the Moral Majority were controversial, not
just among Christians and media commentators but also among social
scientists and scholars. Neither the man nor the organization ever
ranked very high in public approval polls. In deciding to bury the
name, Falwell apparently reasoned that more was to be gained by
jettisoning it than in bearing its liabilities. At least that seemed apparent from his press statement:

. . . The press for six years has bloodied and beaten the name,
Moral Majority. There are a lot of people who will say yes to
everything we are saying, but they dare not stand with us on

particular policies for fear of getting tarred, hurt—that is, picking up baggage the media has dumped on us.[22]

So, like a giant corporation deciding that a new name would be good for business, Falwell said his organization would henceforth be the Liberty Federation.

Most commentators responded to Falwell's change of name with seeming indifference. Many media people believed the name change was a way of camouflaging the demise of an ineffectual organization. It was almost a nonevent. There were only brief notices and little analysis of the reasoning behind the change—a strange response considering the tens of thousands of column inches that had been printed about the Moral Majority over the previous six years.

Among the few national commentators to write on the passing of the Moral Majority was *Washington Post* columnist Mary McGrory. She saw it as a victory of centrist politics over extremism. ". . . [E]xtremism never does very well for very long in this country," she wrote. America had become fed up with Falwell's "holier-than-thou" behavior. "[I]f Falwell wishes to realize his goal of making this a 'Christian nation,'" McGrory stated with confidence, "it will not be enough to change the name of the Moral Majority to Liberty Federation. He must change his own."[23]

Most of the media had long believed that Falwell and his band of "religious zealots" were neither moral nor a majority. So they moved on to another story. But such a response falls far short of understanding what the organization was or the contribution it made to the New Christian Right social movement in America.

Jerry Falwell had very good reason to kill the Moral Majority, one he only skirted with his statement about the name's negative press image. And, contrary to the general impression, it was actually success that led to the slaying of the goose that laid the golden egg.

From the beginning, Falwell masterminded a media machine that gave him a platform to comment on public issues and to encourage conservative Americans to get involved with those issues. And he had always been vulnerable to the possibility that the media equivalents of Dorothy and her companions in Oz would one day step around behind the curtain to discover that the Great Wizard's powers were

largely a façade, more amplified-voice-and-wind machine than sub-stance.

There were bits and pieces of evidence along the way to support the image of a paper tiger. For example, during the 1980 presidential campaign, Falwell claimed that the Moral Majority had between 2 and 3 million members. Yet the circulation of the tabloid *Moral Majority Report* was only 482,000. Since this magazine was widely distributed without charge, why wouldn't it be sent to all of the 2 or 3 million members?[24] Further, the executive director of the Washington State Moral Majority, which the national office in Lynchburg verified to be the largest state chapter, said that he had 12,000 members. A little simple arithmetic, and other morsels of information like this one, belied Falwell's claim of a significant grass-roots organization.[25]

Jerry Falwell was able to create the appearance of a large grass-roots organization by tapping into already-existing religious groups with whom he had a natural fundamentalist affinity. Some of these groups were large urban "superchurches."

Falwell claimed that support for the Moral Majority was broadly based among Protestants of every denomination, as well as Catholics and Jews. Yet a study of its leadership—based on a directory in the *Moral Majority Report*—revealed that forty-five of the fifty state chairmen were Baptist ministers. Further, twenty-eight of them were affiliated with a single small alliance called the Bible Baptist Fellowship.[26]

The authors conducted a systematic analysis of the contents of all the issues of the *Moral Majority Report* for the years 1985 and 1986 and uncovered little evidence of sustained ongoing activities or projects by state chapters.[27] More than half of the reports from state chapters came from the South (i.e., the Bible Belt); one-third of the states in the East and West never sent even one report. Most important, nearly half of the state chairmen's reports were about *future* efforts rather than about activities they had done or were doing. The authors tried to follow up and see if any of these plans were actually carried out but could not confirm a single one.

The price Falwell paid for being able simply to wave his wand over preexisting local organizations (many of them church-based) and claim them as Moral Majority chapters was that he quickly built the appearance of a widespread organization but had little control over its

parts. Sometimes local enthusiasts were so aggressive in the name of the organization or said things so outrageous that they embarrassed Falwell. People such as the West Coast chapter leader who told the press that homosexuals should be executed helped give the Moral Majority and Falwell a reputation for being far more radical than the real Jerry Falwell.

Some of Falwell's closest advisers counseled him early on to proclaim that the Moral Majority had served its purpose and no longer was needed. Falwell was reluctant to let go. But by the end of 1985, he felt that the game had just about run its course. He was anticipating supporting George Bush's bid for the presidency in 1988. Both he and Bush were concerned that the Moral Majority might be more of a liability than an asset.

More important, Falwell had turned fifty and was going through a period of assessing his life goals and priorities. It became clear to him that his top priority was the development of Liberty University into a quality institution of higher education.

Falwell is a man of action. He has little interest in theories or long philosophical discussions of the implications of various courses of action. History may well bear out his prophecy that the 1980s would be a Decade of Destiny.

As a central figure in the New Christian Right's campaign to reshape America toward political and social conservatism, Falwell has seldom paused to reflect upon his actions. Inaction, he believes, is a greater sin than incorrect action. Mistakes tend to be corrected either by greater self-awareness or by the others possessing keener understanding. But inaction is abdication of the responsibility for the destiny of oneself and one's country.

For all of Falwell's emphasis on doing, he is acutely aware of the importance of education. And he recognizes that changing the direction of American history will not be accomplished in a single decade, even a single generation.

An hour's drive northeast of Lynchburg stands the University of Virginia, believed by Thomas Jefferson to be among his most important contributions to the new nation he helped create. Faculty members at the university refer to the founder with awe and reverence—and always, simply as *Mr.* Jefferson. Thomas Jefferson thought degrees

and titles were pretentious. Falwell prefers that people just call him "Jerry," although at church it's all right to call him "Preacher." But titles are strictly for ceremonial occasions.

To anyone steeped in the traditions of Mr. Jefferson at the University of Virginia, it is discordant to hear Jerry Falwell refer to the Founder as "Old Tom Jefferson." But the words that follow reveal Falwell's deep understanding, appreciation, and even reverence for education and for the role Mr. Jefferson's "academical village" has played in shaping America's destiny for more than 200 years. "Old Tom Jefferson," Falwell says, "had the right idea. If you want to shape history, you shape the minds of young people. And that's what we want to do here at Liberty University."[28]

During 1985 and 1986, as Jerry Falwell was reassessing his priorities and reallocating his time to reflect his renewed commitment to the university and to his congregation in Lynchburg, he could not possibly have imagined what lay in store for him in 1987.

It happened so quickly. When Jim Bakker resigned and asked his friend Jerry Falwell to step in and help to set the PTL Network and Heritage USA back on a stable course, Falwell instinctively recognized the credibility crisis all religious broadcasters would be facing and accepted the challenge.

Falwell was immediately criticized both by his fundamentalist colleagues and by Bakker's Pentecostal loyalists; a Baptist simply has no business "meddling" in the affairs of a charismatic camp. Falwell, the man of action, hesitated when Jim Bakker wrote him a month later that, "Due to the unrest in the charismatic world . . . I feel that it is time now for you to turn the PTL ministry over to charismatics. . . ."[29] But after a weekend of agonizing over whether to back away from a mammoth crisis, Falwell fired Bakker's closest associates and took firm control.

From the outset, the Falwell-installed board was top-heavy with fundamentalists, and it became even more so after the firing of former Bakker aide Richard Dortch and the resignations of Rex Humbard and James Watt. Still, there was a clear ecumenical motive and thrust to Falwell's words and deeds. He promised that neither Heritage USA nor the PTL Network would be stripped of their Pentecostal origins, but both would build on the ecumenical tendencies that already were present. Heritage USA would be open to the public and the PTL

Network would broadcast programs reflecting a broad array of theological persuasions.

To the question of how a fundamentalist could preside over a charismatic ministry, Falwell said, first of all, that he was not seeking to make the ministry his own. He was there because Jim Bakker had asked him to come and because he believed that God wanted him there, "at least for the time being." "There is a great distrust out there that we must, must heal. . . ." he told a press conference at Heritage USA after the April 28 board meeting:

There are 400,000 churches in America; 110,000 of them are evangelical and fundamentalist. My personal feeling is that every one of them, before this calendar year is out, will have felt it [the PTL scandals] in their budget.[30]

Jerry Falwell, the man who once ranted and raved against other Christians who didn't believe as he believed, had matured a great deal since he stepped into the national limelight. Not even the most cynical observer can escape the fact that in taking on the task of trying to clean up a ministry riddled with corruption, Falwell was risking a great deal.

But Falwell had already taken risks when he created the Moral Majority.

As noted earlier, the "new ecumenism" of the religious right in America has emerged around projects rather than the union of groups with disparate theological orientations. It would be difficult to overestimate the degree to which the many evangelical traditions in America have fought among themselves during the twentieth century. But today an unmistakable move toward unity is taking place.

The sense of being a beleaguered minority in a culture increasingly overrun by immorality—or, if you will, secular humanism—has served as an external source of unity. Threatened by these external forces, they must pool resources to fight back.

The new ecumenical thrust is by no means a solid front. The political coalition Falwell sought has materialized only to a degree. Bob Jones III, whose grandfather founded Bob Jones University, sternly rejected Falwell, accusing him of helping to establish the conditions for the rise of the Antichrist. To Falwell's challenge to become involved in

worldly affairs, Bob Jones III made it clear that he was quite happy to "seek the soul-satisfying contentment of being a scriptural minority."[31]

In short, Falwell has faced the same dogmatic, world-rejecting crowd that Carl Henry and the founders of the National Association of Evangelicals wanted to distance themselves from back in 1942. But it is clear that the number of self-aggrandizing, sanctimonious separatists is shrinking.

Among evangelical traditions that are less doctrinally dogmatic, there are plenty of nay-sayers rejecting alignment with any partisan cause. They prize their duty to exercise responsible free will. To ally with any movement would compromise their independence. They did not become warriors in Falwell's Moral Majority and they are not likely to become champions of Pat Robertson's presidential candidacy. Still, they are committed to the social and moral agendas of Falwell and Robertson.

In a very profound sense, Jerry Falwell's role has been analogous to that of John the Baptist, proclaiming the coming of a new age and a vision of Christians working together in the secular wilderness. And, like John the Baptist, Jerry Falwell never really had any messianic pretensions. From the very beginning, he saw the Moral Majority as a means to a much broader social movement, not an end in itself. Falwell would be the first to confess that he has been in a lot of scrapes; on more than one occasion he must have felt as though his head was about to be delivered on a platter to jeering newspeople, angry mainline Christians, and hostile secularists. But Falwell has self-confidently ducked every effort to mortally wound him or the many projects he has promoted.

Jerry Falwell may long be the man whom liberals love to hate. And he will probably remain a man they do not understand, leaving them content to live with stereotypes that are, at best, bare hints of the man who is helping to change America in ways they perceive as very threatening.

Jerry Falwell's Moral Majority really was the golden egg. He chose to use the glitter of that egg to attract the attention of the media and promote his cause in the press rather than invest the egg in building grass-roots organizational clout. But that was effectively utilizing the

resources at his command. The Moral Majority was a success. It served Falwell exceedingly well in helping to raise the consciousness of conservative Christians and giving them a vision and hope that America might be restored. Falwell's personal charisma served to arouse a great many independent Baptists. But it did a lot more. It energized and gave a sense of common purpose to literally hundreds of conservative social-movement organizations.

But Falwell's influence extends beyond the alliance of warring fundamentalist factions. In fact, his spirit of a "new ecumenism," consolidating religious conservatives, played better outside the fundamentalist world. Falwell has helped forge working alliances with Roman Catholics, Mormons, Southern Baptists, and Jews. He has appeared on a Unification Church–sponsored platform and on the "Phil Donahue Show" with Mose Durst, president of the American branch of Reverend Moon's church, in the common defense of religious liberty. The fighting fundamentalist has learned that there is much to be gained by joining with other conservative traditions in pursuit of common goals.

There is a certain irony that M. G. "Pat" Robertson has now moved to center stage as the leader of the New Christian Right. Socially, the two men are worlds apart. Falwell is the son of a bootlegger, Robertson the son of a ranking U.S. senator. While Falwell's father was financially successful, he was an uneducated, working-class man who pulled himself up by his own bootstraps. And his son did the same. While Pat Robertson is also a self-made man, his ancestry includes presidents and early Virginia colonists.

Robertson and Falwell are worlds apart theologically as well. While Robertson was ordained as a Southern Baptist minister, he believes in and practices the charismatic gifts of the Pentecostal tradition. Although Falwell assumed interim leadership of PTL and Heritage USA after charismatic Jim Bakker was forced to resign, the practice of the charismatic gifts remain doctrinally heretical to him.

To Falwell, George Bush would make a good president, a logical successor to Ronald Reagan. There is reason to believe that he announced his support for Bush early as a way of discouraging Robertson from throwing his hat into the ring.

There is no question that even the *consideration* of a Robertson

candidacy would have been impossible without Falwell's efforts among conservative Christians in America.

And it is also clear that neither could have become significant figures in late-twentieth-century America without the television programs that gave them access to the audiences they gradually transformed into constituencies.

10

Pat Who?

We have enough votes to run the country. . . . And when the people say "we've had enough," we are going to take over the country.
> —M. G. "Pat" Robertson, President, Christian Broadcasting Network

Pat *Who?*" exclaimed Democratic National Committee Chairman Paul G. Kirk, Jr., upon receipt of a staff briefing on Pat Robertson, founder and president of the Christian Broadcasting Network and host of its flagship program, "The 700 Club."

"I couldn't believe that this relatively unknown man could be a major, if not leading, candidate for president," wrote Kirk in a seven-page fund-raising letter to fellow Democrats in November of 1985. But after reviewing reports from his staff, Kirk ominously concluded, "Pat Robertson has the most powerful political organization in America."[1]

Deliberate hyperbole calculated to raise money to replenish Democratic coffers? Probably. But that didn't matter to the writers of the news. Religion and politics, mixed with a hint of impending danger from an army of religious zealots and a pinch of cynicism on the side, makes for good copy.

Stories about the possibility that Pat Robertson might run for president had already begun to appear as early as March 1985, when the *Saturday Evening Post*, a conservative, family-oriented magazine, published a cover story. Some months later, Richard Viguerie's *Conservative Digest* also produced a cover story. One of the sidebars was

a collection of several dozen quotes from conservative luminaries. The strongest came from Paul Weyrich, president of the Free Congress Research and Educational Foundation and the Iron Man of the New Right:

> Robertson, more than anyone else on the scene, is likely to be the national conservative figure who could not only equal what Reagan has accomplished, but can far exceed it. . . .[2]

No doubt it was this kind of enthusiasm on the part of New Right operatives that caught the attention of Paul Kirk's staff. Editors took the bait of Kirk's fund-raising letter and sent reporters out to learn more about Pat *Who*. But the tone of much of their coverage suggests that most reporters merely assumed Kirk's words were calculated to squeeze the pocketbooks of faithful Democrats. In the early flurry of stories about Pat Robertson, no one seemed to have checked in at Democratic headquarters to see whether Kirk's staff knew something that other people did not know.

If the Kirk letter was intended to help the Democrats at Robertson's expense, it backfired badly, garnering the kind of attention he needed to catapult into national visibility. The words and pictures began to flow. And Robertson knew how to work this coverage to his fullest advantage. He quickly graduated from the covers of *Conservative Digest* and the *Saturday Evening Post* to cover and feature stories in high-circulation weeklies such as *Time*, *TV Guide*, and *People*. National talk-show appearances followed, including "Face the Nation," "Meet the Press," and (of course) "The Phil Donahue Show."

The Kirk letter also brought Robertson lots of attention from Republicans who had never heard of Pat *Who* either. Republicans didn't need much coaxing to invite him to address their state and national committee meetings. And, everywhere he spoke, Robertson inserted the Kirk letter in the press packets distributed to audiences. Penciling in rebuttals to information he felt to be misleading or inaccurate, Robertson was able to plant in the minds of Republicans the idea that he might indeed be a formidable candidate.

In mid-March of 1986, Robertson was still getting good mileage out of the Kirk letter. Turning his guns on Kirk and accusing him of religious bigotry, Robertson upstaged six other presidential hopefuls

who appeared with him before a national gathering of GOP party leaders in Nashville's Opryland Hotel.

But Robertson's time for attention as a serious political candidate, at least as far as the mass media were concerned, had not yet arrived. Editors know a good story when they see one, but they also know the difference between a serious story and a human-interest or novelty story. In early 1986 the Robertson candidacy was certainly viewed as the latter. No editor in the country believed that Pat Robertson could mount a serious campaign for the Republican party's nomination for the presidency.

Nor would any editor want to be the last to cover a story that had already peaked. The press usually does have a very keen sense of how long a story will play, but in the case of Robertson, they badly miscalculated. Before the Robertson presidential story gathered a full head of steam, editors concluded that they had gotten about all they were going to get out of this one. It was time again for a requiem on the television-preachers-and-politics story.

This premature conclusion was precipitated in the early spring when both Robertson and Falwell made business decisions that were interpreted as evidence of weakness. On the last day of March, the Associated Press reported that Jerry Falwell was laying off 225 employees, canceling his toll-free line, and increasing fees and cutting scholarships at Liberty University. Three days later, another wire story with a Virginia Beach dateline reported that Pat Robertson was selling three television stations, dropping his toll-free number, and laying off forty-one employees.

Like a school of fish, editors all over America killed their investigative pieces on the evangelical presidential hopeful and sent reporters out to find corroborating evidence that the mixing of religion and politics had hit the superstars of televangelism in the pocketbook to the point of putting them on the ropes.

There was scarcely a shred of evidence to support this interpretation of the cutbacks. Television ministries have a long history of laying off people temporarily as a means of dealing with seasonal cash-flow problems. CBN's decision to sell three television stations was part of a long-range business decision to redirect its resources toward developing cable broadcasting. Falwell's decision to raise tuition and fees at Liberty University was also part of a long-range plan to move the

school toward self-sufficiency. For both ministries, the decision to cut toll-free lines was a hard-nosed business decision and not an act of financial desperation. (The media never reported that CBN later found other means to cut costs and never discontinued their toll-free numbers.) And so it went with the other cost-saving measures the two television ministries initiated. These decisions were evidence of prudent management, but, almost uniformly, the press approached this story with a pessimistic angle and a set of presuppositions. The secular press had been expecting the collapse of the televangelists' broadcasting empires for years. The Falwell and CBN news releases seemed to provide the evidence they had anticipated. Although the facts did not point to the demise either of the broadcasting empires or of Robertson's shot at big-time politics, stories of the collapse of the two TV ministries were still appearing in mid-May as the first acid test of Robertson's political acumen approached.

The scene was the state of Michigan; the date was May 27, 1986, the deadline for filing to be a county precinct delegate, the first step in a long, drawn-out process for selecting delegates to the 1988 GOP presidential nominating convention. The delegate selection process in Michigan is easily the most complex and attenuated of any state. Furthermore, at no point along the way can delegates be bound to a candidate. Most Republican hopefuls decided to bypass the early phases of the Michigan process in the hope that they would be able to round up a few delegates closer to the date of the convention.

Normally, the filing deadline for this first phase would scarcely draw local news coverage, much less national and even international attention. But, as it turned out, the Michigan primary process took on tremendous significance in 1986. There were three reasons why this was so.

First, the Michigan GOP, hoping to draw attention to itself, began the delegate selection process before anyone else. Even though it was rather like putting up Christmas decorations in June, there was simply no way the press could ignore presidential politics—even though the election was two and a half years away.

Second, George Bush was anxious to establish himself as the heir-apparent to Ronald Reagan. Over the years, the vice president under a retiring president has rarely been denied the nomination. In fact, the last such time was in 1924, when Herbert Hoover outdistanced

Calvin Coolidge's vice president, Charles G. Dawes, for the nomination. Even so, Bush wanted to get a head start. Michigan was the place where the long march began. And Bush, keenly aware that this was the one state where he beat Ronald Reagan in the 1980 primaries, was keyed up and ready. He knew there would be obstacles along the way and wanted to face them head-on. For example, a lot of conservatives have always seen Bush's conservatism as mere expediency and have been unwilling to support him. Bush designed a strategy to deal with that sentiment early and decisively. He also believed that Reagan's good friend Senator Paul Laxalt might decide to become a candidate and, thus, compete with the vice president for the president's endorsement.

Bush recognized that the process was set up to favor a small cadre of party regulars, a situation ideally suited for a sitting vice president to round up the support of most of the delegates. It looked like an opportunity to blitz a big state with a lot of delegates and simultaneously create the image of Bush as an unbeatable front-runner. In a word, the Michigan delegate selection process was important because Vice President George Bush chose to make Michigan a test of his strength. But Bush's enthusiasm to get out in front early may have been the beginning of his undoing.

A funny thing happened on the way to Bush's Michigan blitzkrieg. A couple of unlikely challengers showed up for the fight. The first was Jack Kemp, the former NFL quarterback and conservative congressman from New York. The other was a TV preacher from Virginia named Pat Robertson.

The state party organization and George Bush were two of the factors infusing the Michigan contest with special significance. The third was Pat Robertson. He calculated that his grass-roots strength would enable him to walk away with at least a handful of delegates. And in so doing, he would garner some national attention for his candidacy.

Initially, no one gave the television preacher even a prayer of challenging George Bush or of running well against Kemp. Kemp had long been a darling of conservatives, and many thought he had the best chance of beating out Bush for the nomination.

The day after the May deadline for filing, the Bush and the Robertson organizations each claimed to have registered about 4,500 delegate candidates, while Kemp forces were claiming 3,400. That adds

up to 12,400 delegates, or about 38 percent *more* than the state GOP party claimed were registered. And this, of course, does not allow for the fact that some unknown percentage of delegate candidates were truly "uncommitted." In reality, since delegates were not required to reveal who they intended to support, it was impossible to determine how many delegates each presidential hopeful had lined up.

In the early stages of presidential primaries, winners and losers are determined not by how much strength the candidates have mustered but, rather, by the interpretation of their performance by the media's political pundits. Since analysts didn't expect Robertson to make any kind of showing, the fact that he might have signed up nearly as many delegates as Bush, and more than Kemp, was interpreted as a stunning victory. There were even rumors that Robertson had beaten Bush but was sandbagging his strength.

Whatever the truth, the combination of Bush's insistence on making Michigan a test and Robertson's unexpected strength drew attention to the primary on August 5. The minister's potential presidential candidacy was the hot item as media coverage soared.

August 5 came and went without clarifying the strength of the candidates in the race for delegates. As with the precinct contest in May, there was no statewide tabulation of who was selected to proceed to the congressional district caucuses. Hence, there would be no official results when the polls closed—only the claims of the candidates.

Several forces moved in to fill the information void. And if ever there was an example of Gresham's Law (bad currency driving out good currency), it certainly was operative in Michigan on that primary Tuesday. First, the Bush operatives rushed in with proclamations of a landslide victory. "[T]he vice president's support is a mile wide and a mile deep," announced the state chairman of Bush's Fund for America's Future. Later the Bush staff revised its estimates downward from a clear majority to a plurality. But never mind.

Second, the news media, hungry for information but unable to conduct a standard exit poll (i.e., "Who did you vote for?") because the delegates were not formally tied to a candidate, elected to conduct candidate-preference polls.

The polls conducted by NBC/*Wall Street Journal* and the Detroit *Free Press* lent credibility to the Bush camp's claim of victory. And no one challenged these polls' appropriateness for gauging candidate

strength. So the reporters filed their stories and headed home, believing that Bush had beaten back the challenge of the evangelicals. A sampling of the national coverage of the primary showed near-consensus that Bush had won.

But not everyone was certain. *New York Times* columnist Tom Wicker, understanding the complexity of the process, wrote:

> What actually happened, though nothing may have, was possibly that some Republicans elected some delegates, some of whom may or may not have been pledged to one or more of the three candidates. These delegates in turn, though they might be pledged to somebody, don't have to stay pledged even if bought; but that doesn't matter because they won't vote for any Presidential candidate anyway but only for some other delegates, who will in turn vote for still others. [3]

If Bush won a majority of the delegates in Michigan (and it eventually became clear that he *did not*), it was immediately evident that he failed to win a decisive victory. In fact, in failing to gain the big victory he wanted, Bush actually lost. He lost the opportunity to gain the decisive edge and establish an early bandwagon. He also lost face. He intended to assert his image as a strong front-runner capable of "kicking a little ass" if anyone got in his way. Michigan revealed to all would-be challengers that George Bush was vulnerable. Nothing could alter the inescapable reality that by failing to win decisively, George Bush lost big.

Meanwhile, Pat Robertson won big, regardless of how many Michigan delegates would eventually support him. Robertson captured an edge in the pursuit of delegates, gained some valuable campaign experience, and attracted more media attention than even his own forces might have imagined.

Michigan didn't transform Robertson into a front-runner. In fact, the national media, having done a flurry of "novelty candidate" stories, seemed reluctant to give him much attention for many months. Not so in Michigan, as the delegate-selection process rolled slowly toward the sending of seventy-seven delegates to New Orleans to the 1988 Republican nominating convention.

The first major evidence of Robertson's strength came at a statewide

Republican convention in Lansing, Michigan, on February 20 and 21, 1987. When the convention was over, Robertson loyalists had claimed sixty-three of 101 seats on the Republican State Committee. The *Washington Post* gave only passing mention to this development; the *New York Times* downplayed it, leading with acknowledgment from Bush strategists that they had earlier overestimated their candidate's strength.

Michigan's major newspapers were more candid, and Sunday morning editions bannered the Robertson triumph. Hugh McDiarmid, chief political writer for the Detroit *Free Press*, put it on the line in his column:

> Let's face it. The "Get George Bush" fundamentalists won the Republicans' big jihad, or holy war, in Lansing this weekend, making Pat Robertson the presidential front-runner in Michigan for 1988 . . . whether top party leaders like it or not.[4]

And two months later, after another GOP State Committee meeting produced a brouhaha between the Robertson newcomers and the Old Guard loyal to Bush, McDiarmid wrote that there was no longer any doubt about the strength of the Robertson forces. Looking ahead to the January 1988 selection of delegates, McDiarmid wrote:

> [T]he big question is not whether Bush will lose in Michigan in January, but by how much. And the corollary is not whether Pat Robertson, who will field a plurality of state convention delegates, will win, but by how much (and whether he will share some of his delegates with his ideological blood brother, Kemp)?[5]

And George Weeks, political writer for the *Detroit News*, wrote, "The ruling Robertson-Kemp coalition socked it to the Bush camp Friday night in a stunning show of who's running the Michigan GOP."[6]

If the national press tended to ignore these developments, the Michigan media made much of the Robertson-Kemp coalition. But as the Robertson camp counted, it was firmly in control even without the Kemp alliance. Robertson's staff members had every reason to play ball with the Kemp forces; in fact, Robertson early mentioned Kemp as a vice-presidential running mate. But it was clear that they intended to play hard ball from a position of strength.

Pat Robertson's early successes received some help from George Bush whose own eagerness to get out in front of the rest of the pack contributed to his undoing. But, in truth, George Bush was outsmarted, outmaneuvered, and overpowered in Michigan by Preacher Pat. Beating a sitting vice president on his first outing was no small accomplishment even if the political pundits seemed not to take notice.

There may still be a lot of questions about Pat Robertson come GOP National Convention time. But one thing is certain: Robertson's candidacy was not a lark. He wants to be president. And, like it or not—and clearly a lot of Americans don't like it—the man has to be taken seriously. Pat Robertson's presence in the GOP presidential sweepstakes is the most important factor in shaping the 1988 campaign.

So . . . who is this man Pat Robertson?

The stereotype of Preacher Pat healing hemorrhoids and praying away hurricanes is part of the cultural context in which we know him. It is a stereotype that says something very important about who *we* are—a modern secular culture profoundly skeptical of people who take their religion seriously and practice their faith in ways unfamiliar to those in the antiseptic pews of mainline Protestantism.

As long as we see Robertson on these terms, we will not know him as he sees himself and as he is seen by millions of Americans who are very excited about his candidacy.

Robertson is a man who believes that he and we have a date with destiny.

Marion G. "Pat" Robertson is the son of the late U.S. Senator A. Willis Robertson and the late Gladys Churchill Robertson. He is a descendant of the Harrison family of Virginia, which boasted a signer of the Declaration of Independence and two U.S. presidents. He is also a descendant of John Churchill, second Duke of Marlborough and ancestor of Winston Churchill. Pat Robertson is a true American blue blood. And he has the know-how to utilize all the advantages that accrue thereto.

Graduating Phi Beta Kappa from Washington and Lee University in Lexington, Virginia, Robertson studied briefly at the University of London before he earned a J.D. at Yale Law School in 1955. Before deciding to study for the ministry, Robertson participated in a management training program with the W. R. Grace Company, and he was a partner in an electronic components business in New York.

After graduating from New York Theological Seminary, and serving briefly as a pastor of an inner-city church in Brooklyn, Robertson purchased a dilapidated television station and founded the Christian Broadcasting Network with a mere $70 initial capital. In 1985, the combined revenues of the Christian Broadcasting Network and its affiliated broadcasting enterprises were estimated at $230 million.

Until September 1986, Robertson was the host of "The 700 Club," CBN's flagship program. Shortly before he gave up this post to devote more time to his presidential quest, the A. C. Nielsen Company reported a weekly audience of 12 million for the program—29 million cumulative viewers over the course of a month.[7]

Even though Robertson has never held elective office, he is not exactly a political novice. He grew up on Capitol Hill, where his father served for thirty-four years, climaxing his career as chairman of the Senate Banking and Currency Committee. And, while a law student, Pat was a staff investigator for the Senate Appropriations Committee. Pat Robertson knows how things work in Washington.

A lot of people feel that Pat Robertson's lack of elective-office experience is a big detriment to his candidacy for the highest office in the land. Being a senator or a congressman is considered an important prerequisite for the presidency because it provides an opportunity to learn about foreign affairs, especially if the opportunities arise for foreign junkets.

Pat Robertson's broadcasting empire does business in forty-six nations. He has traveled in at least forty-four countries, including approximately fifteen trips to the Middle East. Robertson does not have to go to the House or the Senate to learn about foreign affairs. He already knows more heads of state than do most veterans of Congress.

Of course, most people's first objection to a Robertson candidacy is not his lack of political experience—that usually comes up later—but his relationship to God. Pat Robertson talks to God a lot. This doesn't strike him as anything very extraordinary. A conversation with God, Robertson insists, is merely prayer. A very large majority of people tell Gallup pollsters that they, too, pray.

But Robertson is confident that he receives some rather explicit information and directives from Up There. This seems to disturb many people because they don't enjoy this personal a relationship with the Almighty. Robertson insists that the only thing that separates him

from other praying Christians is that he *believes* that God will respond.

Compared to those who consider themselves to be in the mainstream of American religion, Robertson has views that are not orthodox. Robertson would insist, however, that in historical context, his views and understanding of how God moves are clearly in the mainstream. Ronald Reagan is helping give credibility to this claim. Furthermore, Robertson is confident that revival is sweeping across the land. It is only a matter of time before his views are once again considered orthodox.

Robertson holds a providential view of American history. He believes that God has had a plan for this land from the beginning. He also thinks that God may now be calling upon him to help fulfill His divine purpose for America. A glimpse of this confidence appears in his 1982 book, *The Secret Kingdom*. The book opens with a sense of serenity as Robertson views a yellow moon over the Atlantic from the corner of Cape Henry on the Chesapeake Bay, near where the first band of settlers arrived in 1607 to establish a permanent colony. Three days after they landed, Robertson reminds us, the settlers:

> . . . carefully carried ashore a rough, seven-foot oak cross and plunged it into the sand. As they knelt around it, their spiritual leader, an Anglican clergyman named Robert Hunt, reminded them of the admonition of the British Royal Council, derived from the words of the Holy Scripture: "Every plantation, which my Heavenly Father hath not planted, shall be rooted up."[8]

The settlers reboarded their boats, sailed around the cape, and took up residence on a river they named after their monarch, King James.

As *The Secret Kingdom* winds toward its conclusion, Robertson reveals to his readers how he was miraculously led to purchase the land upon which the Christian Broadcasting Network would be built. CBN is located just ten miles from the spot where:

> . . . the first permanent English settlers in America had planted a cross on the sandy shore and claimed the land for God's glory and the spread of the gospel. After 370 years, the ultramodern television facility with worldwide capabilities began to fulfill their dreams.[9]

But there's more. Those first settlers had planned to found Henrico College, "a school to teach the gospel and train young men and women for Christian service, hoping to reach the world through education."[10] Plans for the college were never realized. But Pat Robertson is a descendant of one of those who arrived in 1619 to build Henrico College. In 1977, Pat Robertson founded CBN University, which a decade later had approximately a thousand graduate students in five programs, including a law school that opened in the fall of 1986.

Pat Robertson holds other views that many Americans do not regard as orthodox or mainstream. In the name of Jesus, Pat Robertson even commanded Hurricane Gloria, which was bearing down on Virginia Beach in 1985, to change its direction:

> In the name of Jesus, we command you to stop where you are and move northeast, away from land, and away from harm. In the name of Jesus of Nazareth, we command it.[11]

Whether in response to Pat's command, or merely in keeping with the often fickle and unpredictable behavior of hurricanes, Gloria abruptly stopped, changed course, and headed northeast. The studios of the Christian Broadcasting Network and the people of the tidewater Virginia area were safe from potential devastation.

Pat Robertson saw this event as a sign from God. It proved that not only does God answer prayers, but the inner voice he hears really is God's and not merely the dark side of his own blind ambition.

Lesser men would be hauled off to the psychiatric ward, at least for observation and evaluation, if they admitted that they had commanded a hurricane to change its course. But Pat Robertson is not about to hide his convictions or betray his providential view of history for the sake of a few supporters. To borrow the title of his first book, he is determined to "shout it from the housetops."

About nine months later, Robertson spoke candidly and soberly about the significance of this event with "700 Club" co-host Denuta Soderman:

SODERMAN: How important was Hurricane Gloria in this crystallization process?
ROBERTSON: It was extremely important because I felt, interest-

ingly enough, that if I couldn't move a hurricane, I could hardly move a nation. I know that's a strange thing for anybody to say, and there's hardly anyone else who would feel the same way, but it was very important to the faith of many people.[12]

Robertson's comment implies that his viewers and potential supporters will take the change in the hurricane as a sign that God supports Robertson's candidacy.

Robertson's adversaries hastened to pin the "crazy" label on him. The first time he was invited to be on the national news talk show "Meet the Press," the producer opened the program with videotape footage of that emotional prayer scene. Robertson didn't wince. Nor was he ruffled by a score of implicitly hostile questions. At the conclusion of the program, anchor Marvin Kalb turned to the other panel members and said, "I had the impression listening to Pat Robertson that we have obviously interviewed *a rather extraordinary man* [emphasis added]."[13]

Media people view Robertson's candidacy with mixed feelings. On the one hand, a novel candidate on the scene makes for interesting news copy. On the other hand, even the remote prospect of having a preacher for president—especially one who talks to God and claims that God talks back—is disconcerting to most journalists. Could an evangelical preacher be trusted to honor the separation of church and state? Wouldn't he attempt to impose his values on the rest of us? Dare we risk the possibility that he would behave recklessly in foreign affairs, believing that nuclear war is a prerequisite to the second coming of Christ?

Frightening thoughts, these. But they are offset by the fact that almost no one thinks of Robertson as a serious candidate. He may have caught party regulars off guard in Michigan, but as political novices the Robertson forces would certainly be outmaneuvered by the pros early in the campaign. But just in case, Robertson's ideological adversaries were assembling resources and sharpening their pencils to prepare to do battle in earnest. And People for the American Way has accumulated a lot of ammunition that they are now passing out to all soldiers prepared to do battle with Robertson.

"People For," or PAW, which claims 270,000 nonpartisan members

devoted to the protection of constitutional liberties, videotapes "The 700 Club" and otherwise monitors Robertson's activities.

Before the *Washington Star* folded in 1981, Jim Castelli was that newspaper's religion editor. One of the most able religion reporters in America, Castelli now works for "People For" as a writer and political strategist. He thinks the New Christian Right political movement is on the downswing, but he doesn't want to take any chances. If Pat Robertson wants to run for the presidency, Jim Castelli wants the nation to know that there is more to the man than meets the eye. He describes Robertson's personal manner as "smooth, polished, smiling, reassuring—it is not threatening." But behind the enormous grin and "baby face," Castelli sees "an extremist whose views place him well outside the mainstream of both the Republican party and the nation."[14]

"People For" doesn't deny the right of religious people to mix religion and politics, but the organization has some strong ideas about how the two should go together. In 1986, PAW issued five guidelines that all political candidates and their supporters ought to follow. They should: (1) never claim unique qualifications because of their beliefs or affiliation; (2) refrain from claiming divine or scriptural sanctions for their views; (3) refrain from questioning the morality of religious faith opponents; (4) refrain from claiming God supports their quest for public office or opposes their opponents; and (5) disavow any supporting activities that exhibit religious or other forms of bigotry. In a position paper entitled *Pat Robertson: Extremist*, Castelli detailed how Robertson, he felt, had violated each of these guidelines.

Some journalists would like to bag a "two-fer" while Robertson is on the scene. They think "the other reverend" should also stop trying to play politician. In 1984 it was difficult to criticize Jesse Jackson for fear of being accused of racism. But with two preachers in the contest, it is somewhat easier to go after them in tandem.

William Safire, *New York Times* syndicated columnist, launched the first volley at the two reverends. "Neither man is in fact a candidate for president; both are candidates for Bloc Leader." Incensed that either had a right to play in The Big Sand Box, Safire wrote:

If either were serious, he would run for winnable city or state office first; with that experience and forum, he would have to be

taken seriously as a person who could put his views to the test and perhaps put them into government. The poli-preachers can't be bothered with such stultifying preliminaries.[15]

Neither, he thought, had "reached the level of political credibility of Mayor Clint Eastwood."

In his indignation, Safire seemed to forget momentarily that the rules of politics have been radically rewritten over the past forty years and that the mass media, of which he is a stalwart member, have been instrumental in this transformation. And there was no such indignation in the press a few months earlier, when rumors of a possible bid for the presidency by Chrysler chairman Lee Iacocca began to circulate.

Most people know that media exposure and money have replaced the smoke-filled back rooms of party politicians. But some people have still failed to grasp just how important were Ronald Reagan's years of working before a movie camera in preparing him both as a candidate and as a media-wise president.

Pat Robertson has had nearly thirty years of experience in front of television cameras. From 1968 until early 1987 he appeared daily for ninety minutes on "The 700 Club." A good bit of that time was devoted to talking about politics, the economy, and world affairs. Pat Robertson's experience in front of a television camera dwarfs that of anyone else who has ever considered making a bid for the presidency.

America will never be the same as it was before Robertson began convincing his "700 Club" audience that "We have enough votes to run the country. . . . And when the people say 'we've had enough,' we are going to take over the country."[16]

Another Virginian, Senator John Warner, who takes the evangelical Christians seriously and watches them with a careful eye, has told them flatly, "If you Christians ever get organized, there is no piece of legislation in the United States that you couldn't get passed."[17]

The novice Christian politician who took on both a sitting vice president and a ranking conservative congressman in the Michigan GOP primary process, and gave both the scare of their political lives in the first outing of the long race for the 1988 presidential nomination, may be on the verge of getting the Christians organized.

Pat Robertson doesn't want to be a Bloc Leader. He wants to be president. He has been working on it for a long time. Many before him have felt they were called, but the job doesn't get passed around very much and the competition is fierce. By any stretch of the imagination, it is a long shot for anyone who aspires to the office.

It is tempting for the liberal establishment to write off Pat Robertson as a passing opportunist. But that would be a serious mistake. In doing so, liberals would ignore the theological basis of everything Robertson has done and the large contingency of Americans who believe as he does.

Robertson believes in the idea of dominion. Jesus Christ restored the right of dominion to mankind after it had been lost in the Garden of Eden. America, the Christian nation, will be the vehicle for fulfilling the Great Commission. It can do so, however, only after putting its own house in order. That he or someone like him would be "called" to reinfuse our national government with the Christian values it has neglected is as logical in Pat Robertson's view as is his conviction that the CBN conglomerate is part of God's plan to redeem the world.

The truth is that Pat Robertson's chances for taking up residency at 1600 Pennsylvania Avenue in 1988, or some future date, are not as remote as the "slim" and "none" suggested by conservative R. Emmett Tyrrell, Jr., in June of 1986:

Robertson's chances of becoming president of the United States are only marginally better than those of His Royal Highness Prince Louis H. M. Bertrand Rainier III.[18]

Such a sweeping conclusion, barely two weeks after Robertson had rocked the foundations of the Bush and Kemp preprimary campaigns in Michigan, and fully two years before Republicans would gather to select their standard-bearer, reflected the same arrogance as William Safire's diatribe against the reverends Robertson and Jackson. All of the political pundits who are busy writing that Robertson doesn't have a prayer are airing their preference rather than analyzing the resources he can bring to his quest.

What's more, the media's contempt for Robertson actually enhances his chances for success. As long as the pundits amuse rather than

educate their readers, Robertson can go about the business of building his political organization virtually unmolested.

There is another element in Robertson's bid for the presidency— antireligious bigotry. In this era of mass media, bigotry has a way of backfiring against those who express it. Millions of Americans who had little sympathy for Martin Luther King, Jr., and the civil rights movement he led could not help feeling repulsed when they saw the violence perpetrated against nonviolent demonstrators and innocent children.

Initially, antireligious bigotry will probably work against Robertson. But as he gains more media exposure, and people begin to hear his ideas, they will face a classic problem that social psychologists call "cognitive dissonance." Put simply, the "crazy man" image and the image Robertson himself projects do not match. The more agitated the bigots become, the more outrageous their own behavior will be. In time, this may very well lead uncommitted Americans to reject the Robertson critics.

Then Robertson's task will be to transform the rejection of his critics into sympathy for his own candidacy. It's a long shot, but it is not an impossible dream.

Robertson's adversaries, as well as his supporters, need to remember that the negative press he receives parallels remarkably what was written back in 1965 when a movie actor named Ronald Reagan announced that he wanted to be governor of California.

Pat Robertson wants to persuade Americans that he is the logical heir to Ronald Reagan. In 1986 it appeared that there would be a lot of competitors for that title. But the political difficulties Reagan faced after the revelation of the exchange of hostages for arms in Iran and of covert funds for the *contras* in Central America clearly tarnished his reputation.

Many, if not most, candidates sought to put some distance between themselves and the once-very-popular president. But that may have been a mistake. There are still a great many Americans who love Ronald Reagan and believe he acted with integrity and good intentions. If that is hard to believe, recall that a lot of supporters of Jim and Tammy Faye Bakker remained loyal even after the revelations about the shambles they made of their lives and the misuse they made of PTL monies.

Pat Robertson believes that Ronald Reagan has basically been a good president and is proud to be thought of as Reagan's natural successor. Pat Robertson's challenge, not unlike that of John F. Kennedy in 1960, is to persuade Americans that he can be faithful to his religious ideals without being unfaithful to the duty of upholding the traditional separation of church and state.

11

The March of Folly

*A man with a conviction is a hard man to change. Tell
him you disagree and he turns away. Show him facts or
figures and he questions your sources. Appeal to logic
and he fails to see your point.*
　　　　　　　　　　　　—Leon Festinger, *et al.*
　　　　　　　　　　　　When Prophecy Fails

I was . . . brought, in 1818, at the
close of my two years' study of the Scriptures, to the solemn conclusion, that in about twenty-five years from that time all the affairs of
our present state would be wound up," wrote William Miller in his
autobiography, *Apology and Defense*.[1] Initially the New England farmer
was reluctant to share his conclusion with others. In fact, it was not
until after another five years of study and checking his calculations
that Miller began to speak cautiously with a few trusted neighbors
and clergy friends about his forecasts regarding the imminent return
of Christ.

Gradually, private discussions about his prophecy of the coming of
the millennium in 1843 gave way to public lectures. His following
grew steadily, and by early 1843 he was filling the largest halls in the
towns where he spoke. And in Boston, Miller's followers constructed
a tabernacle with a seating capacity of 3,500.

Also growing rapidly was opposition to Miller's heretical views. He
was condemned from pulpits and in newspapers. But followers were
not dissuaded by the negative publicity. By 1843, approximately 50,000
souls, mostly concentrated in New England and the Midwest, were
proud to consider themselves Millerites.

Until that year, William Miller had been vague as to the exact date of Christ's return. Then, on the first day of January, he announced to his followers, "I am fully convinced that somewhere between March 21st, 1843, and March 21st, 1844, according to the Jewish mode of computation of time, Christ will come."[2]

Christ, of course, did not return during that time, nor in the years following, although some of Miller's followers forecast alternate dates.

Common sense would suggest that such a failed prophecy would result in the rapid and widespread dissolution of a movement—especially if the leader were to confess his error and acknowledge his disappointment, as Miller did. But it didn't happen that way. In the face of negative evidence, the ranks of Miller's followers swelled.

There was, ultimately, a limit to the amount of disconfirming evidence that Miller's followers could accept before the movement began to break up. But the idea of Christ's imminent return, even if the precise date was not to be known, as well as several other theological peculiarities, survived. Today virtually all Adventist churches in America can be traced to William Miller. His impact on the spread of premillennial thinking in America has been profound.

Perhaps what is most striking about the Millerite movement is not the fact that Miller's followers persisted so long, but, rather, the almost ordinariness of the phenomenon. The annals of history are filled with such incidents.

One of the most fascinating was studied midway through this century by three social psychologists, Leon Festinger, Henry W. Riecken, and Stanley Schachter. Using the method of participant observation, the three scholars infiltrated a group of people who believed they had been forewarned by extraterrestrials of impending planetary doom.[3]

The founder of the UFO cult, Mrs. Marian Keech, was a housewife who had previously dabbled in several fringe groups, including Theosophy, the I AM movement, and Dianetics (the early form of Scientology). According to her testimony, Mrs. Keech was awakened one night by a strange sensation in her arm. As she seized pencil and paper, aliens allegedly began communicating with her, initially through the spirit of her dead father, by "automatic writing" that allowed her hand to transcribe their message without her conscious effort.

These extraterrestrials from the planets of Clarion and Cerus eventually revealed to Mrs. Keech and her small circle of believers that

the earth soon would be visited by a terrible disaster: the Great Lakes would flood the interior of the United States, the Atlantic seaboard would submerge, a new mountain range would be thrown up in the central states, and not only would Egypt's deserts be made fertile but the continent of Mu would rise in the Pacific.

Specific dates predicted for the arrival of flying saucers to scoop up the faithful came and went without the slightest confirmation. As the group attracted publicity, pressure mounted from fellow believers and the media for them to affirm their beliefs further or to defect. Eventually, the members split: Some persisted in believing in the UFO message and others abandoned it.

Festinger and his colleagues found that what distinguished the faithful from the defectors was the amount of social support they received at the time of disconfirmation. Shared beliefs bring people together; intense interaction works like glue to bind those of common sentiment even closer together. Interacting with people who believe as you do, then, is a powerful antidote against negative evidence coming from outside the group.

As simple as this observation may appear, it is one of the truly remarkable discoveries of the social sciences during this century. Group solidarity and oneness of mind can set people off on noble crusades or lead them down the path to tragedy. It helps to explain much social behavior that is otherwise inexplicable—how a bright young man or woman can fall under the mesmerizing influence of a religious guru; how World War I soldiers could march to their almost-certain death against a wall of machine guns; how a crusading political candidate can be tamed by a Washington bureaucracy.

Given a social milieu in which virtually everyone thinks alike, the newcomer almost always comes to see the world through the lens of the group's conventional wisdom. Those who do not will become disillusioned and drop out of the group, or, if they remain, fail in the performance of their duties as a member of the group.

The whistle-blower in a government bureaucracy or a major defense contracting firm is an archetypical example of someone who refuses to go along with "group think." He is unable to rationalize excess spending, waste, disregard of the environment or of human beings, and so on, and he "tells it like it is." The American mass media love a government whistle-blower almost as much as the British press loves

a sex scandal. But the sad truth is that whistle-blowers rarely win, and few survive unscathed the ordeal of being banished from the group they exposed.

The popular BBC television program "Yes, Minister" portrays a former radical-liberal editor, elected to high political office, struggling to overcome a deeply entrenched and intransigent civil-service bureaucracy. His occasional victories are amusing, even as the evidence of the bureaucracy's awesome power is instructive. Resisting the pressure of the group is not easy. Most of the time, most people come to see the world through the eyes of the groups to which they belong, groups that envelop the consciousness. These groups include coworkers, families, professional organizations and lodges, and, of course, religious institutions.

In *The March of Folly* Pulitzer Prize-winning historian Barbara Tuchman studies why certain governments throughout history have failed to act in their own best interests. Tuchman substantially solves the riddle she poses, but then misplaces the object of her insight. Having examined incidents of "folly" from Troy to Vietnam, Tuchman answers the question in terms of the life of the contemporary chief executive:

> For a chief of state under modern conditions, a limiting factor is too many subjects and problems in too many areas of government to allow solid understanding of any of them, and too little time to think between fifteen-minute appointments and thirty-page briefs. This leaves the field open to protective stupidity. Meanwhile bureaucracy, safely repeating today what it did yesterday, rolls on as ineluctably as some vast computer, which, once penetrated by error, duplicates it forever.[4]

The emphasis here is misplaced because the incumbents of the offices of a bureaucracy, including CEOs and heads of state, understand very clearly that their actions serve their own interests and, often, the interests of the bureaucracy as well. What is missing is a broader context for viewing and understanding a problem.

Later, Tuchman introduces a concept that captures the essence of the social psychologists' concern with the power of the group to create and enforce meaning that molds human behavior. "Wooden-head-

edness," she writes, consists of "assessing a situation in terms of pre-conceived fixed notions while ignoring or rejecting any contrary signs."[5] Bureaucracies function in terms of fixed notions because past experience confirms the workability of those notions. To introduce change is to risk disruption of a system. Those who work within a system have a vested interest in the relative stability of that system.

It is not only bureaucrats who fall into this category, but virtually everyone who functions in terms of preconceived notions. Winning coaches continue to do what they think has been responsible for their past successes. So, also, do the successful businessman and the accomplished sportsman. Teachers repeat lectures they believe were well received by their students. Politicians emphasize those stands that the press, constituent mail, and pollsters suggest are popular.

Thinking and acting in terms of preconceived notions is an entirely natural and normal human activity. And mostly we continue to act "normally" because our lives are entangled in a web of group affiliations. Our social groups reinforce us when we do the right things and write the right thoughts. The price of straying too far from conventional behavior or wisdom is to be banished from or ignored by the social group.

Today an army of political reporters looks at Pat Robertson and, without resorting to Tuchman's language or the concepts of social psychologists, sees him and his spirited followers as a living example of wooden-headedness. When has anyone ever ignored so much evidence that would caution against the folly of running for president? And who but a group of religious zealots, unwilling to abandon their preconceived notions, could so badly misread the mood of the American people?

But "group think" can exist in any group. As evidence began to mount that Pat Robertson was putting together a campaign of considerable significance, the media mostly continued to ignore it. Their certainty that his prospects remained "slim" and "none" suggests that it was *they* who were being duped by collective wooden-headedness.

"The most important thing . . . that we can know about a man is what he takes for granted," wrote sociologist Louis Wirth a half-century ago. "And the most elemental and important facts about society," he continued, "are those that are seldom debated and generally regarded as settled."[6]

Herein lies an important clue to how the media have been victimized by self-inflicted wooden-headedness with respect to Pat Robertson and the Other Americans. "At least since the Enlightenment," write Rodney Stark and William Sims Bainbridge in *The Future of Religion*, "most Western intellectuals have anticipated the death of religion." They continue:

> The most illustrious figures in sociology, anthropology, and psychology have unanimously expressed confidence that their children, or surely their grandchildren, would live to see the dawn of a new era in which, to paraphrase Freud, the infantile illusions of religion would be outgrown.[7]

This belief in the inevitable demise of religion is anchored in a sweeping worldview known as "secularization theory." In a nutshell, secularization theory holds that the Protestant Reformation and the Renaissance set in motion the forces of modernization that swept across the globe and loosened the dominance of the sacred. The technological, industrial, scientific, and cultural revolutions of the Western world are the result. In due course, the theory holds, the sacred shall disappear altogether—except, possibly, in the private realm.

Western scholars have long assumed that this view is the product of rational analysis and objective research. Perhaps, but growing numbers of social scientists are no longer so sure. Notwithstanding, secularization theory has permeated Western culture, trickling down from the mandarins at the apex of higher education until virtually everyone who has passed through any but the most parochial of colleges and universities has been indoctrinated with its assumptions.

When confronted with evidence that religion persists as a vital force in the hearts and lives of men and women in the modern world, scholars, intellectuals, and opinion leaders become incredulous, clinging stubbornly to the fixed notions of the past quarter-millennium.

It is primarily through journalism that we have the opportunity to see the effects of the secularization paradigm in everyday thought. The world is filled with events beyond our firsthand experience, of which we are afforded glimpses through the lens of the mass media. What we know about the world is determined largely by the reporters

and editors who define what is news and by commentators who decide what is worthy of analysis.

In a very profound sense, as Michael Schudson concludes in *Discovering the News*, "the daily persuasions of journalists reflect and become our own."[8] The media give us more than a disembodied message about some event they have judged to be "news." In subtle (and sometimes not-so-subtle) ways, they provide a perspective—a way of looking at and thinking about what they report.

That the carriers of the news also shape the news is not a recent discovery. Fifty years ago, Leo C. Rosten asked Washington correspondents to comment on the possibility of "pure" objectivity in reporting the news. Almost two-thirds agreed that it was "almost impossible to be objective."[9] Still, Rosten found that journalists hold high the ideal of objectivity.

It may come as a surprise that objectivity has not always been a goal of journalists. In fact, before the twentieth century, it seldom occurred to anyone that newspapers *should* report the news objectively. It was taken for granted that newspapers were instruments for achieving the goals set by those who controlled them. One of the reasons the late Walter Lippmann is high in the ranks of America's most revered journalists is that he did much to promote belief in a "new professionalism." And central to that philosophy was a commitment to rational standards and constant vigilance in the pursuit of objectivity.

Lippmann's crusade for objectivity was more than a journalistic goal; it was a moral philosophy. In *American Inquisitor*, written in 1928, he set forth an ideal standard through the voice of "Socrates":

Have you ever stopped to think what it means when a man acquires the scientific spirit? It means that he is ready to let things be what they may be, whether or not he wants them to be that way. It means that he has conquered his desire to have the world justify his prejudices.[10]

From the 1920s to the present day, print and broadcast journalists have struggled with the issue of objectivity. Most have never been completely comfortable with the idea. Objectivity may be the "ideal-

type," but, many contemporary journalists find, the concepts of "fairness" and "balance" are more realistic for their profession.

Fairness from whose perspective? Balance relative to what standard?

For years conservatives have complained about a liberally biased press. And there has been much anecdotal evidence to support the claim. In fact, many liberal reporters have admitted it, but they fail to see it as a problem. As far as they are concerned, they are more capable of sorting through the evidence to present the truth than a mass media in the hands of conservatives.

Only in recent years have there been systematic data to assist in understanding the attitudes, beliefs, and values of American journalists. Stanley Rothman, professor of government at Smith College, is the architect of a study initiated in 1977 to investigate elites in the public-interest movement, the federal bureaucracy, and the media. The study has now expanded into an investigation of elites in a dozen sectors of American culture, and Rothman has been joined by S. Robert Lichter and Linda S. Lichter as co-investigators.

Some of the preliminary findings of their media study began to appear as early as 1981. The first major volume is entitled *The Media Elite: America's New Powerbrokers.*[11] Data include interviews, a survey, psychological tests ("Thematic Apperception Test"), and content analysis of print and broadcast materials.

Lichter, Rothman, and Lichter claim not to be interested in exposing the biases of journalists. Rather, they define their goal as understanding "the relationship between the journalists' perspectives and their product."[12] In short, they are not interested in assessing "blame," but in understanding *how* the backgrounds, beliefs, and experience of journalists affect the final product.

The data confirm the widely held assumption that mass-media personnel are generally liberal. Indeed, the study documents a large chasm between media elites and the general public. But for Lichter, Rothman, and Lichter, the question is Why? The answer is that the media are a fairly homogeneous and cosmopolitan group. They are highly educated and come disproportionately from upper-middle-class homes in the northeast and north-central states.

"The typical journalist," write Lichter and colleagues, "is the very model of the modern eastern urbanite."[13] They are politically liberal

and aloof from traditional norms and institutions, as are most people who possess their demographic and educational profile.

On the behavioral level, journalists have voted overwhelmingly for Democratic candidates. For example, in 1976, 81 percent of the media personnel surveyed voted for Jimmy Carter over Gerald Ford, compared to 51 percent of the general public. And in 1972, an identical proportion picked George McGovern while 62 percent of the general public voted for Richard Nixon. In 1964, 96 percent of the journalists selected Lyndon Johnson over Barry Goldwater.[14]

On a broad range of social and moral issues, journalists express more liberal views than "the man in the street." A few examples of personal-morality issues: Whereas 71 percent of the general public believed homosexuality to be morally wrong, only 38 percent of the media elites agreed. Sixty-five percent of the general public, compared with 35 percent of the media group, believes abortion to be morally wrong. And by a margin of 57 percent to 22 percent, the general public was more likely to view smoking marijuana as morally wrong.

Almost twice as many people in the general public (47 percent to 24 percent) believe that living with someone of the opposite sex outside of marriage is wrong. And, by approximately the same margin (52 percent to 27 percent), the general public believes that divorce should be more difficult to obtain.[15]

On these and a number of other moral issues, only about half as many journalists as members of the general public expressed a socially conservative point of view. Media elites would likely interpret these data as evidence that they are *more tolerant* of individual choice in a pluralistic society. But through the eyes of conservatives who feel strongly that abortion, premarital sex, and drug use are morally abhorrent, the data provide proof positive of the press's tolerance of immorality.

The study also shows that media elites are on the average much less active religiously and less orthodox in what they believe, confirming another suspicion of evangelical conservatives. Furthermore, it is quite probable that the average person of deep religious conviction will attribute the media's "tolerance of immorality" to their lack of religious values.

Comparison of the religious behavior of the media elites with a

national survey conducted by the Gallup Organization during roughly the same period reveals further dramatic differences. Whereas half of the media sample professed no religious affiliation, 68 percent of the national sample reported being church or synagogue members. More than nine out of ten in the national sample expressed a preference for a religious group. In an average week in 1981, Gallup reported, 41 percent of the national population attended church. Only 8 percent of the media elites said that they attended religious services weekly; 86 percent reported they seldom or never attended.[16]

These figures add up to some whopping differences between the values and behavior of media elites and the general public. But the data do not prove that the generally more liberal values of media elites on social issues, and high levels of alienation from traditional institutions and authority, result in a distorted presentation of these issues in their reports. Nor does their low level of religious involvement mean that they are either overtly or subtly biased against religion in a way that would affect their ability to assess objectively the role of religion in the political process.

At the same time, the possibility of systematic bias cannot automatically be ruled out. Lichter, Rothman, and Lichter bring some fascinating data to bear on the issue as a result of their testing. A Thematic Apperception Test is a psychological test that measures the impact of underlying values. Researchers present a series of pictures and ask individuals—in this case the media elites—to construct a story about each one. The pictures are deliberately ambiguous so that the stories people tell are projections of their own consciousness, a mirror of what they think is important and how they understand the world. Lichter, Rothman, and Lichter argue that this technique is useful for understanding journalists because it shows how they "fill in the gaps between what they know and what they assume when confronting a new situation."[17] Here is what they found:

When the journalists were shown a picture that could be interpreted as an authority figure, they "tended to evoke fantasies about abuse of power in the form of greedy businessmen, deceitful lawyers, conniving politicians, intimidating policemen, and sadistic military superiors."[18] On the other hand, when presented a picture interpreted to be an average man, the media elites tended to see individuals victimized by "malevolent higher-ups or an uncaring social system."[19]

The researchers conclude that these subconscious projections of social reality are, at least in part, a demonstration of how reporters see and interpret stories. The journalist's presuppositions are at work from the beginning of every assignment: (1) What is the nature of the story? (2) Who qualifies as an expert or resource person in investigating the topic? (3) What is sorted out as a peripheral idea or not a credible source? (4) What constitutes an interesting angle on the story? (5) How do preexisting values and attitudes affect how the story is finally shaped in the writing stage?

Lichter and his associates thus conclude that journalists are not the tough-minded, independent thinkers they like to believe themselves to be, but, rather, "captives of conventional wisdom [and] carriers of intellectual currents whose validity is taken for granted."[20] Whether they define their own goal as *objectivity* or *fairness and balance*, they are not apt to step outside of themselves, so to speak, and see the extent to which they are captives of their own values and the values of those whom they trust. "Even according to an arbitrary standard requiring that each side receive equal coverage," report Lichter *et al.*, "the results were consistently one-sided."[21]

And how do the media elites respond to this assessment of their work? A theory emerged from Festinger's investigation of the UFO cult members called the "Cognitive Dissonance Theory," which contends that when individuals are confronted with dissonant or contradictory information (that is, two things that don't logically fit together) they will experience discomfort, then do something to reduce the dissonance. There are three possible types of action: (1) *change* their beliefs, opinions, or behaviors so that the contradiction is reduced or eliminated, (2) *acquire new information* that may reduce the dissonance, or (3) *forget, ignore,* or *deny the validity of the information* that produced the dissonance in the first place.[22]

Smoking when there is evidence that it causes cancer is as good a way of illustrating the dynamics of cognitive dissonance as it was three decades ago when the theory became popular in the social sciences. The discomfort produced by the knowledge that smoking causes cancer can be reduced by (1) ceasing to smoke, (2) concluding that the evidence is not yet clear (the posture promoted by the tobacco industry), or (3) denying the validity of the research and avoiding contact with those who transmit the dissonant information.

Festinger's theory of cognitive dissonance lays out the options for journalists confronted with the Lichter, Rothman, and Lichter study. Changing their own behavior is difficult at best. Nor are they likely to change the opinions of the study's authors.

There remain two more options. First, the study does not claim to be an indictment of bias, merely an analysis of how values affect reporting. In fairly short order, then, it can be ignored and forgotten. That is not too hard to arrange when the media elites substantially control whether the study receives wide or scant attention in general and who will review the work in particular.

There can also be a call for new information, such as the testimony of other experts and reviews by recognized authorities on the subject that dispute the findings. Discrediting the authors is another means; if they can be successfully labeled as conservatives, then their findings can be dismissed as a biased attack on journalism.

In fact, the media elites employed a bit of all of these strategies to deflect the discomforting notion that they might be responsible for some distortion or systematic slanting of the news. Perhaps the slickest cognitive trick of all was to extract a radically different message from the study: Rather than showing them to be way out of step with the masses, the data prove instead that journalists are more tolerant, more committed to pluralism, and therefore more in step with the traditions and values of American culture.

And that leads to another very important conclusion of the media elite story. The media, according to Lichter, Rothman, and Lichter, try to uphold two contradictory self-images that are not easily rec-onciled. On the one hand, they see themselves as cool, nonpartisan reporters struggling to get the news. But beneath the veneer of the objective reporter coexists a social reformer. The problem is not just that journalists all went to the same schools, read the same newspa-pers, and, hence, all operate from the same narrow liberal paradigm. "Probably just as important" is that a fair proportion "*desire to exert moral power*, as patrons of outsiders and victims with whom they identify, against traditional restrictions and institutional authority [em-phasis added]."[23]

This is a subtle but consequential characteristic. Even Walter Cronkite, perhaps the most beloved broadcaster in the history of television, has failed to recognize its power. Once asked whether journalists were

biased toward a liberal perspective against established institutions, he said no but added that his profession was prone "to side with humanity rather than authority."[24]

One may reasonably ask, So what? The answer rests in an understanding of how these beliefs and behavioral patterns affect the way religion is reported in the news or analyzed as an element of the political process. Journalists are not, as a group, very religious; some of them even disdain religion. Furthermore, they interact daily with colleagues who also feel indifferent or negative about religion. Thus, living in a subculture that shares their ambivalence or hostility toward religion, they come to believe their viewpoint is normative and widely shared by the general public.

There are many reasons why the media have misunderstood and misreported the story of an ascending New Christian Right. Clearly their liberal bias is an important factor. But if Lichter and his colleagues have correctly characterized journalists as "closet reformers," there is another crucial ingredient in the mix. Like-minded reformers can be championed. Reformers with different but not antagonistic goals can be tolerated. But reformers of a different stripe pose a threat of immeasurable proportions.

When Jerry Falwell was discovered by the mass media and believed to have a huge following, he was terrifying. Only after his image was trimmed down to size were his presence and his message tolerable within a pluralistic society. The dissonance was reduced by the information that Falwell did not have the television audiences and Moral Majority following he claimed.

Now comes Pat Robertson, and the mechanisms for reducing cognitive dissonance are being summoned anew. But it is more difficult this time. The media's interpretation of the resources Robertson has available to launch a significant campaign clashes badly with the overwhelming evidence. And therein lies the essence of their woodenheadedness—they assess religion in terms of their own preconceived, and mutually held, notions of its irrelevance in the modern secular world. From this follows the belief that the New Christian Right could never be a force large enough to upset the status quo. And because these views are reinforced during interaction with other media people, they are inclined to ignore, discount, or reject evidence that would suggest the contrary. In the U.S. bicentennial year, Jerry Falwell

staged a series of patriotic I Love America rallies, which he took to the steps of all fifty state capitol buildings as well as the U.S. Capitol in Washington, D.C. During the same period, the Reverend Sun Myung Moon and his tiny band of followers gained lots of attention with their patriotic rallies.

A charismatic Korean prophet whose followers believed him to be God was a "sexy" story. But a Baptist preacher holding patriotic rallies was just another humdrum story. Falwell and his operatives were utterly frustrated by their inability to attract media coverage, even in April 1980, when the Washington for Jesus rally drew at least a quarter-million people to sing, pray, and lobby.

The Republican National Convention in July of 1980 was a critical turning point for Falwell. His Liberty Baptist Singers appeared in prime time, and Falwell and his right-wing preacher colleagues met with Ronald Reagan. Finally Falwell had the attention he had been seeking. The media concluded he must have some clout.

A month later, Reagan helped reinforce that perception when he accepted the Religious Roundtable's invitation to address the National Affairs Briefing. Suddenly the press became really curious. They showed up 250-strong for the two-day briefing, reinforcing the 100 or so who were traveling with the candidate.

Reagan sounded a lot like the people he came to address. At a press conference, he said he doubted the theory of evolution and that if it is to be taught, "the biblical story should also be taught." In his speech to a packed Reunion Arena, his harangues against the Supreme Court; the Department of Health, Education, and Welfare; the Federal Communications Commission; the Department of Labor; the National Labor Relations Board; and IRS "bureaucrats" were as strong as anything the preachers, right-wing military generals, and New Right operatives had been dishing out. He decried the government becoming "morally neutral." He linked rising crime, drug abuse, child abuse, and human suffering to the education of our youth without ethics.

Most of the press corps probably doubted the sincerity of Reagan's speech. But that he would address such a radical group, and employ their rhetoric, was scary stuff.

From that moment on, Jerry Falwell and the other politically minded televangelists had little difficulty getting media attention. The Moral Majority and the sudden appearance of millions of Christian zealots

was one of the hot items in the campaign and in the post-election analysis.

The media, thus, were slow to discover the presence of a conservative movement in America.

The media's liberal bias helped keep a big story bottled up for a long time. Once the story finally broke, the bias kept right on working, as clearly evidenced by their failure to ask the right questions. Another indication is their failure to seriously analyze Reagan's role in encouraging the development of the New Christian Right movement. When this question does occasionally arise, the media seem more interested in Reagan's own religion. Again, the wrong question. Reagan's personal religious views are simply not very important. Throughout his presidency, Reagan has periodically invoked pious religious rhetoric. Even if he is insincere and uses religion for his own political aims, his ongoing courtship of the New Christian Right has been a big boost to their own commitment and enthusiasm. And, as noted earlier, he has repeatedly addressed conservative religious groups while ignoring mainline Protestantism. The press has consistently failed to deal with the political implications of this.

The media have focused on two questions. First, How big is the movement? Lacking any background on the movement, the media first tended to accept the claims of its leaders, especially Falwell, uncritically. And he assured them that the answer was "very big." Falwell claimed television audiences in the range of 17 to 50 million for his "Old Time Gospel Hour" and 3 to 5 million members of the Moral Majority, and he took credit for registering 4 million voters. When the election was over, he claimed credit for the Reagan landslide and the defeat of liberal congressmen and senators.

Every social movement that is perceived as powerful can be expected to face organized opposition, both from preexisting organizations and, almost always, new organizations that emerge specifically for the battle. People for the American Way and Americans for Common Sense were the most visible of a dozen new organizations created ttle the right-wing threat of the Moral Majority, the Christian table, and Christian Voice. Common Cause and the American erties Union were the most visible existing organizations to attention to "saving America from religious zealots." New Christian Right had a vested interest in persuading

the media that they were very large, so also did the countermobilization organizations. Unless the Moral Majority was indeed a serious
threat to society why would anyone give money to People for the
American Way? So they repeated Falwell's claims and made up some
statistics of their own to show that the threat was real.

Implicit in the formation of a countermobilization effort is a second
question, namely, How unconventional is the threatening movement?
And the answer (no matter what the cause or the nature of the group's
activities) is always "very unconventional." If not, there would be no
need for a countermovement, since they could simply be accepted as
one of the many competitive interest groups in the political arena. By
labeling them unconventional in the extreme, the opposition aims to
brand new movements as illegitimate. If allowed to operate un-
checked, the argument goes, they would constitute a grave threat. In
this case, the New Christian Right is seen as a threat to the very
stability of the political system.

The perception of the New Christian Right as very large—coupled
with the perception that their beliefs about religion and politics were
very unconventional—led to a brief period of hysteria, when it seemed
as though America was in grave danger of being overrun by fundamentalists. Gradually, the exaggerations became evident. When that
happened, the media radically restructured the "born-again Chris-
tians-turned-politicians" story to make it consistent with the new evidence that they were not so dangerous after all. Jerry Falwell was
recast as a bit player rather than a star.

But Jerry Falwell has refused to get off the stage. On a rather steady
basis, he does things and says things the media cannot ignore. So, the
media flip-flops between warning Americans about the dangerous zealot
from Lynchburg and announcing his impotence or imminent fall.

When Pat Robertson got the attention of the national media with
his prospective presidential bid, the media returned to the same questions they had earlier asked of Falwell. First, How big is his audience
(Or, alternatively, How many evangelicals are there in America?) A
second, How unconventional are his views about religion and po

On the face of it, the answers are again the same. Robertso
large audience (or, there are a lot of evangelicals) and his
and political views are highly unconventional. But, as w

these are the wrong questions. Or, at the very least, they are questions of misplaced emphasis.

The number of viewers of Robertson's "700 Club" is not unimportant, but it is secondary to the total array of resources—of which his television audience is only a part—he can bring to bear on a presidential bid. Similarly, the question of how many evangelicals there are in America is relevant, but more important is the likelihood of his coalescing those evangelicals into a solid voting bloc.

What about Robertson's beliefs? Compared with the media, there can be no question that his theological and political views are unconventional—very unconventional. But this is a supreme example of wooden-headedness. Comparing Robertson's views with those of the media can be terribly misleading. As we have seen, the views of the media are not very representative of the public at large.

Obviously, it makes much more sense to examine Robertson's beliefs (theological and political) in light of the views of the general public than some standard of conventionality established by the media and by Robertson's adversaries.

If the press were to take that task seriously, a door would open to the understanding that they are more out of step with the general public than Pat Robertson is. Anything short of a successful presidential bid can be retrospectively judged as a march of folly. But that judgment may miss the more fundamental reality that Robertson's candidacy has served to solidify a nascent religious coalition not previously mobilized. And, further, that coalition could have a significant impact on American politics well beyond the Reagan era. Should that happen, history will surely judge the media as the ones on a march of folly in 1987–88 because they refused, even in the presence of overwhelming evidence, to recognize the importance of Pat Robertson's candidacy and the significance of the constituency he represents.

12

Is There Not a Cause?

A prince, says Machiavelli, ought always to be a great asker and a patient hearer of truth about those things of which he has inquired, and he should be angry if he finds that anyone has scruples about telling him the truth.
—Barbara Tuchman,
The March of Folly

On June 11, 1986, the Supreme Court of the United States struck down, by a vote of 5-4, a Pennsylvania law that regulated abortion, and in doing so upheld the 1973 *Roe* vs. *Wade* decision, effectively legalizing abortion on demand. Pro-choice forces initially were jubilant. Claimed Janet Benshoof of the American Civil Liberties Union: "This is a tremendous pro-choice victory . . . an absolute rejection of the Reagan Administration's request to the Court to overturn that landmark decision."[1]

But the pro-life forces also responded as if they had won. "The thing that jumps out at you is that it's a 5-to-4 decision," noted Douglas Johnson, the National Right-to-Life Committee's legislative director. "We're very encouraged,"[2] he told a *New York Times* reporter. "We're just one vote away from a Court which may be prepared to abandon *Roe* v. *Wade*."[3] (The vote on the 1973 decision was 7-2. In a harshly worded dissent to the Pennsylvania decision, Chief Justice Warren Burger stated, ". . . every member of the *Roe* Court rejected the idea of abortion on demand.")[4]

Two days after the decision, Pat Robertson drew enthusiastic plause when he sharply attacked the Supreme Court at the N Right-to-Life Committee convention in Denver. Referring t

tices as "despots," he called on the assembled to become more active in politics and thereby help "rid this country of the runaway excesses of five unelected men."

But Robertson also wryly noted the narrowness of the margin and the importance of Justice Burger's dissent: "That means with the wonderful process of mortality tables only one more is needed to get a judicial reversal."[5] Robertson's reference was to the aging court and likelihood of President Reagan's having the opportunity to make at least one more conservative appointment to the Court—which is in fact exactly what happened with the retirement of Justice Powell in 1987.

Eleanor Smeal, president of the National Organization for Women (NOW), also recognized that the "good news" for her forces could be short lived. "It is shocking how close we are to losing legal abortion and birth control," she told a gathering of NOW, meeting in Denver just a few blocks away.[6]

Smeal wasted little time in utilizing the decision to rally support for her organization and the pro-choice issue. In a direct-mail appeal she wrote:

> You and I . . . the *majority*—have been overshadowed and ignored while the so-called "right-to-lifers" march en masse on the White House, scream about "baby killing," intimidate and threaten legislators, and *terrorize* innocent women at abortion clinics all across the country.[7]

"This is no time to remain silent," Smeal said as she called on pro-choice advocates to "wake up" and "raise hell."[8]

Interestingly, her letter assumes the posture of the majority position: "The vast majority of Americans want to keep abortion and birth control safe and legal." And elsewhere the letter states, "The clear majority of Catholics support legal abortion."[9]

Is she correct? Or does it matter? Couldn't Eleanor Smeal simply search until she finds a poll to suit her point of view or even make up numbers if she wanted? She could, but she didn't. There are a variety of polls on abortion that support her conclusion.

America has moved beyond fascination with public opinion polling to near-obsession. For almost any conceivable subject, someone has

done a poll. To know how others feel, or to be asked our opinions, is a kind of quasi-enactment of democracy. To cite public opinion statistics is to speak with authority.

Public opinion polls reveal a lot about the subject of this book. Polls can indicate whether a religious conservative such as Pat Robertson has simply fantasized potential support for a political race or whether it indeed exists. Polls can help us determine whether Robertson and other leaders of the New Christian Right are extremist or are actually in touch with mainline America.

Abortion is the single most emotional and publicized moral issue among conservative Christians as well as many other Americans. It is an issue on which every presidential candidate has to take a stand, and that position can affect the presidential race. It is worth considering abortion polls in some detail.

What is it that gives a survey authority and credibility? Social scientists have formulated a set of rules that are codified in research textbooks, but not everybody follows them. You don't need a license to conduct a poll. Anybody can do a poll and publicize the results. How is the public to know which polls are reliable? Often it is not easy.

The first thing to remember is that *how* the question is asked can make a vast difference in the response. Consider, for example, the following items in a *New York Times*/CBS poll conducted in August 1980:[10]

	Yes	No
1. Do you think there should be an amendment to the Constitution *prohibiting abortion*, or shouldn't there be such an amendment?	29%	62%
2. Do you believe there should be an amendment to the Constitution *protecting the life of the unborn child*, or shouldn't there be such an amendment? [emphasis added to both questions]	50%	39%

Both questions get at the same subject (an amendment prohibiting abortion), but the different wording produces very different results. Almost two-thirds (62 percent) say they are opposed to an amendment prohibiting abortion, but exactly half (50 percent) say they favor an amendment protecting the unborn.

The different wordings were deliberately included in this poll to demonstrate the problem. But the fact that wording can influence a response doesn't mean that all polls are tricky, or that no polling result is to be trusted. Rather, it instructs us to approach the world of opinion polling with caution.

Another problem with polling data is interpreting what numbers mean. What people say and what they do are often very different. Also, the intensity of their feelings about an issue may not be evident in the response categories. Someone may say that he is opposed to abortion, for example, but a follow-up question (pollsters call them "probes") about how important the issue is may reveal that it is not very important at all.

In addition to bad data, ambiguous data, and data that may have alternative interpretations, one also has to contend with the problem of *no data*. No data? That's right. Today's garbage is wrapped in yesterday's poll. We may or may not have read that poll. We may or may not remember correctly what it said. In this hazy world of fleeting information, there are mountains of claims regarding what polls have proven.

Claims are not necessarily made with the conscious intent to deceive. But everyone tends to interpret information in a way that is consistent with his or her values or best interests. Also, we are more likely to remember information that supports what we think, so the one poll in ten that supports what we believe may be the only one we remember.

Consider Eleanor Smeal's claim that those who support a woman's right to have an abortion are the *vast majority*, and that even among Catholics *a clear majority* [authors' emphasis] support legal abortion. Is that what the polls say? Again, not surprisingly, it depends on how the question is asked, and how one chooses to interpret the data.

A good figure to cite to refute Smeal's claims appears in an impressive study conducted in 1981 for the Connecticut Mutual Life Insurance Company and entitled *The Connecticut Mutual Life Report*

on American Values in the '80s: The Impact of Belief (hereafter, *Connecticut Mutual*).[11] In this study of 2,018 randomly selected adults, 65 percent said they believed that abortion is morally wrong.[12] Or, one could cite a *New York Times* poll published in February 1986 in which 55 percent said that abortion is the same thing as murdering a child.[13]

These numbers suggest not a huge majority but a solid majority with reservations about abortion. Notwithstanding this abstract moral opposition, a number of reliable polls demonstrate that a large percentage of Americans would permit abortion under certain circumstances. What kinds of circumstances? A recent poll conducted by the National Opinion Research Center (NORC) found that 88 percent of a U.S. sample approved of abortion if the woman's health was in danger; 74 percent approved if there was a significant chance of serious birth defect; and 74 percent said abortion was OK in the case of rape. In those instances, three-quarters or more of the Catholic subsample also gave its consent to abortion.[14]

Eleanor Smeal may have these kinds of issues in mind when she says "vast majority." Furthermore, she might be recalling that a lot of people think that making abortion illegal will not solve all of the problems that result from legal abortion. For example, Gallup found that 88 percent agreed that if abortion were made illegal, "many women would break the law by getting illegal abortions"; and 87 percent believed that many women would be physically harmed in abortions performed by unqualified people.[15] In further support of Smeal's position, one could note a 1985 *Los Angeles Times* poll that found that a majority (51 percent) would oppose a law to prohibit use of federal funds for abortion.[16]

One could make a case that these numbers add up to tacit public support for abortion. But without looking at the numbers in a broader context, one would likely misunderstand the mood of the country. When it comes to abortion on demand, without consideration of anything but the woman's wishes, the American public does not stand with the pro-choice advocates. Let's examine more data.

For more than a decade, the Gallup Organization has been asking questions for *Newsweek* about abortion. The polls reveal that approximately one-fifth (21 percent in 1985) of the American population would permit abortion under all circumstances, and an identical proportion

(21 percent) believes that abortion should be illegal under all circumstances.

Furthermore, this distribution of public opinion has hardly changed in the years since *Roe* vs. *Wade*. Those with strong pro-life and pro-choice beliefs may feel even more strongly today than they did a decade ago, but they have scarcely budged the majority in the middle at all, as shown in Table 1.

Table 1. PROPORTION FAVORING AND OPPOSING
ABORTION IS HIGHLY STABLE OVER PAST DECADE[17]

	Favor Abortion, All Circumstances	Only Certain Circumstances	Disapprove, All Circumstances
1985	21%	55%	21%
1983	23	58	16
1981	23	52	21
1980	25	53	18
1979	22	54	19
1977	22	55	19
1975	21	54	22

We have already noted the circumstances in which the public approves of abortion—the mother's health endangered, serious birth defect possibilities, and rape (or what are sometimes referred to as *medical* reasons). The NORC poll found that, by small majorities, Americans *disapproved* of abortions performed because (a) the couple didn't want any more children (56 percent), (b) the mother was not married (54 percent), and (c) the couple felt they could not afford any more children (52 percent).[18]

When asked if they favored or opposed a ban on all abortions except in cases of rape or incest, or when the mother's life is endangered, 58 percent of Americans told Gallup in 1985 that they favored such a ban.[19]

There are three important tendencies evident in the survey data on abortion. The first is that the majority of Americans neither approve of abortions under all circumstances nor reject it under all circumstances, although their allegiance sometimes is claimed by believers on either extreme of the issue. Second, there is a tendency to view

abortion as a moral issue and to reject it under circumstances other than catastrophic, life-endangering, or life-debilitating circumstances. Third, the available evidence suggests a small but increasing proportion of Americans who reject abortions simply at the "convenience" of the mother (see Table 2).

Table 2. A GROWING NUMBER OF AMERICANS
ARE REJECTING CONVENIENCE ABORTIONS[20]

People Who Say No to Abortion Because Mother . . .	1972–82	1984	1985
Wants no more children	52%	56%	58%
Cannot afford more children	46	52	55
Is not married	50	54	57

To the extent that the data permit one to speak of a majority sentiment in the United States, that sentiment is on the side of a conservative, cautious posture toward abortion. However, the large majority of abortions performed are for so-called nonmedical reasons, i.e., for reasons of personal preference rather than for life-threatening or debilitating reasons. In 1983, Irvin M. Cushner, M.D., testified before the U.S. Senate Committee on the Judiciary that only 2 percent of all abortions are performed for medical reasons.[21] Others have placed the figure as high as 5 percent. In either case, it is clear that the overwhelming percentage of abortions performed in the United States are for reasons that would not be judged as catastrophic and life-threatening.

Thus, one can find some evidence to support whatever claims one wishes to make, but the weight of evidence does not support Eleanor Smeal's claims regarding public sentiment on the abortion issue.

Abortion, of course, has been high on the list of concerns of the New Christian Right. Jerry Falwell has frequently used his "Old Time Gospel Hour" television program to promote the pro-life position, and his Moral Majority has frequently cooperated with other groups on this issue. There are a dozen significant pro-life groups that are, on the whole, better organized and more active than many of the more visible New Christian Right organizations.

In 1981, *Time* called abortion "without question, the most emotional issue of politics and morality that faces the nation today."[22] That assessment seems just as appropriate now as it was then. Insofar as the

weight of public opinion is concerned, the "pro-lifers" would seem to have public sentiment and time on their side.

This perspective runs contrary to the general impression communicated by mass media. On abortion as with other issues, the media have generally portrayed the New Christian Right as being out of step with general public sentiment. But the evidence shows that the New Christian Right is closer to the general public than are journalists.

Consider Jerry Falwell, who is generally depicted as a zealous fundamentalist envisioning the most sweeping transformation of church-state relations of all the televangelists. Falwell has long claimed that the majority of American people agree with him on important moral issues, even if they don't back him personally or the Moral Majority to any great degree (which he blames on the media's distorted portrayal of him as a radical, far to the right of general public sentiment).

It is not possible to examine all of the moral issues Jerry Falwell has identified as part of his platform with the same detail as abortion. But even in a somewhat-abbreviated discussion, it is possible to see that mass media have either subconsciously ignored the question of where the general public stands on the issues, or they have deliberately "stacked the deck" in order to present Falwell as a man outrageously out of touch with American public sentiment.

When Jerry Falwell formed the Moral Majority in 1979, he identified four principal concerns. The organization, he said, was (1) pro-life, (2) pro-family, (3) pro-morality, and (4) pro-America. Having assessed the pro-life concern, let's briefly consider the others.

Pro-Family. Pro-family values mean "traditional" family values and, simultaneously, a rejection of all forms of family life other than the marriage of a man and a woman. Implicit in this affirmation is a rejection of divorce, because Falwell believes that marriage is for life. Homosexual and common-law marriages are explicitly condemned.

Public opinion polls have consistently shown that the family ranks as a top priority among individuals. Likewise, the overwhelming majority of people report that they are "very satisfied" or "mostly satisfied" with their family life.

These sentiments notwithstanding, the divorce rate in America is high and increasing. The paradox affects people of every religious persuasion. The Connecticut Mutual study reports that 52 percent of

Americans believe that obtaining a divorce should be made more difficult and only 21 percent think it should be easier. But when confronted with the hypothetical situation of being unhappily married and unable to reconcile problems, 56 percent say they would be willing to seek a divorce. And to add yet another dimension of complexity, 67 percent say they believe that the high rate of divorce in the United States is the result of people "not trying hard enough to stay together."[23] In short, these sentiments add up to an affirmation of the institution of marriage, but a recognition that it doesn't always work.

Only 29 percent said that they preferred a traditional family, one "in which the husband is responsible for providing for the family and the wife for the home and taking care of the children." Sixty-three percent of the total sample said they preferred a marriage in which husband and wife share responsibility equally.[24] Even among the most religious group in the Connecticut Mutual study, 56 percent said they preferred the shared responsibility to the traditional-family option.[25]

Such are the realities of the changing family in America today. Scripture says, "The husband is the head of the wife just as Christ is head of the Church: let wives be subject to their husbands as to the Lord." When sociologist Patrick McNamara sat down with evangelical and fundamentalist Christians and asked if this was true of their families, they overwhelmingly agreed that it was. But as he explored the process of family decision-making and division of labor in the household, he found them to be remarkably like nonevangelical families.[26]

McNamara's ethnographic research reveals a gap between what families say and what they do. The doctrine of the traditional family is a meaning system that gives coherence and structure to their lives. It is adhered to in principle even if not in the practical matters of day-to-day living. Evangelicals are just about as likely to have an egalitarian, task-and-decision-sharing family structure.

Evangelical Christians do differ significantly from nonevangelicals in their perceptions of what is right and what is wrong. People who score high on the Connecticut Mutual index of religiosity, for example, are much more likely to say that divorces should be harder to get, are less likely to approve of getting a divorce if problems can't be reconciled, and are more likely to believe that divorce is common because

people aren't trying hard enough to work out their problems. Similarly, they are much more likely to disapprove of premarital sex, adultery, unmarried couples living together, and homosexuality.

But perhaps most significant is the extent to which the general public affirms values associated with the traditional family. The Connecticut Mutual survey found that 85 percent of the adult public felt that adultery was morally wrong.[27] That statistic is confirmed by a 1985 NORC survey, in which 88 percent said that "a married person having sexual relations with someone other than their married partner" was "always wrong" (74 percent) or "almost always wrong" (14 percent).[28]

Similarly, nontraditional sex partners are considered wrong. In the Connecticut Mutual study, 71 percent rejected male homosexuality as morally wrong and 70 percent rejected lesbianism.[29] In the most recent NORC survey, 73 percent said that sexual relations between two adults of the same sex was "always wrong," and an additional 3 percent said it was "almost always wrong."[30]

In contrast, a 1986 *Los Angeles Times* poll found 53 percent saying that homosexual relations between consenting adults in the privacy of their home should be legal, while 35 percent said it should be illegal.[31] But, presumably, saying that homosexual relations between consenting adults should be legal does not preclude many respondents from believing that it is immoral.

Taken together, poll findings indicate a certain amount of tolerance for families that have strayed from the "traditional" pattern, and the emergence of a new egalitarianism; but also a strong endorsement of the traditional family. Jerry Falwell would no doubt be less accepting of divorce when couples have made an honest effort to work out their differences, but his views about the traditional family do not appear to be all that different from those of a sizable majority of the American public.

Pro-Morality. The pro-morality plank, as articulated by Falwell in the early days of the Moral Majority, referred almost exclusively to opposition to pornography. In his antipornography campaign, Falwell was portrayed in the media as representing an ideological fringe group that was prepared to encroach on the First Amendment rights of the majority of Americans in order to impose the prudish standards of a minority.

Back in the late nineteenth century, Anthony Comstock led a cru-

sade that resulted in the passage of federal legislation in 1873 prohibiting the use of the mail for obscene materials. From that date forward, legislators and the courts periodically have wrestled with a definition of just what is obscene or pornographic. In a series of Supreme Court cases between 1957 and 1973, the Court failed to define the subject matter, but their efforts had the net effect of liberalizing social practice. The problem of determining what is pornographic was essentially left to the local community.

In 1970 the Presidential Commission on Obscenity and Pornography failed to find any scientific evidence that would causally link pornography to antisocial behavior. The combination of scientific legitimation and the Supreme Court's unsuccessful attempts to draw an empirically definable boundary resulted in a rapidly expanding availability of sexually explicit materials during the 1970s. Fifteen years later, when Reagan's Attorney General, Edwin Meese III, created another commission to study pornography, it was assumed—even before the commissioners were identified—to be a sop for the New Christian Right. It was also assumed that the findings would refute those of the 1970 presidential commission. There was widespread apprehension that it would bring censorship and the abrogation of First Amendment rights.

The American Civil Liberties Union loudly protested the Meese Commission's findings and warned against its recommendations. But their voice was drowned out by four factors. (1) The commission produced evidence that linked antisocial behavior to violent pornography, and it published the results in graphic detail. (2) The widespread existence of child pornography and the abuse of minors that the report detailed were shocking. It wasn't easy for the ACLU to find a spot where they could drive in a wedge for First Amendment rights in the face of the sexual abuse of children. (3) Feminist objections to pornography had been changing the way a lot of people thought about the subject. A broader coalition was voicing the argument that sexual violence in pornography is causally related to the violent and degrading treatment of women. (4) Perhaps most important, a significant majority of Americans had simply grown tired of what they perceived to be the excesses of pornography. Any way you shuffle or interpret the public opinion poll numbers, it is clear that Americans have very serious objections to pornographic material.

Meese Commission member Park Dietz is a psychiatrist who also

holds a Ph.D. in sociology and is professor of law at the University of Virginia. In a personal statement about the report, he noted the public policy tensions represented in his several disciplines. As a sociologist, he acknowledges that all the evidence may not be in. As a law professor, he feels the importance of protecting First Amendment rights, and he acknowledges the ambiguity of the Supreme Court's efforts to determine what, if anything pornographic, lies outside the protection of the law. But, as a physician, he is compelled to make a clinical judgment, even in the face of uncertainty. And as a clinician, Dietz concludes:

> I, for one, have no hesitation in condemning nearly every specimen of pornography that we have examined in the course of our deliberations as tasteless, offensive, lewd, and indecent. According to my values, these materials are themselves immoral, and to the extent that they encourage immoral behavior they exert a corrupting influence on the family and on the moral fabric of society.[32]

By significant margins, polls indicate that Americans support Dietz's thinking. In 1985, according to a NORC survey, more than half (54 percent) of Americans favored legislation that would outlaw pornography for persons under eighteen years of age, and an additional 40 percent favored laws banning pornography entirely.[33] That's 94 percent of the population supporting a total or partial ban on pornography.

It is not simply that pornography is offensive. Again, according to a 1984 NORC survey, a majority (61 percent) of Americans believe that pornography contributes to the breakdown of morals and 55 percent believe that pornography leads people to commit rape.[34] A Gallup poll conducted for *Newsweek* in early 1985 found even greater proportions agreeing that explicit sexual materials have pernicious effects. Two-thirds (67 percent) told Gallup that it is "true" that sexually explicit magazines, movies, and books "lead to a breakdown of public morals"; 73 percent say these materials "lead some people to commit rape or sexual violence"; and 76 percent say they "lead some people to lose respect for women."[35]

Whether pornography does have such effects is unclear. What *is*

clear is that people are concerned that it does. This concern has led the American public to conclude that at least some types of pornography should be banned. Furthermore, there is overwhelming support for removing virtually all kinds of pornography from public display.

One out of five (21 percent) Americans would outlaw magazines that show nudity; two in five (40 percent) would outlaw X-rated movies in theatres.[36] Sexual violence is the most abhorred form of pornography. Seventy-three percent of Americans favor laws that would *totally ban* magazines that show sexual violence; 68 percent would ban movies that depict sexual violence, and 63 percent would ban the sale or rental of video cassettes featuring sexual violence.[37] As is dramatically demonstrated in Table 3, the large majority of Americans would like to see pornography of virtually every kind either out of sight or outlawed altogether.

For a person whose views are supposed to be on the fringe of American culture, Jerry Falwell seems to have a lot of company on the issue of pornography.

Pro-America. By saying he is pro-America, Jerry Falwell is expressing both general patriotism and support for a strong national defense.

Ronald Reagan campaigned on a platform calling for the strengthening of America's defenses. The 1981 Connecticut Mutual survey found that 73 percent of Americans believe "it is important for America to have the strongest military force in the world, no matter what it costs."[38] When Reagan was elected, every major public opinion polling organization that had been asking about defense expenditures over a period of time found public approval for increased military spending was at an all-time high. Americans were with Reagan on this issue early in his presidency.

After several years of increased military expenditures, and increasing pressure to cut domestic programs rather than raise taxes, public sentiment has shifted away from further expanding the military budget. In 1982, for example, President Reagan's proposals to increase military spending rated 69 percent approval in a national poll conducted by the *Los Angeles Times*. That shrank to 54 percent by 1985—but still a majority.[39]

Part of this decline stems from Americans' belief that the military has been successfully strengthened during the Reagan administration. For example, 67 percent of the American population told the Gallup

Table 3. AMERICANS FAVOR OUTLAWING OR
RESTRICTING PUBLIC DISPLAY OF PORNOGRAPHY[40]

	Outlaw	No Public Display	Outlaw Plus Ban Public Display
Magazines that show nudity	21%	52%	73%
Magazines that show adults having sexual relations	47	40	87
Magazines that show sexual violence	73	20	93
Theatres showing X-rated movies	40	37	77
Theatres showing movies that depict sexual violence	68	21	89
Sale or rental of X-rated cassettes for home viewing	32	39	71
Sale or rental of video cassettes featuring sexual violence	63	23	86

Organization in 1985 that "the ability of the nation to defend itself militarily has gotten better as a result of Reagan's policies."[41] And a CBS News/*New York Times* survey conducted at about the same time found 75 percent of Americans agreeing that "Reagan has significantly strengthened the country's military budget."[42]

Furthermore, 83 percent of Americans told Gallup that "building the strongest military force in the world" would be "very important" (46 percent) or "fairly important" (37 percent) in determining America's strength twenty-five years from now.[43]

It is quite clear that Jerry Falwell is not too far out of the mainstream on national defense, either.

While Falwell has never formally amended or expanded the agenda of the Moral Majority, he has spoken out on a wide range of social and moral issues. In addition to the four original goals of the Moral Majority, a later brochure identified another four "vital issues": affirmation of the separation of church and state; opposition to illegal drug traffic; support of the state of Israel and Jewish people everywhere; and support of equal rights for women while rejecting the Equal Rights Amendment as the appropriate vehicle for obtaining this goal.[44] Let's examine these issues very briefly.

Separation of Church and State. Falwell's critics (and now Pat Robertson's critics) to the contrary, Falwell has stated on numerous occasions that he believes in the separation of church and state. On the other hand, he doesn't think that Christians should be disenfranchised from participation in the political process. He believes that they, like any other interest group, have a right to petition the government.

By substantial margins, the polls show that Americans approve of the separation of church and state. Only 14 percent (albeit 31 percent of white fundamentalists) told the *Los Angeles Times* that they favor a constitutional amendment to make Christianity the official religion of the United States.[45]

Opposition to Illegal Drug Traffic. "An epidemic is abroad in America, as pervasive and as dangerous in its way as the plagues of medieval times," wrote *Newsweek* editor-in-chief Richard M. Smith in an introduction to that magazine's second cover story on drugs within three months in mid-1986.[46] Americans perceive that their country is in the midst of a drug crisis.

It's a big story for the mass media as attention shifts quickly from the Central and South American drug sources, to the crime wars for control of the estimated $25 billion-a-year growth industry, to the destruction of respectable upper-middle-class people's lives, to questions of the constitutionality of requiring government employees, airline pilots, and athletes to take drug tests, to Nancy Reagan's "just say no" crusade, to the ever-expanding array of new drugs.

While it is conceivable that a Jerry Falwell or a Pat Robertson might be to the right of most Americans on drug-related issues, it seems

highly unlikely. Their hard-line position on drugs is now the norm, not the exception.

Support of Israel. Jerry Falwell's biggest risk in supporting Israel was the possibility of alienating fundamentalists theologically to his right. It is a posture in line with both American foreign policy and public opinion. Since Israel's founding following World War II, U.S. foreign policy has always been pro-Israel. Political scientist Kenneth D. Wald has noted that in addition to a considerable pro-Israel lobby that consists of more than 200 groups (most of them Jewish) and the typically "moralistic" posture our nation takes in its foreign policy, most Americans—leaders and voters alike—see a strong Israel as serving America's foreign-policy objectives.[47]

Support of Equal Rights for Women. Fundamentalist Christians as well as some other evangelical groups have claimed all along that they support equal rights for women but believe that the Equal Rights Amendment was the wrong vehicle. If there should be another Equal Rights Amendment passed by Congress and sent out to the states for ratification, the issue could again become a source of public dispute between conservative Christians and ERA supporters. If not, it's a dead issue. Feminists may disagree with conservative Christians, but it's hard to sustain the battle—especially when the conservative Christians say their only disagreement is with the means, not the ends.

Now there is one final item to examine—an item that may fool some people.

School Prayer. Jerry Falwell is foursquare in favor of a constitutional amendment to put prayer back into public schools. In 1963, the Supreme Court found a Pennsylvania statute requiring the reading of Bible verses, followed by the Lord's Prayer, to be unconstitutional (*Abington* vs. *Schempp*). The decision was not popular then, and almost a quarter-century later, a majority (56 percent) of Americans say they disapprove.[48] Falwell does more than simply disapprove; he links the decline in public education to that decision.

> The Bible states, "The fear of the Lord is the beginning of knowledge." (Proverbs 1:7) I believe that the decay in our public school system suffered an enormous acceleration when prayer and Bible reading were taken out of the classroom by our U.S. Supreme Court.[49]

On the side of civil libertarians who favor removing all evidence of religion from public schools, there is some hope in poll data showing that the percentage approving the Court decision has slowly increased (from 29 percent approval in 1971 to 44 percent in 1985).[50]

Nevertheless, when the issue is raised in other ways, it is obvious that a large segment of the American public has difficulty with barring all religion from school. A 1983 Gallup survey found 85 percent of Americans saying that they favor an amendment to the Constitution that would allow for voluntary prayer in public schools.[51] A CBS News/ *New York Times* poll in 1984 found 68 percent favoring a constitutional amendment permitting organized prayer in schools. And of those approving, 77 percent said they would still approve of the amendment if it meant that the prayer used was from a religion other than their own.[52]

Together, all of these polls strongly suggest that Jerry Falwell is not all that radical compared with the rest of the American public, even if his positions appear extreme in the eyes of the media.

Of course, one can locate elaborations of Falwell's positions in sermons and speeches that suggest very dogmatic views on these issues. But one can also find much interview material in which his posture seems quintessentially pluralistic.

The leadership of the civil rights movement, including Martin Luther King, Jr., made some rather strident statements along the movement trail. And we have heard some pretty ugly words from fired-up rhetoricians: feminists, gay rights advocates, environmentalists, antiwar protesters, anticultists, and striking labor leaders.

All movement leaders are prone to hyperbole when rallying their constituents or in the heat of battle with their adversaries. Pat Robertson is no different from other movement leaders and spirited political candidates in this regard. From the very beginning of his exploration of a presidential bid, the mass media endeavored to label him an extremist, just as they attempted with Ronald Reagan when he first sought political office. Robertson makes no bones about being a conservative, but he rejects the label of extremist.

One thing is clear: Pat Robertson does not have the option of flip-flopping on issues to accommodate public opinion trends. He has repeatedly addressed almost every potential campaign issue on "The 700 Club." These commentaries are available on videotape. The Amer-

ican public is the arbiter of the struggle to determine whether Robertson is a mainstream conservative in the Reagan mode, or the dangerous extremist his critics claim.

Ironically, it was the archenemies of the Other Americans who took the Robertson candidacy seriously from the outset. For example, "skin" magazines such as *Penthouse, Hustler*, and *Genesis* warned of the certain moratorium on First Amendment liberties that a conservative Christian government would impose.

The May/June 1987 issue of *The Humanist* included an article—complete with an illustration of Gestapo goons wearing the cross in place of swastikas—that stated emphatically that Robertson is a firm opponent of church-state separation. Painting Robertson as something akin to a neo-Nazi, its authors concluded:

> Our only hope is that the majority of Americans will, through Pat Robertson's brazen presidential bid, see the obvious implications of the religious right agenda and therefore decide that this country doesn't need theocracy.[53]

Ronald Reagan has been called The Great Communicator. Pat Robertson, too, needs to do some slick communicating. The public opinion poll data suggest he may not be as far away from the mainstream of America as the media have characterized him. A *Los Angeles Times* poll found that 69 percent of Americans believe that "life today is getting worse in terms of morals."[54] If Robertson plays it right, his so-called extremist views on morality constitute one of his strongest assets.

To be a serious candidate for the presidency, the first issue he has to deal with is the widely held belief that religion and politics should not be mixed. In 1984, the Gallup Organization asked people if they favored or opposed "the separation of Church and State as described in the U.S. Constitution." By a margin of seven to one, those with an opinion affirmed the principle of separation (71 percent to 10 percent).[55]

But another question in the study revealed that many Americans are confused about what the Constitution says regarding the separation of church and state. A mere majority (55 percent) correctly identified the relevant passage in the Constitution: "Congress shall make no law

respecting an establishment of religion, or prohibiting the free exercise thereof." Forty-five percent said they believed the Constitution says: "The state shall be separate from the church, and the church from the school." This statement is actually taken verbatim from the Constitution of the Soviet Union.

By a margin of 52 percent to 30 percent, Americans expressed the view that it is wrong for religious groups to work actively for the defeat of political candidates who disagree with their position on certain issues. Fifty-four percent felt it is wrong for political candidates to bring in their own religious beliefs in discussing issues. And 64 percent believe it wrong for clergymen to air their own political beliefs in their sermons.

A national poll conducted for the *Los Angeles Times* in mid-1986 suggests that Americans' views on these issues have not changed much since the 1984 poll.[56] An identical proportion (54 percent) disapproved of political candidates bringing in their own religious views in discussing issues, and 62 percent disapproved of clergymen introducing their own political views in sermons.

Furthermore, 67 percent of those polled for the *Los Angeles Times* agreed with the statement, "We must maintain the separation of church and state." And by a margin of 2.5 to 1, people said they would be *less* likely to vote for a candidate who described himself as "an evangelical Christian." By a margin of more than two to one, respondents rejected a candidate who differed from his opponent only in the fact that he was a Protestant minister.

The average American appears to have strong reservations about mixing religion and politics; and having a preacher doing the mixing is worse. That is the conclusion reached by George Skelton, the *Los Angeles Times*'s Sacramento bureau chief who reported on the political implications of the poll:

> Although most Americans today say they are religious and worried about declining standards of morality, they are in no mood to launch a moral crusade through the national political process.[57]

So, what of the prospects of Pat Robertson becoming president? It's just not in the cards, as Skelton reads the numbers, and he quotes

the *Times* poll director I. A. Lewis to back him up. *"Pat Robertson is not a viable presidential candidate* [emphasis added]," concluded Lewis after analyzing the study results.[58]

Pollster Lewis has some impressive numbers to back up his conclusion. First of all, only 17 percent of the national sample were identified as fundamentalists and half of them did not have enough knowledge to form an opinion of Robertson's prospects as a presidential candidate. While those who did know him had a favorable impression by a three-to-one ratio, white fundamentalists rejected his presidential candidacy by a ratio of six to five. And among all registered Republicans, Robertson was rejected by a whopping five-to-one margin.

Still, Pat Robertson is a very pragmatic man. In his business operations at CBN, he has been quick to kill projects that just weren't working out according to the business plan. If the odds are so stacked against a bid for the presidency, why has he walked away from "The 700 Club," which he says he loves doing, and risked the financial stability of the show and CBN?

In the Old Testament, a giant called Goliath appeared on the scene of battle between Israel and the Philistines, and virtually the entire Israelite army fled. When David the shepherd learned of this, he went down to the battlefield and slew the giant with a slingshot. His brother scolded him for leaving the sheep unattended, but David replied, "Is there not a cause?" (I Samuel 17:29).

David did not fear the giant because he had faith that God would protect him just as He had protected David when the young lad battled the lions and bears that attacked his father's sheep.

The New Christian Right has used the imagery of David and Goliath to portray their struggle against a society that has become a secular giant. The Christian Roundtable, one of the significant social-movement organizations of the New Christian Right, has used "Is there not a cause?" as the motto of their organization. It captures the sentiment of evangelical and fundamentalist Christians who see their cause as noble and their troops as meager in the face of the Secular Humanists.

For Pat Robertson, a presidential campaign is a matter of doing what he thinks God would have him do. But his perceptions of how God speaks are not as unorthodox as he sometimes sounds on "The 700 Club" and as his adversaries would have us believe. On "Meet

the Press," in response to interviewer Ken Bode's question about the specific instructions Robertson receives from God, he replied:

> There are a number of ways that God speaks to people. He speaks through circumstances. He speaks through the advice of friends. And he speaks primarily through an inner peace that people get that what they are doing is right and proper.[59]

A lot of people skeptical about Robertson's candidacy will concede one point: Considering the odds, it must be an act of faith that pushes him forward.

But there is more than faith. When he was president, John F. Kennedy once said that after prayer, one has to get up off one's knees and hustle, because on this earth God has no hands but ours to do his bidding. Faith figures centrally in his operations of CBN, but so does hustle. There are probably few corporations in America where solid market research and rational decision-making play a more critical role.

Is Pat Robertson hiring different pollsters who are giving him different results than the *Los Angeles Times*, the *New York Times*, and the *Washington Post*? Yes and no. He commissions a lot of polling for CBN in programming and research, and sometimes he includes questions that are not explored in other polls. But, for the most part, Robertson reads the same polls as everyone else. He just reads the results differently.

Take, for example, that *Los Angeles Times* finding that by a margin of 2.5 to 1 people would be less likely to vote for a candidate describing himself as "an evangelical Christian." Reporter George Skelton found in that question what he was looking for. But Pat Robertson found something else—something *he* was looking for. Skelton reported the margin correctly, but he neglected to cite the precise figures of 27 percent and 10 percent respectively. That camouflages another important statistic: A majority, 57 percent, say that it wouldn't make any difference. Furthermore, 30 percent of those who are fundamentalists (white and black), and a third who vote conservatively, report that they would be more likely to vote for someone who identifies himself as "an evangelical Christian."

When Pat Robertson reads this poll question, he sees a natural three-to-one edge among conservative voters. Equally significant, he sees that a sizable majority are not *dis*inclined to vote for someone because he identifies himself as an evangelical Christian.

There are a lot of other questions in that survey that Robertson would read differently than Skelton. Robertson certainly would disagree that while most Americans are religious and worried about declining moral standards, "they are in no mood to launch a moral crusade through the national political process."

Robertson is very much persuaded that there is a religious revival taking place in America today—a revival that parallels in order of magnitude and significance the Great Awakenings of the eighteenth and nineteenth centuries. The significance of the poll data for Robertson is that they confirm a high degree of discontent. More than two-thirds (69 percent) of all Americans believe that "life today is getting worse in terms of morals." Only 17 percent believe that the moral fiber of the nation is improving. The percentage who believe things are getting worse runs two-thirds or greater for Democrats, Republicans, and independents; approximately four out of five fundamentalists and blacks believe that moral standards are declining.

For a preacher-turned-political-candidate, these numbers represent an enormous opportunity. The challenge is to mobilize a generalized discontent into a social movement.

George Skelton apparently sees at least three factors that persuade him that Americans are not in the mood for a moral/political crusade. First, there is a low level of support for Robertson's candidacy. Second, Americans express strong support for the separation of church and state. And third, there is general disapproval of preachers getting involved in politics.

Again, Pat Robertson's assessment of these matters is rather different. First, in mid-1986 he was not particularly concerned that he had such a low level of support even before declaring his candidacy. In the early stages of a campaign, mere name recognition is important, and he wasn't doing badly. According to the *Los Angeles Times* poll, he ranked third among Republican hopefuls behind Vice President George Bush and former Secretary of State Alexander Haig and ahead of former Senate Majority Leader Howard Baker, current Senate Mi-

nority Leader Robert Dole, New York Congressman Jack Kemp, and former U.N. Ambassador Jeane Kirkpatrick.

Second, Pat Robertson also believes in the separation of church and state. He wrote a book in 1986 about the church-state relationship in American history,[60] which he hopes clarifies his stands on a number of important issues and also helps focus attention on what he believes as opposed to what others say he believes. Some of the views he expresses will not be popular with liberals, but, on balance, he believes that his views on church and state separation can be a net political asset and not a liability.

Third, Pat Robertson has seen other polls regarding people's attitudes about clergy involvement in politics. As a general proposition, people say that they don't think clergy ought to mess around with politics. But this general stance tends to break down under examination of specific issues and context. When people know the preacher, and his views happen to agree with their own, they don't think his involvement in politics is a bad idea. For example, liberals thought Martin Luther King, Jr.'s, involvement in the political process was an effective way to express the legitimate grievances of black Americans. Conservatives disagreed, but they didn't object if their preacher got up in the pulpit and denounced the activist clergy.

When Billy Graham was the quasi-official White House chaplain to Republican presidents, Democrats howled that Graham was legitimizing conservative political ideologies. Republicans didn't see anything wrong with that.

Blacks have generally approved of mixing religion and politics because black preachers have traditionally been the leaders of their communities. Whites tended not to object—unless the black preachers were effective.

Liberal Catholics were glad when their bishops spoke out against the nuclear arms race; conservative Catholics wasted no time in letting the bishops know that their pastoral letter on economics exceeded the bounds of their competency.

In general, people object to preachers being involved in politics if they are on the other side. If the preacher is on *my* side, he has obviously considered the issues carefully and is acting in a morally responsible and courageous manner. Public opinion polls consistently show disapproval of clergy involvement in politics because the general

question tends to make people think of those sanctimonious SOBs on the other side.

Pat Robertson took a long hard look at the poll numbers before making his decision to enter the presidential race. And he concluded the poll numbers were sending a message that the pundits were missing—a message that would be critical to victory in 1988.

13

The Road to the White House

There's only one job in the United States and in the world, I suppose, that would give me any more opportunity to do good for my fellow man.
—M. G. "Pat" Robertson, President,
Christian Broadcasting Network

Cervantes's classic character, Don Quixote, fancied himself a knight-errant. On his broken-down old nag, with a kitchen pot for a helmet, he tilted at windmills, thinking them to be ogres and dragons. Insisting on perceiving everything around him in terms of chivalry and medieval ballads, he usually ended his efforts in catastrophe.

By modern standards, he was psychotic. But to sixteenth-century readers, he was a tragic, romantic figure. As medieval society was giving way to a totally different social order, with chivalry one of the casualties, Don Quixote's doomed attempts to resurrect it had a certain nostalgic appeal. But readers also knew his lunacies could not be taken seriously. Common sense told them the world had changed.

And common sense tells late-twentieth-century Americans that the world has changed. Ours is a rational and pragmatic social order. Religion is fine as long as people keep it to themselves. But in the public arena, religion can be a mischievous and unwelcome intruder. Technology and the imperative of scientific management define what is desirable and essential in corporate and governmental bureaucratic order; and private morality is the god of the educated and sophisticated.

240

Media savants take for granted that we all live in a secular world. In their view, Pat Robertson's vision of America is simply out of touch with these realities. He is an anachronism. Robertson's adversaries see him in quixotic battle with a new order he cannot possibly hope to change. He represents a dying breed of American with archaic beliefs and simplistic solutions. Any presidential campaign run by him would be a hopeless gesture.

It was suggested earlier that Barbara Tuchman's concept of wooden-headedness might be a useful tool for understanding why the mass media have not been able to grasp the significance and permanence of the conservative movement in America. Wooden-headedness may also be an obstacle to understanding why the media and America's liberal elite cannot move beyond their images of Pat Robertson as the kook who thinks he can shrink hemorrhoids and move hurricanes. But still there is something unnerving about him. When Robertson is the subject of cocktail conversation, laughter usually gives way to anger.

Both are manifestations of quiet anxiety.

The reason Pat Robertson is not a pathetic and laughable character is that his candidacy is no more a fluke than is the broadcasting empire he has built. The critical mistake made by media pundits and political professionals is that they assess Robertson's potential strength through the lens of an outmoded model of the political process. They continue to assume that political parties still are important and that party support is critical to gaining a nomination and winning an election.

Since their zenith in the late nineteenth century, political parties have been in a steady decline, resulting from "a loss of their near-monopoly over several significant tasks that must be performed in a democratic society," notes David Everson in "The Decline of Political Parties."[1] Those services included dispensing patronage, providing services through precinct captains, running elections, and serving as a locus for social activities.[2]

Most significant has been the progressively diminishing role of political parties in the selection of candidates. Once the privilege of insiders and top party leaders, accomplished in closed-door, smoke-filled rooms, the process gradually became democratized. The spread of primary elections, which began in the early twentieth century in various states, was evidence of both cause and effect.

Primary elections in themselves didn't immediately weaken party

leaders' influence. Until recently, caucus-convention and primary elections were still heavily locked within the party framework. Candidates without party support—and who had not put in their time as staunchly loyal activists—had little hope of winning more than minor local office.

As late as 1960, only fifteen states held presidential primaries. That number had increased dramatically by 1980, to thirty-seven. Democrats and Republicans don't necessarily select delegates in the same manner in each state. Not surprisingly, the Republican party has leaned toward control by an elite. In 1988 there will be thirty-seven states (including the District of Columbia) where Republicans will select delegates by primaries. More important, delegates selected by primaries will account for approximately 60 percent of the total.

In addition to the democratization of the primaries, three factors have contributed to the shrinking power of political parties over this century. These factors are (1) the development of mass media, (2) the emergence of a professional class of political campaign consultants, and (3) public funding of campaigns.

More than anything else, mass media have revolutionized the way we "do politics" in America. Where once the party machinery was the citizen's main conduit for news about candidates, the overwhelming proportion of campaign information is now transmitted via the mass media of television, newspapers, magazines, and direct mail. They are used both to transmit information and fund the process.

If a candidate can communicate directly with the communicators (mass media), or, better yet, directly with the voters, the party's role in selling candidates is diminished. How to do so more effectively is the business of political consultants, who, as Larry Sabato has documented so brilliantly, "have replaced party leaders in key campaign roles."[3] They communicate with the mass media, they develop advertising campaigns to communicate directly with voters, they develop strategies for combatting their candidate's opponent, and they raise money to pay for all of it.

High-tech mass-media campaigning is expensive. Laws governing campaign spending have tended to spread the giving around and further democratized the process. Campaign financing has become exceedingly complex since the Federal Elections Campaign Act of 1971. Political Action Committees (PACs) are created explicitly for the pur-

pose of supporting candidates financially. Originally envisioned as an instrument for organized labor, they have become, with subsequent revisions of the law, a tool of virtually every kind of interest group.[4] As extremely effective—yet completely independent—instruments for financing political campaigns, PACs constitute yet another powerful blow to the control of political parties in America.

Many scholars, including Sabato, have cautioned against portraying a golden age when political parties were omnipotent. In retrospect, the clout they once possessed seems to have been exaggerated. But whatever the limits or weaknesses of the political parties of yesteryear, it is difficult to imagine parties as nearly impotent as they are today. The political boss, and the political party with real muscle, passed from the American scene when Chicago's Mayor Richard Daley died more than a decade ago. In most parts of the country, party leaders are like barkers in front of the Bourbon Street striptease joints in New Orleans on a January night; they beckon passersby to check out their candidates. And, like the barkers, the party leaders are out in the cold while the action is inside.

The political party's impotence was abundantly evident in the para-party organization created by Richard Nixon for his reelection in 1971; the Committee to Re-elect the President "functioned virtually as a surrogate party." Notes Sabato:

> It had its own internal advertising agency; a direct mail operation with four mailing offices; 7 computer centers; 10 regional head-quarters and separate branches in the states and many localities; 250 telephone bank outlets; many group divisions (youth, labor, ethnic, etc.); and a rather unique security outfit that all Americans became well acquainted with. CREEP even appointed its own precinct workers, leaving all the "party" candidates to fend for themselves, and brooked no interference in its affairs, undertaking no action (for the general good of the Republican party or anything else) that might interfere with its supreme goal of electing one candidate.[5]

Perhaps Neil Staebler's forecast that "elections will increasingly become contests not between candidates but between great advertising firms" is too pessimistic and simplistic.[6] But his framing of the

question dramatically highlights the shift in American politics from parties to campaigns managed by professionals.

So pervasive is the clout of the consultant that political scientist Nelson Polsky states bluntly:

> Interest groups that organize themselves around such anachronisms as state and local party systems are bound to lose out to those that are skilled in currying favor with reporters and news media gatekeepers.[7]

Pat Robertson's candidacy, as well as possible candidacies by evangelical Christians in the future, must be understood in the context of the decline of traditional political-party strength and the rise of the mass media and high-tech political consultants.

Once upon a time, name recognition, one of the most indispensable resources for a candidate, was almost always achieved by working within a political party. But, as many people are failing to notice, this began to change back in the 1950s, when both major parties courted World War II hero General Dwight D. Eisenhower to head their ticket. Then there was an astronaut named John Glenn, and a movie actor named George Murphy, who used their careers outside of politics to boost them into the U.S. Senate. And, more recently, another Hollywood actor won the governorship of the nation's most populous state and used that as a launching pad for his flight to the White House.

Political pundits fasten on reasons that each of these cases are exceptions rather than barometers giving a sound reading on the new rules. But the exceptions are far too numerous to be dismissed as anomalies. Pat Robertson understands that the game of politics is being played according to new rules. And the playing field is one on which he is very comfortable.

Even if they don't understand how the game is played, the media savants see themselves as the contest gatekeepers. "No man cometh unto the people but by us" is their unspoken creed. The price for violating it is ridicule. Robertson would rather have a friendly press corps, but he knew before he began his presidential quest that such a development would be unlikely.

Feeling confident that he is more in touch with the genuine values

and religious sentiments of tens of millions of Americans, Robertson
is bemused by the media's treatment of his candidacy. He thinks he
knows who is wearing blinders. Half-laughing, he told the authors:

> The first thing I see is an absolutely unbelievable lack of sophis-
> tication among the media. They don't understand. They don't
> take me seriously. So they deal with false perceptions and smoke
> and mirrors.[8]

He paused, and then added, "It's probably just as well, because they
haven't caught up with what's happening." Pat Robertson knows that
he needs media attention, lots of it, to build a solid campaign. But he
also knows that the longer it takes the media to take him seriously,
the easier it will be to grab the delegates and run.

If there is any lesson to be gleaned from the history of declining
party influence and the rise of paraparty politics, it is that Robertson's
initial core constituencies can be formed without relying on traditional
parties. This has been increasingly true since the advent of electronics,
particularly television. Perhaps his candidacy will finally help Americans understand that the road to big-time political careers no longer
begins with the local precinct.

By the time Pat Robertson officially entered the race, a few political
analysts were beginning to recognize he was a serious candidate. He
already had in place an impressive organizational structure, but almost
no one was willing to give him a real chance at winning the nomination.
As students of contemporary American religion and the sociopolitical
movement of the New Christian Right, the authors were persuaded
early on that his chances were much greater than his sharpest critics
feared or most of his closest associates realized.

Of course, anyone who runs for president is traversing an open mine
field. Candidates face incredible scrutiny of their professional record
and personal biography by reporters and by the hostile research staffs
of other candidates.

The perceived unorthodoxy of Robertson's religious views, and the
fact that he has not previously run for office, contribute to even more
careful scrutiny. Beyond that, the chances of his running a flawless
campaign are remote. Virtually every candidate for the presidency
miscalculates on some critical issue. Sometimes there are develop-

ments utterly beyond their control that have a decisive effect on their campaign.

Former Michigan Governor George Romney seemed to be doing well in 1968 when, upon his return from a fact-finding trip in Vietnam, he dealt himself a fatal blow by claiming that he had been brainwashed.

Former Maine Senator Edmund Muskie's presidential hopes wilted overnight when he broke down and cried in front of television cameras when discussing vicious rumors Republican operatives had spread about his wife.

And, perhaps more than anything else, it was an errant moment at Chappaquiddick that rendered forever improbable a bid for the presidency by Senator Edward Kennedy.

For former Colorado Senator Gary Hart, it was a failure to recognize that the rules of accountability had been changing. It wasn't so much what he did in his private life, but that he lied about it and attempted to project a fraudulent image of traditional family values.

Wise individuals attempt to assess the potential damage of "skeletons" in their personal closets before they commit themselves to the lure of presidential politics. And, quite probably, a lot of otherwise able people choose to turn back. Democratic vice-presidential nominee Senator Thomas Eagleton, who had been institutionalized briefly with mental-health problems, apparently did not anticipate the impact of this event on his candidacy. Nor, obviously, did Senator George McGovern, who chose Eagleton as his running mate in 1972.

Early in Pat Robertson's exploration of a presidential bid, rumors began to circulate that he used his senator-father's influence to avoid combat duty when he was a marine in Korea.

The source of the rumors was traced to a letter written by former California Congressman Paul "Pete" McCloskey to Indiana Congressman Andrew Jacobs. Jacobs subsequently shared the letter with two syndicated newspaper columnists who used the material. Robertson recognized the damage such accusations could have on his candidacy, so he acted decisively to put them to rest. Labeling the allegation "wanton and reckless," Robertson sued Jacobs and McCloskey, accusing them of spreading false statements "for the purpose and with the effect of injuring, disgracing and defaming [Robertson's] good name and reputation." He asked for damages of $35 million from each.

On July 24, 1987, federal judge Joyce Hens Green dismissed the claim against Jacobs, finding neither malice nor reckless disregard of truth in his sharing the letter. McCloskey also filed a motion for summary judgment to dismiss the suit, but Judge Green denied the motion and handed the case to a jury for consideration because of evidence that McCloskey may have willfully disregarded information supporting Robertson's position when he wrote the letter to Jacobs.

By taking the offensive, Robertson neutralized a potentially damaging issue. If he could win a judgment, it would represent an important political gain. A public retraction from McCloskey would similarly represent a victory. In his deposition, McCloskey made comments with the appearance of at least a partial retraction. And sources close to the case advised the authors that McCloskey's attorneys offered a public retraction in exchange for dropping the suit. But Robertson refused.

Why would Robertson insist on pursing the libel suit? From his vantage point, there are four important reasons. First, it is a matter of honor: his and his father's. Second, it is a matter of principle. Robertson believes that McCloskey's comments were a deliberate and malicious effort to damage his political aspirations. Third, his aggressive pursuit of one who has attempted to malign him serves as a warning to others who might consider similar action. Fourth, hanging tough on this case is a way of demonstrating that he is strong-willed, decisive, and capable of leadership.

The scheduling of the trial for March 8, 1988, the date of the Super Tuesday primaries, came as a blow to Robertson. He needs to be on the campaign trail, not tied up in a courtroom.

If the stumbling blocks along the campaign trail are often unanticipated—and the scheduling of the McCloskey libel trial could well be one for Robertson—the break that lifts a candidate into the limelight doesn't just happen. Surges of interest, events calculated to stimulate momentum, are usually well planned.

Pat Robertson is a decisive man who leaves little to chance. A year before his announcement and more than two years before the second Tuesday of November 1988, Pat Robertson's game plan was in place.

"I know what I'm going to do, and exactly how I'm going to do it," boasted Robertson's chief campaign strategist, Marc Nuttle. And as

the campaign began to take shape, Nuttle's confidence seemed warranted. Robertson staged as flawless a precampaign game plan as a candidate could realistically expect—a textbook operation.

Does he have a viable game plan? You bet he does. Consider the following. Political scientist James W. Davis, an expert on presidential primaries, has outlined what he called "the winning formula" for a successful candidate or aspiring nominee.[9] As Larry Sabato warns, "There are literally hundreds of 'how to win your election' books and manuals in circulation, and in the main their recitation of 'do's' and 'don't's' is uninspired and tedious, not to mention repetitious."[10] But Davis's work is neither a "how-to" nor theoretical speculation. His conclusions are based on a careful analysis of recent elections. He identifies seven ingredients for a successful campaign:

1. An early start;
2. Grass-roots organization;
3. Decisive early fund-raising;
4. Early media impact;
5. A staff knowledgeable about primary laws;
6. A need for pluralities rather than majorities;
7. A high-risk strategy.

It is important to recognize, says Davis, that the process of winning delegates to the nominating convention is a very different process from winning the general election. This simple but profound observation cannot be overstated or repeated too often: *The process of winning delegates to the nominating convention is a very different process from winning a general election!*

And it is crucial to winning delegates. Winning the nomination by no means guarantees winning the general election, but without it, there is not even a viable chance.

In 1964, former Governor Nelson Rockefeller spent more money than anyone before him had ever spent in pursuit of the presidency. But Senator Barry Goldwater beat him in the primaries, in the state caucuses, and at the nominating convention. Goldwater proved that people who are motivated by commitment to a cause are more zealous workers than those who are motivated by money or prestige. And

Goldwater also proved that the key to winning the nomination is securing delegates for the national convention.

To run in the national election for the presidency, you don't have to be ideologically in the middle of your party. You don't have to be a loyal party worker. You have to secure delegates who will vote for you at the nominating convention. Pure and simple. Barry Goldwater understood this. George McGovern understood this. Jimmy Carter understood this. Ronald Reagan understood this. So does Pat Robertson.

An Early Start. "In recent years," says political scientist Davis, "the successful party nominee for president has invariably developed a long-range campaign strategy long before his formal announcement of candidacy."[11] If one were to do case studies of a couple of dozen candidates who have entered a presidential primary over the past two decades, it would probably be difficult to pinpoint exactly when each one really started running. In Washington, congressional staffers, political consultants, and reporters tend to view virtually everybody's behavior in light of a future presidential bid. It's a game, but it is also more than a game. Lots of people are strategizing, calculating, and otherwise trying to imagine a scenario wherein they or their boss might have a chance for the Big Race.

As already mentioned, Pat Robertson vehemently denied that the 1980 Washington for Jesus rally had anything to do with politics. And a few months later, he recoiled from the media hype of the National Affairs Briefing in Dallas. Quietly resigning from the Religious Roundtable, he gave Jerry Falwell a wide berth to assume titular leadership of the New Christian Right. And, one might add, to draw the flak from liberals and mass media.

Robertson simply went about his business quietly, without fanfare or the watchful eye of the mass media. In 1981, a year after he resigned from the Religious Roundtable, Robertson created The Freedom Council as a "low-profile" grass-roots organization.

Freedom Council literature defined its purpose as defending, restoring, and preserving religious liberty in America. A mission statement affirms The Freedom Council to be a Christian organization, and, within this context, it would seek to "encourage, train, and equip Americans to exercise their civil responsibility to actively participate in government."

The Freedom Council was a tax-exempt organization so its activities necessarily were bipartisan. This was made explicit in the organization's statement of strategy: "It will not support or oppose any candidate for elected office or participate, directly or indirectly, in any campaign for public office."

Freedom Council literature and staff emphasized the dual tasks of motivating Christians to get involved in the political process and training them to be active participants. Noted Freedom Council staff member Allan Harkey:

> Many churches make the mistake of getting people fired up and motivated to impact the governmental process, but they don't tell them how it works. And that only leads to frustration and ineffectiveness. [12]

The Freedom Council was certainly effective in motivating people and getting them involved in Michigan. A record number of people obtained enough petition signatures to qualify to be delegates to the first round in the complex process of naming delegates to the Republican National Convention. Robertson's Freedom Council, and later Americans for Robertson, registered as many, if not more, delegates as the partnership of George Bush's Fund for America's Future and the Bush-controlled Republican National Committee.

In the process, the claim that The Freedom Council was mobilizing nonpartisan Christians became strained. Technically, the people signed up by The Freedom Council were uncommitted. Some may indeed have been supporters of other candidates, most likely Congressman Jack Kemp. But in the final analysis, the overwhelming majority of those who were stimulated to get involved in politics by The Freedom Council would be Robertson supporters.

After the May deadline for delegate-filing in Michigan, Robertson formed his exploratory committee, Americans for Robertson (AFR). Technically, AFR and the Committee for Freedom, Robertson's political action committee, ran the partisan efforts to get people to the polls to vote for the people who had been registered as delegates by The Freedom Council. In reality, the distinction was, at best, messy. And, for the most part, the press made no distinction at all. To bolster

the nonpartisan nature of The Freedom Council, $5,000 was contributed to the Michigan efforts of Jack Kemp.

Robertson's adversaries, especially Bush operatives, have complained that The Freedom Council crossed over into partisan political activity. Perhaps so. But evenhanded observation ought to note that Bush's control and use of the Republican National Committee to bolster his partisan interests has the aura of heavy-handed establishment politics.

As far as Robertson and his staff are concerned, The Freedom Council scrupulously followed the letter of the law in Michigan. But Robertson's decision to establish an exploratory committee for his own candidacy strained The Freedom Council's ability to function as a bipartisan group. Thus, roughly on the schedule planned, The Freedom Council folded in the fall of 1986.

There is no way to directly trace Americans for Robertson volunteers to prior involvement with The Freedom Council, but it is clear that there were enough to give a hefty boost to Robertson's quest for 3 million petitions. Two days prior to his self-imposed one-year moratorium, Robertson announced he had 3.3 million signatures. It seems unlikely that this goal would have been achieved without The Freedom Council volunteers.

Whether or not Pat Robertson knew when he founded The Freedom Council that he would one day offer those who joined the opportunity to work for his candidacy, the outcome was the same. Any way you look at it, the net effect is that Pat Robertson was out of the gates and running early. His game plan was substantially in place even before there were rumors that Pat was praying and seeking God's will about a possible candidacy.

Grass-Roots Organization. Grass-roots organization is the key to election success. When political parties were in their heyday, they could reach from the top of the organization down to the precinct, and even the block, to communicate with voters. Today parties don't have enough clout to reward loyalty with turkeys at Christmas or a job for a favorite nephew.

Notes James W. Davis, "In recent years no presidential contender has won the nomination without first setting up an effective campaign organization in at least half of the presidential primary states and in a sizable number of caucus-convention states."[13]

Notwithstanding their diminished power, political parties still play a vital role in the electoral process. A small proportion of the citizens in every community are active party members. Party participation does for these folks what civic clubs and church participation do for others, providing a source of identification and loyalty.

Whereas a campaign can be organized independently of these existing structures, they offer a convenient work force. They also represent an important communications network. Typically, a prospective candidate will not plug into the party organization as such. Rather, he will court a few people who, in turn, attempt to sell others on the idea that Candidate X is a winner and ideologically attuned with them.

George Bush is the only candidate officially plugged into this organizational and communications network. For all intents and purposes, he controls the Republican National Committee. State party elites desire to be involved in national party affairs. The Republican National Committee may not be able to move the masses, but it has a lot of influence with the state elites who, in turn, can use whatever muscle they have to move congressional districts and county party organizations.

In Kansas, presumably, the party apparatus is loyal to former Senator Bob Dole; former Senator Howard Baker might expect a similar loyalty in Tennessee, should he take leave of his White House chief of staff role and seek the nomination. But when these men move beyond their direct constituencies, they either have to convince the state leadership that it is in their interest to break with the initiatives of the Republican National Committee or they have to create their own grass-roots organizations.

All of the prospective candidates have an interest in dulling the clout of George Bush and the RNC. There will be behind-the-scenes battles to win the support of key state party operatives or at least to check their power. Where state party chairs are known to be loyal to Bush, leadership challenges will occur. Failing in this effort, candidates have the option of winning over subsectors of the party, or turning elsewhere to recruit people who have not previously been active in the political process.

In the 1986 election campaign, Pat Robertson took every opportunity to be active in the Republican party and to lend his support to

party nominees. And outside of the campaign, he has spoken at scores of Republican gatherings. He hoped that such activities would help break down some of the hostility toward his candidacy, but it seemed clear that he would not make a serious bid for the Republican party's nomination by courting party regulars. At least not at the outset.

Pat Robertson's grass-roots strength is grounded in the conservative Christian community which has been recruited into the political process over the past seven years by the New Christian Right. Back in 1976, a Southern Baptist Sunday school teacher named Jimmy Carter awoke the sleeping giant and persuaded a lot of evangelicals and fundamentalists that it was all right to get involved in politics. For nearly ten years—with high visibility for the last seven—Jerry Falwell stormed across America telling conservative Christians that it is their *duty* to be involved. While the Moral Majority was more of a media organization than a grass-roots effort, it also succeeded in motivating people and enhancing communications networks.

For five years The Freedom Council was an important instrument for educating evangelical Christians and encouraging them to become involved. It served, as Council staff person Allan Harkey put it, "as a glorified civics teacher." But there are literally hundreds of New Christian Right organizations across America that have moved beyond civics instruction to engagement in the political process, taking up voter registration efforts, organizing rallies and protests, lobbying, and so on. Beverly LaHaye's Concerned Women for America claims a half-million members. Her husband Tim's American Coalition for Traditional Values (ACTV) claims to have registered 2 million new Christian voters for the 1984 elections. ACTV's executive committee and board members include Ben Armstrong, Jim Bakker, Bill Bright, Kenneth Copeland, Paul Crouch, James Dobson, James T. Draper, Jerry Falwell, John Gimenez, Richard Hogue, Rex Humbard, D. James Kennedy, James Robison, Adrian Rogers, Charles Stanley, Jimmy Swaggart, Robert Tilton, Jack Van Impe, and Don Wildmon.

Like Falwell's Moral Majority, the grass-roots strength of CWA and ACTV probably is exaggerated. It would also be an exaggeration to assume that all Pat Robertson needs to do to obtain the enthusiastic support of these people is to put out the word. Robertson must work hard to consolidate conservative Christian support. But it is evident

that Robertson achieved some measure of success in plugging into this network. And early successes made it easier for him to tap this latent reservoir of support.

There are two other important bases for building grass-roots organization. The first, of course, is local churches. For decades, the black church has been a focal point for political organization. Liberal Protestant churches were a locus of political organization during the civil rights movement and the protests against American involvement in Vietnam; today, some are involved in the antinuclear movement and the sanctuary movement. In the past decade, the foundation has been laid for engaging conservative Christians in the process.

The other important pillar of grass-roots support was virtually overlooked by the political commentary on Robertson's "almost announcement" of September 17, 1986, that he would seek the signatures of 3 million people pledging prayers, financial support, and labor. That petition represents a mailing list of prospective campaign volunteers that would be the envy of any presidential candidate.

The petition goes beyond the pledge to work. Signers are asked to check how many of a half-dozen types of campaign jobs they are willing to do, giving a computerized list of people willing to work door-to-door, man phone banks, display signs and bumper stickers, and so on, for every zip code in America, which can, in turn, be translated into precincts.

Quite simply, the petition was an ingenious move. For recruiting volunteers, it is more valuable than any list that might be assembled from the computers of the Republican and Democratic parties.

Decisive Early Fund-Raising. In 1972, George McGovern financed his campaign with early waves of direct-mail solicitations, which asked many people for only modest contributions. This sort of political "March of Dimes" greased the wheels of his momentum in key primaries. His campaign, observes James Davis, demonstrated "that it was possible for an unknown candidate to come from out of nowhere to win the nomination—if he had adequate campaign funds to underwrite the drive."[14]

The fund-raising acumen of televangelists is almost legendary—and Pat Robertson's Christian Broadcasting Network and related enterprises heads the pack in fund-raising skills. In 1986, they reported income of $230 million.

On the surface, it would appear that raising big bucks would be the least of Pat Robertson's concerns, that he or his surrogates can go on "The 700 Club" and raise money for his campaign the way his telethons raise money to support his religious programs. Not so.

And some people presume that skill in raising money for one enterprise will automatically transfer to raising money for another cause. The degree to which this may be so is not clear. Although The Freedom Council was always a low-key operation, it is clear that CBN contributed significantly to its funding. Also, Jerry Falwell was not as successful in raising money for the Moral Majority as for "The Old Time Gospel Hour" and its related activities.

The truth is that a lot of people who are inspired by the preaching and programming of religious broadcasters are simply not turned on by the televangelists' this-worldly political agendas.

Robertson's petition drive was a critical step in building the financial foundation for a campaign. The audiences in the 216 auditoriums that received a satellite feed from the September 17, 1986, gathering in Constitution Hall in Washington, D.C., were given petitions and a "personal gift form." With a patriotic color scheme of red, white, and blue, the form read, "YES, Pat! I/we want you to be the next President of the United States." Below this boldface banner, the copy read:

> Enclosed is a contribution of:
> ____$100 (individual)
> ____$200 (husband and wife)

And below this appeared a checklist of how the gift would be transmitted: by check, by billing, or by credit card.

Two weeks before his official announcement, Robertson claimed his goal of 3 million signatures had been exceeded by 300,000. To achieve this goal, Robertson had to go to the telephone banks. Still, this is no small accomplishment. And with the telephone banks in place, he set a new goal of 6 million signatures.

Consider the implications of these petitions for fund raising. The petitions didn't just ask people for pledges of support; they asked for work, prayers, and *gifts*. If each petitioner contributed $100, Robertson would have a campaign war chest of *$300 million*—an unprecedented figure in American electioneering. Of course, he didn't achieve

anything like this figure during the petition drive phase of his campaign. But when he announced his candidacy on October 1, 1987, he had raised over $11 million. The only other candidate to approach this figure was George Bush.

The petitions represent an unprecedented list of prospective campaign workers and financial contributors. It is doubtful that any candidate ever possessed a better base for direct-mail solicitation. A large proportion of these signers are conservative Christians who regularly give generously to their local church and some television ministry. On a per capita basis, they give away a higher proportion of their money than the average American.

Federal Election Commission laws on campaign spending are keyed to voting-age population in each state. Using 1987 figures, a candidate could spend approximately $27 million in pursuit of his or her party nomination. But this spending limit does not apply if a candidate elects not to accept federal matching funds. Robertson's donor base provides him the potential to forgo matching funds and, thus, outspend the other candidates.

In short, by the time of his announcement, Pat Robertson's campaign was assured of financial viability—even without any support from the big spenders, which he is likely to gain. The conservative new rich in America like Pat Robertson. In May of 1986, Robertson raised more than a million dollars at a dinner in Washington. Attendees contributed between $1,000 and $25,000 per couple. In August, his friend Bunker Hunt invited a few pals to his ranch to meet Pat. They showed up 3,000 strong. Apparently the organizers fell short of breaking the record of raising $3.5 million at a single event, which the governor of Texas set for President Reagan in 1982.

"It's going to take an awful lot of money," Robertson noted in the spring of 1987 after a successful first round in his bid to take control of the Republican party in South Carolina. Robertson was elated with his campaign's early progress and seemed overwhelmed by the responsiveness he was finding. "If we can raise the money, I think I can win the nomination," he stated.

The latter may not follow necessarily from the former, but no one denies that money is crucial to staying in a presidential campaign. And it is equally undeniable that Pat Robertson has far more expe-

rience in soliciting contributions than anyone else on the campaign trail.

Early Media Impact. With twenty-five years of mass-media experience, Pat Robertson has a pretty good idea of what will and what will not attract media attention. From the very first "rumors" of his interest in the presidency, Robertson has staged a masterful media campaign.

When Jimmy Carter began his lonely trek across America, he was lucky if he found a reporter now and then who would interview him. From the beginning, Robertson had a press corps to meet him wherever he traveled. This provided local and regional coverage, and, with increasing frequency, his comments about current events appeared on the national wire services.

But more important, Robertson "staged" a number of events that have drawn attention. For six months Robertson used the "Pat Who?" letter of Democratic National Committee Chairman Paul Kirk wherever he spoke. But he waited until he appeared on a platform with six other Republican hopefuls in Nashville—thereby ensuring national coverage—to accuse Kirk of being an antireligious bigot. He not only got attention, he upstaged the other prospective candidates.

In July 1986, Robertson addressed the summer convention of the Virginia Press Association and outlined a six-point agenda for a "Post-Reagan Era." Journalists began following the activities of Robertson's Freedom Council if only because it made for unconventional stories. That same summer, Robertson gave the go-ahead for his presidential exploratory committee, Americans for Robertson.

The ambiguity of the Michigan primary/caucus process, coupled with the fact that it was the first official campaign event for the 1988 elections, assured the event would receive media attention. George Bush's decision to make Michigan a test of his personal strength was ready-made for the media-conscious Robertson. By registering as many, or nearly as many, delegates as Bush, Robertson experienced an important surge of media attention between the May filing deadline and the statewide primary in early August.

The gala testimonial in September was another demonstration of skilled media management. There were press conferences and fanfare beforehand, and there was scarcely a major print or broadcast media organization not in attendance at the main event. In addition, the

satellite linkups provided a natural hook for local news coverage. All over America, newspapers ran one story on the Constitution Hall event and another on the local turnout.

A few days before the testimonial, Pat Robertson went to see Jimmy Swaggart. It was reported that Swaggart was intent on dissuading Robertson from making a bid. Instead, Robertson received Swaggart's endorsement, which was announced immediately after the September 17 event.

A few days later came a black-tie gala celebration with fireworks to commemorate CBN's twenty-fifth anniversary. Broadcast live on CBN, the event also drew a sizable national press corps. The emcee was Gavin MacLeod, popular captain on the long-running television show "The Love Boat." And in the front row, reminding the audience of their roots, were Jim and Tammy Faye Bakker of the PTL Network.

In the time between the first rumors and the "almost announcement," Robertson went from "Pat Who?" to cover stories and guest appearances in major secular print and broadcast outlets.

A Staff Knowledgeable about Primary Laws. As difficult as it is to grasp how the complex Michigan nominating process works, it is much more difficult still to grasp how fifty state parties select their delegates.

Caucuses and primaries are the two major delegate-selection methods, but within this seemingly simple structure is an ever-changing jigsaw puzzle.

Knowing the rules for each state, and keeping on top of changes, requires considerable expertise. How a candidate approaches a state primary depends on the nature of its rules, and in some states it is critical that a candidate get involved in the rule-making process. Standing on the sidelines can result in the adoption of rules favoring one candidate, usually the establishment candidate, over the others. Unless a candidate has a good chance of winning, putting time and money in one of the winner-take-all contests is questionable. When delegates are distributed proportional to the number of votes received, it usually makes sense to go for what you can get. It also matters whether a primary is binding for one, two, three, or more ballots—or is merely a preferential poll.

The same can be said of the maze of federal elections laws. They pose a formidable mountain of red tape and restrictions requiring a

small army of accountants. A modern presidential campaign requires an expert staff to steer its way through these regulations without committing some sin of omission or commission, however inadvertent, in reporting contributions and expenditures.

Robertson has a staff monitoring his strategy in light of separate state primaries, but their inexperience in election laws became apparent in December 1986. The Internal Revenue Service turned its attention to the Christian Broadcasting Network conglomerate to see if Robertson's various organizations, such as CBN itself, The Freedom Council, the Committee for Freedom, and Americans for Robertson, had provided incomplete or false information.

Money did flow from one organization to another, and records appear not to have been always consistent and in order. "Mistakes were made, confusion did reign," Thomas A. Bruno, a Freedom Council lawyer, told the *New York Times* in admitting that there had been some "sloppy" bookkeeping. But, he added, "there was no attempt to defraud. There were no tricks or gimmicks."[15]

If nothing else, Robertson's problems with the IRS demonstrate that it is not enough to have a staff expert in mapping out the best ways to garner delegates in various state primaries. Post-Watergate elections laws demand legal accountants with the sophistication to keep on top of ever-changing and increasingly detailed federal regulations and requirements.

A serious presidential campaign must: (1) understand the primary procedures of each state, (2) develop strategies to maximize the chance of winning delegates within each state's selection procedures, (3) constantly monitor the ever-changing rules, (4) to the extent that one has any party strength, support or resist rule changes depending upon whether they will help or hurt, and (5) quickly adjust strategies to exploit favorable changes and control damage when rule changes are unfavorable. There is almost no way for a candidate to wander into the primaries a few weeks or months before filing deadlines and expect to do well just because he or she may be riding high in public opinion polls. Colorado Congresswoman Patricia Schroeder demonstrated an understanding of this fundamental principle when she decided, after 75,000 miles of barnstorming around the country, not to seek the Democratic nomination. "[It's] too late to get in and . . . catch up,"

she told supporters and reporters on September 28, 1987, in Denver.[16]

The benefits of running for the presidency while occupying the vice presidency are enormous. George Bush was able to use the resources of the Republican National Committee to plan and coordinate his campaign with state GOP party leaders. From his position of national leadership, Bush was able to twist arms for campaign support and for beneficial state rule changes, such as rules that automatically entitle certain elected officials to be delegates. Elected officials, be they members of Congress, state legislatures, or elected party officials, are more likely to benefit from something Bush has to offer than are private citizens elected by some democratic procedure. Hence, they can more readily be counted upon to be loyal to the "incumbent."

One Robertson staff member estimated that in the worst scenario, George Bush could tie up about 25 percent of the 2,235 Republican National Convention delegates merely by manipulating the rules, without ever winning a delegate through open general public primaries. Clearly, "incumbency" has its rewards.

One thing that Robertson had going for him was that every other presidential hopeful had the same interest in resisting rule changes that would favor Bush. Another advantage was the series of changes that moved almost all of the caucuses and primaries of the southern states to the same date (March 8, dubbed Super Tuesday). Clearly, this initiative was meant to strengthen the conservative influence of the southern states. What was not anticipated when Super Tuesday was conceived was that it would provide Pat Robertson and Jesse Jackson, playing to their respective strengths with evangelical and black voters, the opportunity to emerge as the front-runners of their respective parties.

A Need for Pluralities more than Majorities. Most people, notes James Davis, think of electoral victories in terms of majorities, but in presidential primary politics, *pluralities* (winning more votes than any other candidate although less than a majority) are often more important.

Quite often, no single candidate receives a majority of the votes in a presidential primary. In most states, delegates are awarded proportionately to candidates, based on the votes they receive. However, in some states, the winner of a plurality of votes receives *all* of the

delegates. This "winner-take-all" policy is more common in GOP primaries than in Democratic ones. In both cases, the candidate's goal is to win as many delegates as possible. It doesn't take a majority of *votes* to enter the national convention with a majority of the *delegates*.

Both Jimmy Carter in 1980 and George McGovern in 1972, for example, depended on pluralities to secure the Democratic nomination. In fact, Carter registered an absolute majority in only eight of his seventeen primary triumphs.

What's more, early plurality wins can be critically important in helping establish a candidate as a front-runner. For example, in 1976 Jimmy Carter won only 29 percent of the precinct caucus vote in Iowa (38.5 percent were uncommitted), but it placed him 13 percent above his nearest rival, Indiana Senator Birch Bayh. As a result, *Time* and *Newsweek*, the three major television-network evening-news programs, and the press in general focused attention on Carter's campaign, to the relative exclusion of his opponents. Suddenly he was identified as the candidate to beat. Notes James Davis, "Carter's first-place finish in Iowa made him a national celebrity. . . . Carter's media coverage also served to publicize cost-free the 'new face' image he sought to project across the country."[17]

Most analysts who have assessed the Pat Robertson candidacy have tended to think in terms of the straightforward demographics of an evangelical vote. And the way they read the political tea leaves, there just are not enough evangelicals in America to tip the scales in favor of Robertson.

In their rush to judgment, they seem to forget that winning a nomination is a separate task from winning a general election; and that the key to winning delegates is not necessarily majorities but pluralities. And pluralities can often be achieved because of a proportionately higher voter turnout among supporters of a particular candidate. Robertson understands the importance of pluralities. He also understands the importance of getting supporters to the polls.

A High-Risk Strategy. The idea of long-range, carefully calculated strategies seems incompatible with the notion of taking high risks. But in presidential politics, a "play-it-safe" strategy is almost certain to lead to failure. Presidential nominations, says James Davis, "usually go to a candidate who is willing to gamble and risk his political future

on a bold course of action."[18] "Underdogs," "dark horses," and "out-siders" have nothing to lose with bold, high-risk strategies.

"Recent history," adds Davis, "shows that the convention nominee of the out-party candidate has usually been the candidate who was willing to risk big stakes in the primaries."[19] Risks may include spending large sums of money that the candidate doesn't have, taking strident stands on issues to detract attention from well-established candidates, and taking on the front-runner head to head.

John F. Kennedy, as a young senator from Massachusetts, gambled when combatting Minnesota's ranking and popular Senator Hubert H. Humphrey in the latter's neighboring state of Wisconsin. Kennedy beat Humphrey and gained instant national recognition. With the outcome of the nominating convention very much in doubt, Kennedy again challenged Humphrey directly in West Virginia, a state where Humphrey's strong support from labor should have given him a decisive edge. No Catholic ever having won the presidency, Kennedy took a big chance by putting the issue on the political agenda. And he chose Houston, in the heart of the Bible belt, to do so. Without these and other risks, John F. Kennedy would have remained a senator.

Perhaps Jimmy Carter's high-risk roll was in New England. Faced with a financial crisis early in his campaign, he borrowed heavily, putting up his family farming property as collateral. By beating Morris Udall and Henry Jackson, he established himself as a viable candidate, and, thereafter, the campaign contributions began to flow.

Pat Robertson's candidacy, in itself, has to be judged as a high risk. For openers, he has no experience in elected office. While he has other credentials, he has spent most of his career as a television evangelist. Anticipating criticism of preachers in politics, Robertson resigned his Southern Baptist ordination on the eve of the announcement of his candidacy. But that didn't negate the fact that his religious views have been portrayed by the media and by his adversaries as beyond orthodox, leaning toward "radical" and "fanatical." Similarly, his political views have been portrayed as just as far out as his religious beliefs. His bid for the presidency, then, represents a great risk to himself and to the highly successful broadcasting network he left behind.

"I understand this radical thing," he acknowledged in an interview, noting that the secular press has tended to portray him as a right-wing religious extremist. But then he added, "Anyone who wants to promote innovative change has to be somewhat radical."[20]

When Barry Goldwater ran for president, his campaign slogan was, "A choice, not an echo." Robertson knew that his problem would not be being perceived as just another voice. But he needed to take two distinct kinds of risks. First, he would need to persuade people he was not the "kook" he had been portrayed to be. And second, he would have to show himself to be something new and different from the other candidates pressing toward the Republican nomination.

Evidence of his willingness to take risks came early. His libel suit against former Congressman Pete McCloskey and Congressman Andrew Jacobs meant the possibility of losing. The choice of the streets of a poor black neighborhood in Brooklyn for his announcement involved the risk of hecklers, which he got. But he also got videotape that, later in the campaign, would symbolically demonstrate his concern for the poor.

Generally, politicians try to differentiate themselves from other candidates by claiming to have a plan or program that will solve some problem. But conventional wisdom dictates that one does not risk getting bogged down in explaining details, or, for that matter, making details available for others to criticize. From early in his campaign, Robertson demonstrated a willingness to take risks in firmly establishing the ways in which he differed from the rest of the candidates. There was no soft peddling of his views, or waiting to see which way the latest public opinion polls were leaning.

More than any man who has run for president since Woodrow Wilson, Pat Robertson is an intellectual. And he has faith in his ability to communicate complex ideas so that a layman can understand them. Robertson understood before he started that political platitudes would not be enough. From the beginning, his campaign took the risk of unveiling concrete programs to deal with problems Washington has ducked for a long time. He knew that many of his proposals would be unpopular with the press and probably would not be initially well received by the public. But his plan was to sell Americans on the necessity of squarely facing and solving problems. And by getting a

lot of issues out on the table, Robertson hoped to draw other candidates away from campaigning-as-usual toward serious discussion of real alternatives for real problems.

Organization is imperative and Robertson demonstrated a great deal of skill in developing grass-roots and staff support. But success depends on his ability to undo the negative stereotypes that early dominated secular news coverage. In the end, success means building an image of himself as not only qualified to be president, but the one logical successor to Ronald Reagan.

14

A Strategy for Victory

Here's what . . . [the people] . . . want in a president.
They want somebody, first of all, that is honest and will
tell it to them like it is. . . .what people want first is
integrity. And the second thing they want is leadership.
They want somebody who will be able to be a leader and
get things done. The third thing they want is a com-
municator. They know instinctively that they need a leader
who can enunciate noble goals for this country and then
mobilize public opinion behind them. That, I think, is
more important, in their view, than political experience,
which they put down relatively low because there is no
experience for that job. . . . So you have to look at all
the other candidates out there and decide which ones fill
these roles.

—Pat Robertson,
Before The Economic Club of Detroit

If Pat Robertson is to mount a suc-
cessful campaign for the presidency, he has to overcome more barriers
than perhaps anyone who has ever made a run for the office. More
than the technical aspects of campaign strategy, Robertson's greatest
challenge is image management. There are six objectives he absolutely
must achieve to perfection:

1. Pat Robertson's highest priority must be to shed the label of
televangelist. This was evident even before the 1987 scandals, but
became even more imperative.
2. To be a successful candidate, Pat Robertson must overcome his
image as a religious fanatic.

3. He needs to build a strong coalition of the highly diverse evangelical and fundamentalist groups in America. A corollary task is to hold the most extreme elements in check so that they don't destroy his efforts to portray himself as a religious and political moderate.

4. A viable candidacy requires that Americans come to identify Pat Robertson as Ronald Reagan's logical and natural successor. That doesn't mean just claiming the label of "natural successor," but demonstrating, in the course of the campaign, that he has the qualities and communication skills to carry on where Reagan left off.

5. Robertson must persuade a majority of Americans that he offers not extremist ideology, but reasonable solutions to problems. Failing here, he may merely trade the label of religious fanatic for that of political extremist. The more it appears that his campaign may be successful, the nastier will be the claims of the political left. To the extent that Robertson succeeds in presenting himself as a moderate conservative, there should be a backlash against the accusations.

6. Robertson needs to transform sympathy for him because he is being treated unfairly by his adversaries and the press into a massive turnout for him at the polls.

These are more or less progressive steps. Robertson's absolute first priority has to be overcoming the image of himself as a "religious wacko." If he loses this one, his candidacy isn't going anywhere. And, at the other end of the list, the transformation of backlash sympathy into votes has to be timed perfectly. Let's examine each of the objectives in turn.

Shedding the Label of Televangelist. The PTL scandal involving Jim and Tammy Faye Bakker had a certain quality of comic relief. The lurid revelations of their misdeeds meant an orgy for the secular press, who paused only briefly to turn their venomous pens on a hapless Gary Hart.

Robertson knew before he embarked on his presidential quest that he would need to shed the televangelist stereotype. But he couldn't have begun to imagine how absolutely vital that task would become.

After Robertson authorized an exploratory committee, he often quipped that he was confident he knew God's will, but that *just in case* he had misunderstood, he was praying that God would send him an unambiguous message. Between Oral Roberts's plea for donations

lest God call him home and the Bakkers' debacle, Robertson must have agonized over the prospect that God was trying to get his attention.

He had gotten a big break when Roberts endorsed his candidacy in September 1986. Roberts had never previously supported a candidate for political office. Now it seemed worthless, perhaps even damaging. But as disgraceful as Roberts's pleas for money may have been, there was still a little room to maneuver and save face. Roberts, after all, was saddled with huge debts and a shrinking audience of aging followers. He may just have run out of time and ideas.

But the PTL scandal was something altogether different, a watershed in the history of religious broadcasting. The colossal sums of money involved, the decadence of the Bakkers' lifestyle, the carnality and unrepentant hypocrisy of the principal actors—all were unparalleled.

If he were free to do so, Pat Robertson should run, not walk, away from any identification with televangelism. Unfortunately, it is not that easy to do. To free up his time, as well as to avoid "equal time" demands from other prospective candidates, Robertson stepped down as host of "The 700 Club" in September 1986. The dilemma is that his absence produced a slump in audience and revenues. At some point along the campaign trail, he may face a choice between jumping back in to protect the viability of a corporation it has taken him a lifetime to build and pursuing the presidential nomination.

Pat Robertson has long said that he doesn't like to be called a *televangelist*, recognizing that the word conjures up negative images. If he could have his way, he would prefer to be seen as a successful businessman whose business is broadcasting, with the content of that broadcasting just happening to be religion.

This is unquestionably sound image-making strategy. In the meantime, the consequences of being typed as a televangelist are obvious. In a poll of the southern region conducted by the *Atlanta Journal* and the *Atlanta Constitution* in the spring of 1987, before the Bakker scandal had broken, 69 percent of the respondents said they would not even consider voting for Robertson. This negative rating exceeded that of all other prospective candidates. Jesse Jackson came closest, with 45 percent.

The 69 percent negative rating is ludicrous, for Robertson's rec-

ognition at the time was barely that high. But the poll reflects the depth of distrust of televangelists—even before the scandals.

But there was a positive side to that seemingly devastating poll. Perhaps most telling, 49 percent said they would be inclined to choose a candidate who was "born again" over one who was not. Only 13 percent preferred the candidate who was not "born again." Further, 49 percent of those polled said they would vote for a candidate who favored a constitutional amendment to outlaw abortion, and 73 percent said they would be favorably disposed to vote for a candidate who would bring back public-school prayer.

These are bread-and-butter issues for Pat Robertson. George Bush may profess support for them, but in their hearts, the voters are not convinced. More than any other candidate, Pat Robertson is unshakably committed to conservative positions that motivate a large core of Americans.

Overcoming the Image of Religious Fanatic. Pat Robertson cannot escape having to deal with the fact that there are millions of people who know little about him but hold a negative image of television preachers in general. And the publicity about Pat's conversations with God convinces them that they don't want anything to do with this preacher in particular.

Since his adversaries have hundreds of hours of videotape of Pat's own words on "The 700 Club," and Robertson has been a rather prolific writer, they can amass lots of video clips and quotations to make the case that he is an extremist.

Most Americans don't practice their religion with the same enthusiasm and emotion as do charismatics and Pentecostals, and many even assume that people who carry on that way could not be of sound mind. The prospect that one of "them" might be a viable candidate for the presidency seems utterly preposterous.

But times change. In 1960, many people thought it inconceivable that a Roman Catholic could be elected president. After all, don't Catholics take their orders directly from the Vatican?

Walter Mondale, along with others before him, tried to pin the "religious wacko" label on Ronald Reagan, but it didn't work. Earlier in 1984, Ronnie Dugger noted in the *Washington Post* that on at least five occasions during his first term in office, the President had made

reference to his belief "that Armageddon may well occur during the present generation and could come in the Middle East."[1]

The fear Mondale attempted to ignite is that someone who believes that Russia is an "evil empire," and that nuclear holocaust is foreordained in Scripture, might "regard his finger on the button as an instrument of God's eternal purpose."[2]

Pat Robertson believes with all his heart that he is not a religious fanatic. But he recognizes that others do see him this way, so he has taken steps to give his own beliefs a mainstream image. In the political consulting business, this is known as "spin-doctoring." Cynically, "spin-doctoring" is presenting some bad or politically damaging information to make it seem like an asset. A less cynical approach would be to say that "spin-doctoring" is the presentation of information in the most favorable light possible.

In the introduction to his campaign book, *America's Dates With Destiny*, Robertson describes his adult conversion experience in April 1956:

> That night, in a plush hotel dining room after years of searching, I discovered my own spiritual roots. That night I confessed Jesus Christ as my Savior and Lord. I felt God's salvation in my life for the very first time. I could see why evangelical Christians called the experience a "new birth."[3]

Two years later, he noted, "God blessed me with another kind of spiritual experience. His spirit entered my life."[4] To make sure that his reader understands that there is nothing weird about receiving the "gifts of the Holy Spirit," Robertson notes explicitly: "In those two *rather orthodox*, biblical experiences, my life was changed forever."[5]

On "The 700 Club," Robertson talked about personal conversations with God. That kind of testimony goes over well with his audience, but it is also the kind of stuff the media use for applying the "wacko" label, so Robertson's appearances on secular television have involved a careful selection of a language more acceptable to mainstream religious. In a 1986 interview, however, Robertson declined to reject the imagery of a one-on-one conversation with God.[6] There is simply

too much videotape suggesting that Robertson has those types of conversations to try to hide the belief just because it may be politically unpopular. Furthermore, to deny the personal relationship he believes he has with God would be to betray his followers who see nothing strange about this.

Enter the Spin Doctor. In early 1986, the Gallup Organization conducted a national survey for the Christian Broadcasting Network that queried the public's understanding of how God communicates with individuals.

A whopping 69 percent of adult Americans told Gallup that God has led or guided them in making decisions.[7] And more than a third (36 percent) believed God directly spoke to them "through some means."[8] Eleven percent claimed to have heard an audible voice. The survey never mentioned Robertson, but George Gallup, Jr., did:

> The public is perhaps more open to a person saying he is receiving guidance from God than the press has indicated, and not just in terms of Pat's statements about hurricanes and so forth but also in a broad sense. . . . The public doesn't reject the concept.[9]

Thus, when Robertson speaks of seeking God's guidance and having confidence that he knows God's will, Gallup says he believes the data indicate that "it strikes a responsive chord."

But Robertson paid for the poll! How can it have credible data? Why would he ask the question unless he were trying to convince people that he is not a religious extremist?

They *are* credible data, because they are gathered by the most credible polling organization in America. Robertson had Gallup ask the question because nobody else has asked it. And Robertson has frequently called upon Gallup to do polling for CBN.

Coincidentally, Andrew Greeley, the Catholic priest who writes best-selling novels and also happens to be a very good sociologist, recently replicated a study of paranormal experiences he had first conducted in 1973.[10] The results support George Gallup's conclusions. Greeley found a phenomenal rise in the proportion of Americans reporting paranormal experiences. The percentage of all adults reporting contact with the dead rose sharply from 27 percent in 1973 to 42 percent in 1986.[11] Widows and widowers reporting contact with de-

ceased spouses increased from 51 percent to 67 percent. Reports of extrasensory perception rose from 58 percent to 67 percent, and *déjà vu* experiences similarly jumped from 59 percent to 67 percent. But perhaps the most startling finding of all was a 350 percent increase in the reporting of visions. In 1973, only 8 percent said they had experienced a vision, versus 29 percent in 1986.

What's happening? Is the whole country going nuts? Father Greeley doesn't think so. In fact, Greeley tested people who had had some of the deeper mystical experiences and found them to score very high on a standard test of personality health.[12]

The statistics cannot be explained away as the result of bad research or fudging data. The data were collected by the National Opinion Research Center, a top-flight academic polling organization affiliated with the University of Chicago. Greeley claims never to have had a psychic or mystical experience and notes that the Roman Catholic Church's posture toward the paranormal is currently one of "profound skepticism."[13]

How are we to account for the phenomenal growth in the proportion of people claiming paranormal experiences in a period of a dozen years? Greeley concludes that there probably isn't much, if any, increase. Rather, people simply are more comfortable in reporting such experiences, because a lot of highly visible people are openly talking about it.

Religious broadcasting, with its not-insignificant audience, provides a context for reporting and discussing religious experiences in a matter-of-fact manner. Celebrities from sports and entertainment who have had religious conversions are regular guests on the religious talk shows. Shirley MacLaine, who prefers to think of her experiences as alignment with the Universal Energy rather than contact with God, has done much to popularize spiritual movements in the secular culture.

The Gallup survey was a smart move on Robertson's behalf. It represents a step toward demonstrating that his religious beliefs may not be as "off the wall" and extremist as his adversaries claim. Most Americans don't speak in tongues or believe in miraculous healing, but many do. Pat Robertson is unlikely to break out in glossolalia during a press conference, and when his wife, Dede, was diagnosed with breast cancer, they didn't wait to see if prayer would work before electing surgery.

The 1980 Washington for Jesus rally commemorated Abraham Lincoln's proclamation of a national day of prayer and repentance, a powerful reminder that religion in the public square has not been restricted to early American history or the "peculiar anomalies" of Presidents Carter and Reagan. In this century, Woodrow Wilson stated our religious origins as bluntly as any contemporary televangelist:

> America was born a Christian nation. America was born to exemplify that devotion to the elements of righteousness which are derived from the revelations of Holy Scripture.[14]

Franklin D. Roosevelt, perceived as a secular aristocrat, called for a spiritual revival during his presidency:

> No greater thing could come to our land today than a revival of the spirit of religion—a revival that would sweep through the homes of the nation and stir the hearts of men and women of all faiths to a reassertion of their belief in God and their dedication to His will for themselves and for their world. I doubt if there is any problem—social, political or economic—that would not melt away before the fire of such a spiritual awakening.[15]

Scarcely a generation ago, we were reminded of the origins of this nation and human rights by John F. Kennedy in his inaugural address:

> The world is very different now. For man holds in his mortal hands the power to abolish all forms of human poverty and all forms of human life. And yet the same revolutionary beliefs for which our forebears fought are still at issue around the globe— the belief that the rights of man come not from the generosity of the state but from the hand of God.[16]

Robertson's detractors often forget that he is not the first presidential aspirant to suggest that God may be on his side or that a nationwide spiritual repentance is not such a bad idea for a president to endorse. *Building a Coalition of Evangelical and Fundamentalist Voters.* When the secular press considers Pat Robertson's candidacy, they tend to see evangelicals as his sole source of support. Furthermore, many of

them concede this bloc to him. But it is not that simple. Notes Robert Dugan, director of the National Association of Evangelicals' Office of Public Affairs:

> Media reports that evangelicals will give bloc-support to Robertson are unreliable, the endorsements of Jimmy Swaggert, Oral Roberts and others notwithstanding. Many evangelicals have doubts about the appropriateness or feasibility of a Robertson candidacy. Others want to know who else is running before committing themselves. A number of potential candidates are positioned to make a strong pitch for evangelical support.[17]

Dugan has long pressed evangelicals to get involved in the political process. But he thinks they should get involved as individuals, each pursuing the dictates of conscience. He worries that organizational support of a candidate can be divisive and lead to compromise of principles. And he is also concerned that the evangelical community can lose its voice in the political process if that one candidate or party does not win.[18]

Pat Robertson is not foolish enough to take the evangelical and fundamentalist vote for granted. Almost a full year before his announcement of probable candidacy, Pat Robertson invited his televangelist colleagues to a private meeting in Washington to discuss a possible bid for the presidency. He knew he would need their backing if he was to have a chance of pulling together the large bloc of evangelical and fundamentalist voters. While the meeting was cordial, there was underlying tension. Some of them didn't care for the idea of his running for president, and they told him so. And some of them broke their pledge of confidentiality and told the press.

Over the next several months, there was plenty of evidence to support Dugan's caveat. Falwell made public his intention to actively back George Bush. Gary Jarmin, who has worked for Christian Voice and ACTV, made known his support for Jack Kemp.

The National Association of Evangelicals conducted a straw poll of 110 evangelicals attending a Washington workshop on religion and politics. While the attendees could not be considered representative of any group of evangelicals, the leadership, nevertheless, issued a

news release on the results, which was headed, "Evangelicals are widely divided over possible 1988 presidential candidates."[19]

Another sentiment held by many evangelicals was expressed in a cover story on Pat Robertson that appeared in a Seventh-day Adventist periodical:

> [N]o matter how much political clout the New Right amasses . . . —even putting Pat Robertson in the White House—the New Right's plans for a moral America are doomed. They're attempting God's work with man's methods. . . . To mix sin with politics is as fruitless as stabbing at demons, and as unbiblical as the evils they seek to correct.[20]

But if attendance at Constitution Hall on September 17, 1986, can be taken as an indicator of evangelical leadership support, Robertson made an impressive start.

There is another dimension to the evangelical and fundamentalist coalition that has been overlooked by the political analysts. Traditionally, the Democratic party has enjoyed the luxury of taking black voters for granted because of the Republicans' upper-class, conservative image. Republicans are making some inroads, but they are limited to one or two percentage points. Why should Pat Robertson be able to cut into the Democratic lock on the black vote when other Republicans have not?

First, there are a lot of black evangelicals. Second, Robertson has a very good chance of mobilizing them. Something on the order of one-half of them regularly watch religious television. Black preachers are a visible presence at the annual meetings of the National Religious Broadcasters. Frederick Price is the only black preacher who has broken into the ranks of nationally syndicated televangelists, but there are a lot of black preachers on local television and a whole lot more on local radio.

Whether or not "The 700 Club" is a regular part of their television diet, there are few black evangelical television viewers who don't know that Pat Robertson ten years ago gave a break to Ben Kinchlow, a black man from the ghetto, by installing him as co-host of "The 700 Club." Kinchlow, an executive vice president of CBN, heads up the network's "Operation Blessing," a humanitarian outreach program that

distributed an estimated $45 million in aid in 1985. And when Robertson left his regular position on "The 700 Club," Kinchlow took over the top spot.

Third, Robertson's conservative views on many social issues are shared by a large percentage of blacks, presumably including many who are not evangelicals. True, they tend to support liberal social welfare programs, but blacks as a group tend to be quite conservative on many issues. For example, a 1985 survey conducted by the Center for Media and Public Affairs found that 84 percent of blacks favor harsher sentences for criminals, 55 percent support the death penalty for murder, 60 percent oppose letting homosexuals teach in public schools, and 43 percent support a ban on all abortions.[21]

A small shift in the percentage of black votes could make a big difference. And black churches with conservative pastors represent fertile ground for harvesting those votes.

But what about Jesse Jackson's bid for the Democratic nomination? Can blacks be expected to abandon their own *and* cross over to the Republican party? The Robertson people think a Jackson bid helps their cause. Jackson helps mobilize and register black voters. But a vote for Jackson is largely a symbolic vote. A vote for Robertson may be seen as a vote that counts.

The final dimension of maximizing support from fundamentalists and evangelicals is that Robertson "keep in check" the most radical elements of that constituency.

Back in 1984, the presidential candidacy of the Reverend Jesse Jackson was marred by the support he received from another minister, Louis Farrakhan. Farrakhan, of course, is the Black Muslim whose anti-Semitic ravings were widely publicized and caused Jackson significant embarrassment. Jews were understandably infuriated when Jackson refused to repudiate Farrakhan publicly. But Jackson knew that to do so would weaken his strength with a larger segment of blacks in America than just Muslims. He had no choice but to try to straddle the fence.

Fence-straddling is uncomfortable and more dangerous than riding firm in the saddle. But it is part of the price Pat Robertson needs to pay for the support of his televangelist colleagues. The mass media have already served notice that Robertson, like Jackson, can expect to be held accountable for the excesses of his supporters.

The first televangelist to support Robertson publicly was Jimmy Swaggart. And even before the ink on the newspapers carrying the announcement had dried, political pundits were writing that Swaggart would be to Robertson what Louis Farrakhan was to Jesse Jackson.

Swaggart just happens to have the largest audience of any *weekly* syndicated religious television program. Almost 4 million people see his program during an average week, and more than 9 million monthly. In addition, he has a daily Bible-study program that attracts a couple of million viewers per week. Swaggart's endorsement potentially means a lot of votes. But when Jimmy Swaggart gets wound up, this populist Pentecostal's rantings and ravings can sound as intolerant as Louis Farrakhan's. And People for the American Way has publicized a compendium of Swaggart's gems.

Obviously, Robertson needs evangelists' support, but it must be diplomatically balanced by endorsements from other public figures, including more mainline religious leaders.

Persuading America that He is the Logical and Natural Successor to Ronald Reagan. Pat Robertson believes that the strength of the Republican resurgence in the United States during the late 1970s and the 1980s was built on commitment to conservative principles. His campaign is based on a combination of attributing the successes of the Reagan administration to the application of conservative principles and proposals and programs that reach well beyond the Reagan agenda.

"We don't have to apologize for the record of the Republican party," Robertson told a state gathering of Republicans shortly after the 1986 elections. In a mood of optimism and confidence, he continued:

> We don't have to apologize for the fact that the whole nation is moving toward conservatism. There is no reason whatsoever, because of a slight dip in an off-year election and one adventure in the Middle East, why we should hang our heads and say we are losing. We are not losing. We have the long-range program that is touching the needs and the hearts and the interests of the people of the U.S.A.[22]

In Pat Robertson's campaign, Ronald Reagan is seen as the unassailable architect of numerous achievements: a drop in interest rates from 21 percent to 7 percent; a drop in inflation from 15 percent to

2 percent or less; the creation of 8½ million new jobs and 700,000 new businesses; a drop in the top income tax rate from 70 percent to 28 percent; plus a strengthening of our defenses and bringing the Soviets to the bargaining table in sincerity.

In a way, the Iran/*contra* scandal could turn out to benefit Robertson enormously. By disassociating themselves from the questionable, if not illegal, means the president used to support the *contras*, other candidates can also put some distance between themselves and the president's insistence that this is the place to halt communism in the Americas.

Perhaps Robertson alone will stand firmly with Reagan in insisting that America must stand up against communism in Central America. Should that happen, it could be a critical advantage.

Of all the issues in his years as president, Reagan has probably been least successful in convincing Americans and the Congress that our strategic interests are at stake in Central America. This is partly the result of the post-Vietnam nervousness about getting involved where we ought not to be involved. But it also stems from Reagan's inability to communicate effectively *why* it is in our strategic interest. And that may well be the result of inability or unwillingness to master the details of Central American geopolitics, a problem Robertson, with his fact-finding trips to Central America and firm grasp of particulars, doesn't have.

An NBC/*Wall Street Journal* poll conducted in spring 1987 asked what was the most important criterion for selecting a president; 48 percent said, "vision and a plan for the country." A distant second was "record of competence" (24 percent). Third and fourth, respectively, were "strong moral character" (17 percent) and "agrees with you on major issues" (9 percent). The pollsters concluded:

What emerges is a desire for a president with a high degree of comfort with himself and a strong sense of conviction, and someone who impresses them [the voters] with his honesty in attacking the nation's problems.[23]

Because of his effective communication skills and the sincerity of his belief in the accomplishments of Ronald Reagan, Robertson may

end up at the front of the line of all those who would have American voters believe that they are natural successors to the President.

Convincing Americans that Proposed Solutions to Problems are Reasonable Programs. As noted in the last chapter, an outsider has to pursue a high-risk campaign to overcome the incredible advantage of the "incumbent," and Robertson's greatest risk is being labeled as extremist. His position on Central America is clearly a case in point. Robertson could succeed in alleviating concern about his religious beliefs only to pick up the extremist or fanatic label for his political and economic views.

"Pat Robertson," claims People for the American Way strategist Jim Castelli, "is, very simply, an extremist whose views place him well outside the mainstream of both the Republican Party and the nation."[24] A lot of people want to stick that label on Robertson.

Controversial ideas can help draw attention to his candidacy, but Robertson hopes to be able to persuade a large portion of the general public that his views are also sensible.

There are a lot of issues about which the average American knows little or nothing. How and why the Federal Reserve Board ("the Fed") controls the money supply is a case in point. At best, the average citizen knows that the money supply has something to do with whether interest rates and inflation go up or down. Among those who do know something about how the Federal Reserve works, conventional wisdom holds that the Fed operates benevolently and above the influence of everyday politics—another dimension, as it were, of our system of checks and balances.

Robertson has expressed contrary—and controversial—views. He does not think the Fed should exist totally outside the control of elected officials. Rather than being forced to defend his views against accusations of extremism, Robertson wants to proclaim them boldly, in the certainty that a fair hearing will prove them to be workable, reasonable, and in line with the sentiments of the general public.

Below is a hypothetical news release of a Robertson campaign speech. The substance and words are taken verbatim from an interview with Robertson published in *Conservative Digest* in 1986:

> Presidential candidate Pat Robertson today called for the abolishment of the Federal Reserve Board. In an address to the na-

tional convention of the XYZ, Robertson stated that "The Federal Reserve Board must be brought under the control of the elected officials of this country."

The Federal Reserve Board, he noted, has the power to put the nation into a recession or to allow prosperity; it has the power to control our trade; and it can put millions of Americans out of work or create full employment.

Robertson argued that we have a situation where the president, who is elected by the people, directs his administration to drive the car with the foot on the gas, but a man sitting in the back seat has the power to apply the brake at will. "This is schizophrenic," he contended.

Robertson noted that when *U.S. News & World Report* takes its survey of readers, the Federal Reserve chairman, who is *not* an elected official, is named as the second most powerful man in the United States.

Robertson claimed that the Fed, which has the power of life and death over our society, is a creature of the banking elite and it is not even owned by the federal government. There has never been so much as an independent audit of the Fed by an outside accounting firm. "That's shocking in a free country," said Robertson.

The remedy Robertson proposed is to merge the functions of the Fed into the Treasury Department.[25]

These words are certain to send liberals howling that Robertson's views are outrageously extreme. But, in any case, Robertson doesn't expect liberals to vote for him.

Transform Sympathy into a Massive Voter Turnout. Since televangelists became highly visible during the 1980 presidential campaign, they have taken a pretty good bashing in the press. To the viewers and supporters of religious television, criticism of the televangelists is also criticism of them. The supporters of the televangelists mostly try to ignore the criticism. But it will become increasingly difficult to ignore as we move closer to the 1988 presidential elections. The more it appears that Pat Robertson is running well, the more strident will become the attacks against his religious faith.

Some of it will be honest opposition. But a lot of it will represent

irrational antireligious bigotry. This is why, in the end, the evangelical and fundamentalist communities will rally solidly behind Robertson. Notes Bob Dugan of the National Association of Evangelicals:

> Opponents are likely to move from legitimate debate over Robertson's use of religion in politics to insidious attacks on his faith. Such tactics could drive more Christians into his camp. After all, spiritual blood is thicker than political water.[26]

But there exists the potential for a sympathetic backlash beyond the evangelical and fundamentalist communities—even beyond the moderates and conservatives in mainline Protestant and Catholic churches. To win, Pat Robertson must catch that sympathy and transform it into votes.

To be sure, a lot of people do not like what Pat Robertson is trying to sell on the campaign trail. But as Americans listen to Robertson, they are going to find a man who seems likable and sincere. They are going to hear a man who clearly knows a great deal about the subjects he addresses. They are going to see a man who doesn't square up with all the nasty things said about him.

If he reaches out too eagerly for sympathy, he runs the risk of looking not tough enough to take the heat, or, even worse, as though he staged the attacks against himself.

But Pat Robertson will find a right time and a right way to catch the tide of antireligious bigotry and turn it into an opportunity.

15

The American Cultural
Revolution:
The Next Step

> *The most important political idea of the mid-1980s is
> cultural conservatism. Republican or Democrat, the first
> 1988 presidential candidate to genuinely grasp the time-
> liness of this idea—not just make some pro forma utter-
> ances about school prayer and abortion—could very
> quickly find himself with a powerful national constitu-
> ency.*
>
> —Paul Weyrich

It is Ronald Reagan's crowning achievement that he made his conservative agenda America's agenda. What in the 1960s liberal era would have been seen as a right-wing extremist agenda became, under two Reagan administrations, mainline issues for public-policy consideration.

Ronald Reagan took issues such as military preparedness, runaway government spending, income tax reform, Communist influence in the Caribbean and Central America, traditional family values, old-fashioned religious values, and patriotism, and he moved them onto center stage. His stubborn refusal to raise taxes while increasing military spending resulted in record budget deficits. Nevertheless, until his covert dealings with Iran and secret funding of the *contras* sent his approval rating plunging in late 1986, Reagan enjoyed unprecedented popularity. His simple, down-to-earth affirmation of America,

free enterprise, and traditional values struck a responsive chord with a significant majority of Americans.

Liberals remain reluctant to admit that Reagan's agenda has become the nation's agenda. The restoration of the Senate to Democratic control in 1986 brought cries of jubilation that the Reagan Revolution was over. Even as the votes were still being tallied on election evening, NBC's John Chancellor denied that there had ever been a Reagan Revolution. And he cited public opinion polls to support his claims.

For all the gloating about the end of the Reagan Era, liberal political pundits ignored an important and indisputable reality—the Democrats did well in the 1986 elections because they coopted the issues that Reagan had defined as important. Conspicuously absent were politicians campaigning on promises to go to Washington and spend more money. Nor were local politicians suggesting that state and local governments ought to be picking up the slack in funding social programs cut by mean-spirited politicians in Washington. Easy spending was out. Fiscal restraint was in. Americans may not be ready to give up all the government services to which they have become accustomed, but they want a lean government. And that's what they believe they have under the Reagan administration. For a candidate to propose anything else would be to court disaster at the polls.

Careful examination of the 1986 election results shows mixed feelings. On the so-called personal morality issues, voters went both ways, and sometimes in contradiction to traditional patterns. In usually conservative Kansas, for example, voters finally repealed the last vestige of Prohibition in America by voting to allow liquor to be sold by the drink. And in often-liberal Oregon, it was the liberal Protestant Ecumenical Ministries that led a successful fight against a referendum to legalize the possession or cultivation of marijuana for personal use.

The most frequently cited evidence of the repudiation of Reagan and the conservative Republican philosophy was, of course, the Democrats' recapture of the Senate. Eight seats passed from Republicans to Democrats, a shift that clearly affected Reagan's ability to get his programs through the legislative body of government. But to interpret the outcome of the Senate races as a barometer of future American voting patterns may be very misleading.

Almost totally overlooked by the election analysts was the fact that the Republicans lost a mere six seats in the House. This is unprece-

dented in modern political history. Since 1946, the party occupying the White House has lost an average of thirty seats in nonpresidential election years. In the off-year elections of a president's second term, the average number of seats his party lost was forty-eight.[1]

Republicans also did very well in the gubernatorial races, scoring a net gain of eight seats. Furthermore, they won in two traditionally Democratic states, Texas and Florida, which could be important in the 1988 presidential elections.

Perhaps the greatest shortcoming in the 1986 election analyses was the failure to examine the outcome in light of the campaign itself. Most of the Senate races were issueless campaigns without any national theme. Local races tended to produce either slick but bland television commercials or vicious personal attacks. When Ronald Reagan finally jumped in with a late campaign blitz, he, too, pursued an issueless trek across the country. Americans were willing to "stay the course" in 1984, but "win one for the Gipper" just didn't have any zing in 1986.

Republicans were hurt particularly badly in the South, where registered Democrats outnumber Republicans by margins of up to 2.5 to 1 in some states. In the absence of issues, people tend to stay home or return to their "regular" party. A lot of both happened in the South. After a brutal Republican primary campaign in North Carolina, 25 percent of those who voted for Ronald Reagan in 1984 voted for Democrat Terry Sanford, a popular former governor.

The Republicans seemed to be trying to run on the perceived momentum of the 1976, 1980, and 1984 elections. But voters, unable to differentiate the candidates in terms of issues, returned to their "usual" voting patterns.

Yet another element generally ignored in the post-election analysis was the margin of victory in the Senate races. Several incumbents from both parties won by very large margins. Wendell Ford, Democrat from Kentucky, received 74 percent of the votes, and in Kansas, Republican Robert Dole received 70 percent of the votes. But many of the races were quite close. In nine of the thirty-four Senate races, the winner received no more than 52 percent of the votes cast. Republicans were successful in only two of these nine close races (Idaho and Wisconsin). The margin of Democratic victory ranged from 2,979 votes for Kent Conrad in North Dakota to 112,689 for incumbent Alan

Cranston in California, where more than 6 million votes were cast. In five of the seven states, the margin was under 24,000 votes. A strategic realignment of only 32,000 votes would have brought Republican victories in five states. To have won all nine of those close races, and thus retained control of the Senate, the Republicans would have needed a realignment of merely 117,000 out of more than 12.6 million votes cast, less than one percent. A small additional fraction of voter turnout for the Republican candidates would have netted the same result.

The conservative movement clearly lost ground in the 1986 elections. But the big loss of Senate seats was the result of small margins of victories in several states. It is possible that history will mark 1986 as the end of America's late-twentieth-century encounter with conservatism, but it is unlikely. The only real conclusion to be drawn from the elections of 1986 is that there are no firm conclusions. Only in the context of future elections will we be able to determine whether 1986 was the beginning of a decline in conservatism or, like a stock market on a major bull or bear trend, merely a correction or resting-point along the way. Furthermore, when we do analyze future elections, we will need to look carefully at the behavior of the winners and the losers. It is quite possible that we will see Democrats winning because they espouse a philosophy and vote in a pattern consistent with the conservatism that Reagan brought to Washington.

This book is grounded in social-movement theory, a theoretical orientation that cannot answer the question of the duration or the ultimate intensity of the conservative movement in America, but does provide a conceptual perspective for wrestling with the evidence.

Social movements do not necessarily give way to countermove ments, but it is not unusual for new problems to be identified as a consequence of addressing others. The programs initiated to deal with inequality and civil rights during the 1960s and 1970s are now seen as a source of some of the problems of the 1980s. The conservative mood in America today seems almost certainly a reaction to the liberal mood of previous decades. But it is more.

Social movements are not easily sustained for long periods. Maintaining momentum requires more and more resources. The capacity of social structures (public and private) to respond is not without limits. Movements tend to become bureaucratized, and with this they develop survival imperatives independent of the movements. In brief,

movements have cycles. Over time, they lose momentum and must either be regenerated or fade.

These natural tendencies have important implications for understanding (and misunderstanding) the present conservative movement in America. First, a variety of liberal social-movement activities dominated American politics for more than two decades. Whatever the empirical links between the liberal agenda and the current array of intolerable social conditions, there is an *appearance* of causal relationship—an appearance that the New Christian Right has not hesitated to exploit.

There are two problems with viewing the New Christian Right merely as backlash, however. First, it discourages further analysis, and thus is likely to miss other characteristics of a movement that has great potential for mobilizing a broader following.

The second problem is that this fails to recognize the value of old themes as an instrument for mobilizing passive adherents. The civil rights movement and the feminist movement both played heavily on old themes and unfulfilled dreams and promises. The underlying theme of the conservative movement is a covenant broken and promises similarly unfulfilled.

For liberals, as well as a lot of moderates, it is hard to escape the conclusion that conservative Christians are swimming against the mainstream of American culture. The movement seems out of step with emerging values regarding relations between the sexes. And the New Christian Right's long list of personal "vices" include a number of issues that both liberals and moderates feel ought to be left to personal choice.

For conservative Christians, it is a matter of reestablishing the public importance of private virtue. The issue is not only other people behaving in ways that run counter to their values. They object to a liberal culture that flaunts and calls virtuous the behavior they believe to be sinful. And it bothers them all the more that their personal piety is a matter of scorn and the butt of jokes.

It is difficult to measure the size of the hard core of conservative Christians in America who are fighting mad, but social-movement victories do not depend on a zealous minority becoming a zealous majority. Rather, social movements succeed when they are able to put enough pressure on the political system to address their griev-

ances. They have a greater chance when they can present their concerns in ways that are not perceived as a threat to the values of others. And if the general public believes that a movement's cause is just and legitimate, the chances of success are further enhanced.

Over the present decade, the New Christian Right has built a solid foundation for pursuing their agenda. It will gain momentum regardless of Pat Robertson's pursuit of the presidency. Consider three observations about the growth of the New Christian Right movement during the 1980s.

First, the decade has been characterized by a broadening of the base of support among conservative Christians, large numbers of whom have not heretofore been involved in the political process.

Second, the number of New Christian Right organizations has mushroomed. While there are many national organizations, the real movement is occurring at the local, community level.

Third, and equally impressive, is the extent to which the New Christian Right has been building coalitions with groups that share common concerns on both broad and specific social agendas.

It is a measure of the developing maturity and strength of the movement that it is able to put aside ideological differences to work for common goals. Abortion is probably the most significant cause drawing together groups that as recently as the 1970s could not even have imagined sitting down in the same room, much less working together. As late as 1980, it would have been hard to predict that by 1985 fundamentalists, charismatics, Mormons, Catholics, and conservative Jews would be working together.

In time, the conservative Christian movement has the potential to become solidified enough to "take over the country." If the Robertson campaign does not succeed in pulling them together, it will at least demonstrate to conservative Christians the real potential of their movement.

As has been enumerated, the resources of the New Christian Right can be enlisted in the cause of electing Pat Robertson president. These same resources will remain to be harnessed by other conservative Christians, regardless of what happens to Robertson's bid.

In conclusion, let's examine five underlying factors that have lent, and will continue to lend, muscle to the New Christian Right social

movement. Together, these factors add up to enough strength to create a cultural revolution in America.

Loss of Confidence in the Liberal Philosophy. The past quarter-century in America has seen assassination, military defeat, failed leadership, and the persistence of poverty, crime, and drug use.

Other peoples, in other times and places, have faced prolonged frustrations and humiliations and learned to live with them. But the events of the past quarter-century have not gone down well with Americans because we have always thought of ourselves as good, God-fearing people who, with His hand, have the ability to control destiny. As individuals, most of us are doing well. But as we look around us, all the upheaval seems to testify to a deep and fundamental cultural malady.

Sociologically speaking, even if it were possible to step outside our world and objectively assess our cultural condition, it would not matter. People act upon what they perceive to be real. Whether or not our problems seriously threaten our destiny as a people, we *think* they do. Before Ronald Reagan, Americans had lost confidence in the future. He has stoked the flames of hope for a brighter future.

After fifty years of experimenting with the liberal Democratic philosophy, America has entered a period of reassessment. To be sure, the liberal philosophy is not dead. Its contributions to the concepts of human rights and personal liberty are firmly institutionalized, and America is unlikely to retreat very far from these principles. At the same time, it is unable to completely eliminate poverty or uproot the structural causes of social inequality.

Of paramount concern in the years just ahead will be the struggle to define the proper role of government in our lives—what it may and may not do, what it should and should not do, and what it must and must not do. As we struggle for a new consensus on these issues, we will learn that the old labels of *liberal* and *conservative* no longer fit very well. But if the issues don't easily fit our current understanding of liberal and conservative categories, it seems fairly obvious that many of the issues will be resolved in terms more compatible with a conservative rather than a liberal philosophy.

Legitimization of the Conservative Cultural Revolution. The conservative revolution in America has been a long time in coming. Former

Senator Barry Goldwater was out in front, but in retrospect, it is clear that he was not alone. Otherwise, how could he have captured the Republican nomination in 1964? About the same time, Ronald Reagan pulled America's most populous state to the right. Eventually he would move the whole nation in that direction.

People have jumped aboard the conservative bandwagon for different reasons. There were the economic conservatives, the libertarian conservatives, the anti-big-government conservatives, and the anti-communist conservatives. The religious conservatives came late. When Ronald Reagan encountered them, he intuitively understood their role in shaping a cultural conservatism that would broaden the conservative coalition in America.

Ronald Reagan's dilemma was legitimizing a political philosophy that contends government should deliver less, not more. His answer was to delineate a new concept of the moral state. "Getting government off our backs" has been Ronald Reagan's favorite political slogan and his personal moral crusade. A society free of government entanglement in the lives of its citizens is a good society—a morally good society. And the symbol of that achievement during Reagan's years in office would be tax reform without raising taxes.

The concept of less government as moral government is easily linked to religious imagery. Theologians themselves, running the gamut from charismatic televangelist Kenneth Copeland to neo-conservative Catholic lay theologian Michael Novak, have identified free enterprise as *the* economic system most compatible with Christianity. Ronald Reagan has borrowed from this rhetoric. But he has made a more direct, less philosophical, and down-to-earth connection: Big government places heavy tax burdens on individuals and thereby strains the American family's ability to take care of itself. Free from government interference, individuals and families can find their way back to basic values.

Ever so skillfully, Ronald Reagan has equated his policies with morality. Military buildup is justified not in terms of strategic interests, but as the morally correct move in the face of an "evil empire." "The people want a constitutional amendment making it unequivocally clear our children can hold voluntary prayer in every school across this land," Ronald Reagan told the National Religious Broadcasters in 1984.[2] "And if we could get God and discipline back in our schools," he continued, "maybe we could get drugs and violence out."[3]

Perhaps Reagan's strongest equation of religion and morality with his political agenda came in Dallas in 1984, on the eve of his renomination. With the whole world looking on at a prayer breakfast for 17,000 in the Reunion Arena, he offered his immortal counsel on the inseparability of religion and politics: Reagan's comments came in the context of a broader exegesis of the role of religion in American history. But unwilling merely to offer a history lesson, the president went on to define his position on school prayer as moral while labeling those who oppose school prayer as intolerant (i.e., immoral):

. . . the frustrating thing is that those who are attacking religion claim they are doing it in the name of tolerance and freedom and open-mindedness. Question: Isn't the real truth that they are intolerant of religion? That they refuse to tolerate its importance in our lives?[4]

Sometimes subtly, other times not so subtly, Ronald Reagan has used religion to legitimize his new agenda for America. In doing so, he helped legitimize the New Christian Right's social movement. His repeated appearances before evangelical and fundamentalist forums, to the exclusion of mainline groups, underscored this.

The social movement that is being spearheaded by the New Christian Right has provided America with a plausible story line of how we got into the troubles we face, why they are perpetuated, and how we might get out.

To the fundamentalists of the early twentieth century, the enemy was modernism. When the New Christian Right came on the scene and identified the enemy as secular humanism, their cry had a familiar ring. Secular humanism, it seemed, was a mere repackaging of the old modernism. Secular Humanists are responsible for the weakening of traditional values and the family. They targeted education and basic learning—proselytizing that values are relative rather than absolute, insisting that there is no place in the classroom for God, nor for mention of the role of religion in history.

At first, secular humanism appeared to be the shrill battle cry of a few latter-day, know-nothing hicks. But, in time, secular humanism would establish itself as a plausible explanation for what had gone wrong. There are two reasons why this is so. First, while there are

some important parallels between the 1920s and 1980s, there are also some dramatic differences in the social milieu. Second, there are similarly dramatic differences between the messages of the fundamentalists of the 1920s and of the fundamentalists and evangelicals of the 1980s.

In both the 1920s and the 1980s, the nation was trying to rebound from war. They are also two periods shaped by revolutions in social behavior. The "Roaring Twenties" are analogous to the experimentation with alternative lifestyles and drugs in the late 1960s and 1970s. But the responses have been dramatically different.

In the 1920s, Americans were jubilant over victory in Europe, in the "war to end all wars." Modernism meant a new era of confidence, prosperity, and personal freedom. It was not to be feared, but welcomed with gusto. The future was bright, as least for the broader, secular culture. The fundamentalists—with their stuffy lifestyles, untenable biblical literalism, and movement to abolish alcohol—were viewed more as a nuisance than a threat to progress.

In the minds of 1980s liberals, the fundamentalists are cut from the same cloth as their 1920s counterparts. The main difference, liberals perceive, is that they are not quite so laughable because their agenda is much larger and they appear to have the potential to flex more political muscle.

But the differences are actually profound. Whereas America in the 1920s was optimistic about the future, America in the 1980s is not quite so confident. By the end of World War I, Americans were largely persuaded that our engagement was noble. But America never felt very good about fighting in Vietnam, and that sentiment deepened in time. Most believed it was a war that we never should have become involved in. Vietnam was also a staggering blow to our sense of national righteousness and political invincibility.

Now, our inability to deal with terrorism adds to our sense of vulnerability. And Americans of the 1980s worry about the possibility of a nuclear holocaust. In a word, we Americans entered the 1980s much less optimistic or confident of our power to shape the world, or even our own destiny. No one liked it when Jimmy Carter talked about malaise. But deep in our hearts, we knew that everything was not in order; that something had gone terribly wrong.

The message of the fundamentalists of the 1920s ran against the

grain of public sentiment. They saw the future of this world as bleak; salvation was in the world yet to come. The message of the fundamentalists and evangelicals of the 1980s also runs against the grain. But now, they are the optimists. Theologically, they still believe that Jesus is coming soon. But, as a matter of doctrine, they confess that they don't know how soon is soon. In the meantime, prosperity and personal happiness will come to those who profess and follow the Christian path.

That is their personal message of salvation. The new political message is that Christians united can restore America to its former position of greatness and righteousness. It is a promise to restore America's covenant destiny.

While this call is aimed at the fundamentalist and evangelical communities, it is a message with a strong civil religious appeal. One does not have to be an evangelical Christian to believe in the desirability of returning to traditional values, restoring a sense of right and wrong, and reclaiming America's rightful place as a special land in God's scheme of things. Ronald Reagan has gone far in legitimizing these goals and dreams as the goals and dreams of all Americans.

To succeed with their broader political agenda, to assume the undisputed role as leaders in the emerging cultural revolution, the New Christian Right must build upon the legitimacy that Ronald Reagan has bequeathed them. They need to persuade millions of Americans that their cause is America's cause, that their values are America's values, that their dreams for the restoration of a good and decent nation are truly the dreams of all decent Americans.

Monopoly of Religious Broadcasting. The New Christian Right social movement emerged because a small group of religious broadcasters were able to use the airwaves to persuade large audiences that there was a cause that demanded their attention. They sent out the call that brought a quarter- to a half-million conservative Christians to Washington in 1980. They put out the word that brought thousands of pastors to Dallas in August 1980 for two days of hoopla, rallying Christian support for Ronald Reagan. In 1980 and again in 1984, televangelists helped create groups that motivated Christians to register and then to go to the polls to vote.

There can be no question about the centrality of religious broadcasting in making possible Pat Robertson's candidacy. Television was

his instrument for learning and perfecting communications skills; for becoming knowledgeable about social, economic, and foreign-policy issues; for attracting a loyal following; for encouraging and organizing Christians to become involved in the political process; and, finally, for launching his campaign.

No other interest group has ever possessed as much media access for promoting an ideological perspective as the religious broadcasters. The latest figures reported by the National Religious Broadcasters show that there are 1,370 religious radio stations and more than 221 religious television stations in this country. There are currently three Christian networks broadcasting twenty-four hours a day that can be picked up via satellite nationwide, two more scheduled to achieve this coverage, and several other networks with more limited schedules. There are 414 organizations engaged in the production of religious television programs and 596 organizations producing religious radio programs.[5] Arbitron and Nielsen ratings, as mentioned earlier, indicate a sizable audience that will become even larger with greater proportions of American homes wired to receive cable television.

Clearly, religious broadcasters occupy a position of even lower esteem in the eyes of the general public than they did before the Roberts and Bakker scandals. But the balance of power between the liberal and the conservative evangelical traditions is unlikely to be altered in the foreseeable future. The liberal churches have neither the resources nor the inclination to compete successfully. The scandals may result in pressure on the Federal Communications Commission to monitor religious broadcasters more aggressively. But barring even deeper scandals in other major ministries, there seems to be nothing on the horizon that would challenge current FCC policies.

Thus, the instrument evangelicals and fundamentalists have used to mobilize conservative Christians on the New Christian Right agenda is likely to remain intact. And it will continue to direct its audiences toward social engagement. Religious broadcasting will remain a medium for the intellectual growth and development of communications skills for others who follow in the steps of Robertson and Falwell.

Mastery of Fund-raising Skills. No social movement can be sustained for long without access to significant financial resources. Tragedy, violence, heroism, or media events can bring a cause to public attention. And investigative journalism may keep the issue before the public

for a while. But in the absence of social-movement organizations, public visibility and chances to effect change are soon lost. Without money, social-movement organizations fold.

As we have seen, the New Christian Right, with its direct ties to televangelism, has a distinct advantage when it comes to raising money. Without broad-based financial support from their audiences, the television ministries soon would be off the air. So televangelists have developed state-of-the-art fund-raising technology, and their fund-raising know-how is transferable to the social-movement organizations they have created. And to some measure at least, their mailing lists can be used to seed social-movement organizations. Jerry Falwell used "Old Time Gospel Hour" mailing lists to promote the Moral Majority. Pat Robertson supported The Freedom Council with direct gifts from the Christian Broadcasting Network. The American Coalition for Traditional Values is partially supported by gifts from the ministries of the several televangelists who helped found the organization and sit on its board of directors.

Another key source of support for the social-movement organizations of the New Christian Right are a few very wealthy Americans who are committed to conservative causes. It is no secret that there is mutual respect between several of the televangelists and oil-rich Texans. And insurance magnate A. L. Williams has been an enthusiastic supporter of Robertson's political interests for a long time.

Even without adequate data on the extent to which conservative wealth in America is supporting the televangelists' political agenda, it should be evident that this group is capable of providing significant support for a long time. Even temporarily deflated oil prices and collapsed silver markets cannot dry up the discretionary funds of the very wealthy for supporting causes they believe in and causes they believe to be in their own best interests.

In short, the fund-raising base of the New Christian Right is solid. It may suffer periodic setbacks and have cash-flow problems, as occurred in the wake of the Bakker and Roberts scandals, but its sources of revenue are unlikely to disappear.

The Demographic Revolution. There is a fifth and decisive reason why the social movement now being forged by the New Christian Right will continue unabated until a genuine cultural revolution is realized. America is on the threshold of a demographic revolution. The nation

is growing older. The revolutionary impact of this aging process is not easily grasped. But it will be profound and widespread, affecting nearly every aspect of our collective life. And, what's more, the process is inevitable and irreversible.

One way to grasp what is happening is to look at the growing number of Americans who are reaching age sixty-five. As we began the twentieth century, there were only 3.1 million Americans over the age of sixty-five. By 1930, just a little more than a generation, that number increased to 6.7 million. Today there are 29 million Americans over sixty-five, and the Bureau of the Census projects that the number will grow to approximately 65 million by the year 2030.

The size of the U.S. population has also grown significantly, but the number of elderly has grown faster, so they represent an ever-increasing proportion of the population. Whereas the 3.1 million citizens over sixty-five in 1900 represented only 4.1 percent of the U.S. population, the percentage over sixty-five increased to 5.4 in 1930 and then jumped to 11.2 in 1980. In 2030, the percentage over age sixty-five will be 20. That figure represents one in five, compared to one in eight today and fewer than one in twenty at the turn of the century.[6]

Medical advances have made this aging process inevitable. It is also happening in Western Europe and will gradually become a global phenomenon. But the American experience of aging will be accelerated by the post–World War II "baby boom." The "baby boom" was substantially, though not exclusively, a result of deferred fertility during the years of the war. Between 1946 and 1965, there were 76 million births in America. These "boomers" are now twenty to forty years of age. As they begin to move into the ranks of the elderly in the early twenty-first century, there will be a demographic tidal wave.

Never before has a nation had such a large proportion of its population over age sixty-five. An inevitable consequence of the expanding aging population is a shrinking proportion of younger people. The implications of this are staggering. Younger populations will almost certainly be taxed more heavily to support Social Security and health-care benefits for the elderly. While Congress has taken measures to try to keep the Social Security Administration solvent for the next several decades, the technological revolution in medicine is being accompanied by astronomical rises in health-care costs.

To add to this growing health-care burden, the years ahead portend a rapid growth in the number of people who live to advanced ages. According to Bureau of the Census estimates, the number of citizens eighty-five and over will grow from 3 million today to 16 million midway through the next century. The startling implications of these figures are evident in data from the Social Security Administration and a study of Massachusetts citizens conducted at Brown University.[7] According to the Social Security Administration, those who reach age sixty-five today can expect to live an average of sixteen more years. The Brown study indicates, however, that, on average, these same people can expect to be self-sufficient only about ten years; those who reach age eighty-five can expect to live an average of seven additional years but function independently for only three.

One consequence of the demographic revolution will be the conflict of interest between younger generations looking to preserve their own resources and older generations who feel they are entitled to retirement and health-care benefits through government-funded programs. As a result of their large numbers, accumulated resources, and experience, the elderly will wield significant clout in the political process.

While the aging can be expected to vote and lobby for their own interests—which certainly will include social-welfare programs—the major impact of their political engagement will be to support conservative economic and social policies.

Social-science research conducted over the past several decades has demonstrated that older populations tend to hold more conservative political and economic worldviews. For some time it was believed that this relationship could be attributed to the effects of the Depression on those older adults who lived through it. More recent research challenges this connection. Norman Nie and his colleagues have shown that even as many segments of the society have become more liberal, the older segment has generally become more conservative.[8]

Furthermore, the elderly do not "slow down" or withdraw from participation in public life, particularly voting, as was once believed. Earlier studies had shown lower levels of public participation among the elderly. We now know that the lower levels of participation observed stemmed from the lower educational and socioeconomic status of many elderly citizens. Among better-educated and better-off el-

derly, there is hardly any discernible decrease in political participation. Increasingly, the aging will mirror the general population in terms of education levels and socioeconomic status.[9]

In a word, the future will see the elderly playing an increasingly important role in the political process. And their voice will be politically conservative.

Just as people become more conservative over time, there is a strong tendency for people to become more religious as they grow older. Data compiled by the Gallup Organization and its affiliate, the Princeton Religious Research Center, demonstrate a powerful relationship between aging and holding a religious worldview. Gallup's fifty-year survey, *Religion in America*, reveals that people over fifty are more likely than younger age groups to believe religion can answer all or most of today's problems. Those over fifty also report that they have a great deal of confidence in organized religion, and they are more likely to report religious affiliation and participation in a local church or synagogue. And, as noted earlier, the elderly are more likely to be viewers and contributors to one or more of the televangelism ministries.[10]

Social-science research also supports the conclusion that conservative religious worldviews and conservative political ideology go hand in hand. This is not an inevitable correlation but rather a strong tendency.

Ronald Reagan was sixty-nine years old when he became president of the United States. He will be just a few days short of seventy-eight when his successor is inaugurated in January of 1989. Reagan's presidency both personifies and symbolizes the rise to power of an aging America—confident of the validity of their conservative values. And their conservative religion is the foundation of their conviction and determination.

Another potentially significant barometer of the shift toward political and religious conservatism in America is found in a recent analysis of the values and behavior of the "baby boomers." Examining extensive social survey data gathered by the National Opinion Research Center, David Roozen and his colleagues found a decided shift away from liberalism and toward conservatism on social and political issues, *particularly* among the "baby boomers."[11] They also found higher levels of participation in religion among older "boomers" than younger ones.

This is the rebellious generation of the late 1960s. They rejected the authority, values, and lifestyles of their parents and older generations. They scoffed at tradition and experimented with alternative lifestyles to an unprecedented degree. If the data analyzed by Roozen and his colleagues accurately reflect what is happening, the cultural revolution pulling America back to religion and traditional values may be even more profound and swift than we have suggested in this analysis.

Whatever the fate of Pat Robertson's quest for the presidency, the social movement that made it possible will not soon recede.

There is a cause. The New Christian Right is locked in a struggle against the "dark forces" of secular humanism. As they see it, theirs is a battle of right and wrong, of good and evil.

A closing scene from *The Empire Strikes Back*, the second of George Lucas's celebrated *Star Wars* trilogy, offers a powerful metaphor for the Robertson candidacy. The evil lord Darth Vader has captured young Luke Skywalker's friends and thereby set a trap for him. Luke has not completed his training to be a Jedi knight but insists on attempting a rescue. Yoda and Obi-Wan Kenobi are afraid that Luke will be captured and try to dissuade him from the risky mission. Failing, Obi-Wan sighs, "That boy was our last hope." To which the Jedi master Yoda sagely replies, "No. There is another."

Pat Robertson's bid for the presidency may be premature, but there will be other evangelical candidates, perhaps even better qualified, to do battle with the secular political establishment in America. And, in the meantime, Pat Robertson, like Luke Skywalker, can be counted on to put up a helluva fight.

Notes

1. Getting Saved from the Televangelists

Epigraph: Sinclair Lewis, *Elmer Gantry* (New York: Dell Publishing, 1954), p. 424.

1. Ibid., p. 232.
2. Ibid., p. 5.
3. Ibid., p. 447.
4. "Heaven Can Wait," *Newsweek*, June 8, 1987, p. 58.
5. Tom Shales, "The 'Nightline' Coup," *Washington Post*, May 29, 1987.
6. Cited in Harry F. Waters, "A Nerd's Sweet Revenge," *Newsweek*, April 13, 1987, p. 70.
7. Jean Seligmann, "The Inimitable Tammy Faye," *Newsweek*, June 8, 1987, p. 69.
8. Cited in Gordon Witkin and Jeannye Thornton, "Stones Fly in the TV Temple," *U.S. News & World Report*, June 8, 1987.
9. Transcript, Jim Bakker's statement of March 19, 1987. *Charlotte Observer*, March 20, 1987.
10. Cited in Megan Rosenfeld, "Bakker Says His Ministry is at an End," *Washington Post*, May 2, 1987.
11. Ibid.
12. Art Harris and Michael Isikoff, "The Bakkers' Tumultuous Return," *Washington Post*, June 12, 1987.
13. Transcript of ABC's "Nightline," May 28, 1987.
14. "Statements from Bakkers," *USA Today*, April 27, 1987.
15. Ted Mellnik, "Bakker, Dortch Dismissed," *Charlotte Observer*, May 5, 1987.

16. Michael Isikoff and Art Harris, "Old PTL Board Reportedly Took Tens of Thousands in Payments," *Washington Post*, June 5, 1987.
17. Michael Isikoff and Art Harris, "$120,000 for PTL's Washington 'Liaison,' " *Washington Post*, May 13, 1987.
18. Ibid.
19. Art Harris, "PTL's Books Termed 'A Mess,' " *Washington Post*, April 30, 1987.
20. Ibid.
21. Ibid.
22. Jeffrey A. Frank and Lloyd Grove, "The Raging Battles Of the Evangelicals," *Washington Post*, March 25, 1987.
23. Associated Press, "Swaggart Calls Bakker 'Cancer' of Christ," *The Daily Progress* (Charlottesville, Virginia), March 25, 1987.
24. David R. Gergen, "On Christian Understanding," *U.S. News & World Report*, April 6, 1987.
25. Dale Crowley, Jr., Radio Station WFAX, Washington, DC, May 16, 1987. Reprinted in *The Christian News*, May 25, 1987.
26. Art Harris and Michael Isikoff, "PTL Probe Widens," *Washington Post*, June 2, 1987.
27. Russell Chandler, "Bakker Scandal Damages Standing of TV Preachers," *Los Angeles Times*, March 31, 1987.
28. Adam Clymer, "Survey Finds Many Skeptics Among Evangelists' Viewers," *New York Times*, March 31, 1987.
29. Jack Kelley, "Roberts, Bakker in Disfavor," *USA Today*, April 1, 1987.
30. "470 Laid Off at Robertson's TV Ministry," *Washington Post*, June 6, 1987.
31. Chandler, op. cit.
32. Kelley, op. cit.

2. "God Bless Our President . . ." and Other Revolutionary Ideas

Epigraph: From President Ronald Reagan's speech at the Statue of Liberty relighting ceremonies, *New York Times*, July 4, 1986.

1. Abraham Lincoln, A Proclamation for a Day of Humiliation, Fasting and Prayer, April 29, 1863. Reprinted in rally materials prepared by organizers of Washington for Jesus.
2. Audiotape, Bill Bright's address on the Mall, Washington, DC, April 29, 1980.
3. Ibid.
4. Audiotape, Pat Robertson's remarks on the Mall, April 29, 1980.
5. "The Children of Bright," *Newsweek*, June 16, 1980, p. 55.
6. Ninian Smart, "Religion, Myth, and Nationalism," in Peter H. Merkl and Ninian Smart, eds., *Religion and the Politics of the Modern World* (New York: New York University Press, 1985), pp. 15-28.
7. Joseph Campbell, *The Masks of God: Primitive Mythology* (New York: Viking Press, 1959), p. 3.
8. Richard John Neuhaus, *The Naked Public Square* (Grand Rapids, MI: William B. Eerdmans, 1984), p. 80.
9. Oscar Handlin, *The Uprooted* (Boston: Little, Brown, 1951), p. 3.
10. Ninian Smart, p. 15.
11. Cited in Robert Bellah, *The Broken Covenant: American Civil Religion in Time of Trial* (New York: Seabury Press, 1975), p. 15.

12. George Will, "Our 'Patriotism Plus.'" *Newsweek* Special Issue, Summer 1986, p. 116.
13. Pat Robertson, *America's Dates With Destiny* (Nashville, TN: Thomas Nelson, 1986), pp. 281-2.

3. The Electronic Communications Revolution and the Rise of the New Christian Right

Epigraph: Gary North, *Backward Christian Soldiers* (Tyler, TX: Institute for Christian Economics, 1984), p. 219.

1. Marshall McLuhan and Quentin Fiore, *The Medium is the Message* (New York: Bantam Books, 1967), p. 4.
2. Ibid., p. 8.
3. Ben H. Bagdikian, *The Information Machines* (New York: Harper & Row, 1971), p. 18.
4. Gregor T. Goethals, *The TV Ritual: Worship at the Video Altar* (Boston: Beacon Press, 1981), p. 18.
5. Jeremy Rifkin (with Ted Howard), *The Emerging Order* (New York: Ballantine Books, 1979), p. 98.
6. Eleanor Randolph, "Network News Confronts Era of Limits," *Washington Post*, February 9, 1987.
7. James T. Wooten, cited in ibid.
8. Charles G. Finney, Jr., *Lectures on Revivals of Religion*, ed. William G. McLoughlin, (Cambridge, MA: Belknap Press of Harvard University Press, 1960).
9. William G. McLoughlin, *Revivals, Awakenings, and Reform* (Chicago: University of Chicago Press, 1978), p. 125.
10. Bernard A. Weisberger, *They Gathered at the River* (Chicago: Quadrangle Books, 1958), pp. 210-13.
11. Karen Graff, "Billy Sunday's Crusade Against Evil in Springfield," *Illinois Times*, April 15-21, 1982, p. 4.
12. Ralph M. Jennings, "Policies and Practices in Selected National Religious Bodies as Related to Broadcasting in the Public Interest, 1920–50" (Ph.D. diss., New York University, 1968), p. 483.
13. Ibid., p. 484.
14. Ibid., p. 489.
15. Lowell S. Saunders, "The National Religious Broadcasters and the Availability of Commercial Radio Time" (Ph.D. diss., University of Illinois, 1968), p. 20.
16. Ibid., p. 22.
17. Charles M. Crowe, "Religion on the Air," *Christian Century*, August 23, 1944, p. 974.
18. James DeForest Murch, *Adventures for Christ in Changing Times* (Louisville, KY: Restoration Press, 1973), p. 174.
19. Ralph Jennings, p. 490.
20. Ben Armstrong, *The Electric Church* (Nashville, TN: Thomas Nelson, 1979), p. 49.
21. Harold J. Ockenga, keynote address to founding conference of National Association of Evangelicals, 1942.
22. Ibid.
23. Ralph Jennings, p. 317.

24. James Murch, p. 175.
25. Ralph Jennings, p. 312.
26. James Murch, p. 179.
27. Ibid.
28. Ibid.
29. Cited in Peter G. Horsfield, *Religious Television: The American Experience* (New York: Longman, 1984), p. 89.
30. Gary K. Clabaugh, *Thunder on the Right: The Protestant Fundamentalists* (Chicago: Nelson-Hall, 1974), p. 91.
31. Ibid., p. 101.

4. We're Mad As Hell and We're Not Going to Take It Anymore!

Epigraph: Paddy Chayefsky, screenplay of the motion picture *Network*, 1976.

1. Richard John Neuhaus, *The Naked Public Square* (Grand Rapids, MI: William B. Eerdmans, 1984), p. 45.
2. Jeremy Rifkin (with Ted Howard), *The Emerging Order* (New York: Ballantine Books, 1979), p. 197.
3. Richard John Neuhaus, p. 31.
4. Ibid., p. 32.
5. Ibid., p. 49.
6. James Robison, *Attack on the Family* (Wheaton, IL: Tyndale House, 1980), pp. 7-8.
7. Ibid., p. 8.
8. Ibid., p. 17.
9. Donald Heinz, "The Struggle to Define America," in Robert C. Liebman and Robert Wuthnow, eds., *The New Christian Right* (New York: Aldine, 1983), p. 142.
10. John Whitehead, *The Stealing of America* (Westchester, IL: Crossway Books, 1983), p. xi.
11. John Whitehead, *The Second American Revolution* (Westchester, IL: Crossway Books, 1982), pp. 17-42.
12. Ibid., p. 46.
13. Herbert Schlossberg, *Idols for Destruction* (Nashville, TN: Thomas Nelson, 1983), p. 46.
14. John Whitehead, 1982, p. 58.
15. Interview with authors, August 17, 1986.
16. Ibid.
17. Martin Marty, *Context*, 17/19 (November 1, 1985), p. 1.
18. William Safire, "Secs Appeals," *New York Times Magazine*, January 26, 1986.
19. John Whitehead and John Conlan, "The Establishment of the Religion of Secular Humanism and Its First Amendment Implications," *Texas Tech Law Review*, November 1 (Winter), 1978, pp. 1-66.
20. James Davison Hunter, "Humanism and Social Theory: Is Secular Humanism a Religion?" Unpublished paper, University of Virginia. Presented in *Smith et al.* v. *Board of School Commissioners*, Mobile, Alabama, October 7, 1986.
21. Paul C. Vitz, *Censorship: Evidence of Bias in Our Children's Textbooks* (Ann Arbor, MI: Servant Books, 1986), pp. 75-6.
22. James D. Carroll, et al., *We The People: A Review of U.S. Government and Civics Textbooks* (Washington, DC: People for the American Way, 1987), p. vi.

23. Richard Marquand, " 'Secular Humanism' Issues," *Christian Science Monitor*, March 23, 1987.
24. Tim LaHaye, *The Battle for the Mind* (Old Tappan, NJ: Fleming H. Revell, 1980), p. 25.
25. John Whitehead, 1982, p. 38.
26. J. Gordon Melton, *The Encyclopedia of American Religions*, Vol. I (Wilmington, NC: McGrath Publishing, 1978), pp. 155-6.
27. Tim LaHaye, *The Battle for the Public Schools* (Old Tappan, NJ: Fleming H. Revell, 1983), p. 79.
28. *Magazines for Libraries*. 1986 ed. (New York: R. R. Bowker, 1986), p. 586.
29. Tim LaHaye, p. 9.
30. Donald Heinz, pp. 133-4.
31. Herbert Schlossberg, p. 39.
32. Tim LaHaye, p. 30.
33. Richard John Neuhaus, p. 28.
34. Tim LaHaye, pp. 24-5.
35. Ibid., p. 76.
36. Ibid., p. 72.
37. Ibid., p. 78.
38. Richard John Neuhaus, p. 80.
39. Jeremy Rifkin, p. 89.

5. The Other Americans

Epigraph: Richard John Neuhaus, *The Naked Public Square* (Grand Rapids, MI: William B. Eerdmans, 1984), p. 52.

1. Michael Harrington, *The Other America* (rev. ed.) (Baltimore, MD: Penguin Books, 1961).
2. John B. Judis, "The Charge of the Light Brigade," *New Republic*, September 29, 1986, p. 16.
3. Pat Robertson, *Answers to 200 of Life's Most Probing Questions* (Nashville, TN: Thomas Nelson, 1984), p. 197.
4. John Judis, p. 16.
5. Pat Robertson (with Bob Slosser), *The Secret Kingdom* (Nashville, TN: Thomas Nelson, 1982), p. 7.
6. Richard Quebedeaux, *The Worldly Evangelicals* (San Francisco: Harper & Row, 1978), p. 27.
7. Stuart Rothenberg and Frank Newport, *The Evangelical Voter* (Washington, DC: The Institute for Government and Politics of the Free Congress Research and Educational Foundation, 1984), pp. 25-37.
8. Anson Shupe and William A. Stacey, *Born Again Politics and the Moral Majority: What Social Surveys Really Show* (New York: Edwin Mellen Press, 1982), pp. 16-20.
9. Wade Clark Roof, "The New Fundamentalism: Rebirth of Political Religion in America," in Jeffrey K. Hadden and Anson Shupe (eds.), *Prophetic Religions and Politics* (New York: Paragon House, 1986), p. 26.
10. Ibid.
11. Reprinted in James Davison Hunter, *American Evangelicalism* (New Brunswick, NJ: Rutgers University Press, 1983), p. 50.
12. Wade Clark Roof, p. 23.

13. Anson Shupe and John Heinerman, "Mormonism and the New Christian Right: An Emerging Coalition?" *Review of Religious Research*, Vol. 27 (December), pp. 146-57.
14. Walter R. Martin, *The Kingdom of the Cults* (rev. ed.) (Minneapolis, MN: Bethany House Publishers, 1977), p. 198.
15. James Davison Hunter, pp. 73-101.
16. See, for example, Joel Carpenter, "Geared to the Times, But Anchored to the Rock," *Christianity Today*, November 8, 1985, pp. 44-7; Haddon Robinson, "More 'Religion,' Less Impact," *Christianity Today*, January 17, 1986, pp. 4-1, 5-1; Grant Wacker, "Searching for Norman Rockwell: Popular Evangelicalism in Contemporary America," in Leonard I. Sweet (ed.), *The Evangelical Tradition in America* (Macon, GA: Mercer University Press, 1984), pp. 257-88; and George Gallup, Jr., *Religion in America. 50 Years: 1935-85* (Princeton, NJ: Princeton Religion Research Center, The Gallup Report), #236 (May).
17. Pat Robertson, 1984, pp. 187-8.
18. Ibid., p. 188.
19. Robert Bellah, *The Broken Covenant: American Civil Religion in Time of Trial* (New York: Seabury Press, 1975).
20. Ibid., p. 12.
21. Ibid., pp. 162-3.
22. Ibid., p. 162.
23. Robert Bellah, et al., *Habits of the Heart* (Berkeley, CA: University of California Press, 1985).
24. Pat Robertson, *America's Dates With Destiny* (Nashville, TN: Thomas Nelson, 1986), p. 297.
25. Ibid., p. 303.
26. James Davison Hunter, "American Protestantism: Sorting Out the Present— Looking Toward the Future," *This World*, Spring 1987, p. 58.
27. Pat Robertson, 1986, pp. 298-99.
28. Ibid., p. 300.

6. Legitimizing the Movement

Epigraph: Cotton Mather, *On Witchcraft* (originally published 1692, reprinted by Dell Publishing Company, New York, 1972), pp. 13-14.

1. William G. McLoughlin, *Revivals, Awakenings, and Reform* (Chicago: University of Chicago Press, 1978), p. 29.
2. Ibid., pp. 30-1.
3. Historian Paul Johnson says, "Religious evangelism was the first continental phenomenon, transcending differences between the colonies and dissolving state boundaries." Thus, George Whitefield's religious ecumenism, born out of his Arminian theology, "preceded and shaped political unity." See Paul Johnson, "The Almost-Chosen People," *The Wilson Quarterly*, Winter 1985, pp. 78-89.
4. R. C. Gordon-McCutchan, "The Irony of Evangelical History," *Journal for the Scientific Study of Religion* 20 (December), 1981, pp. 309-26.
5. Paul Johnson, p. 82.
6. Cited in Martin Marty, *Righteous Empire: The Protestant Experience in America* (New York: Harper & Row, 1970), p. 7.
7. Wayne Flint, "One in the Spirit, Many in the Flesh: Southern Evangelicals,"

in David Edwin Harrell, Jr. (ed.), *Varieties of Southern Evangelicalism* (Macon, GA: Mercer University Press, 1981), p. 24.

8. Richard V. Pierard, *The Unequal Yoke* (Philadelphia: J.B. Lippincott, 1970), p. 29.

9. The effect of World War I on evangelical Christian Americans is thoroughly discussed in George M. Marsden, *Fundamentalism and American Culture* (New York: Oxford University Press, 1978), p. 141ff.

10. Myer S. Reed, Jr., "An Alliance for Progress: The Early Years of the Sociology of Religion in the United States," *Sociological Analysis* 42 (Spring), 1981, p. 31.

11. James Leuba, *The Belief in God and Immortality* (Boston: Sherman, French and Company, 1916), p. 264.

12. Donald Dayton, *Discovering an Evangelical Heritage* (New York: Harper & Row, 1976), p. 129.

13. Ibid., p. 127.

14. Cited in Haynes Johnson, "Modern-Day Book-Banning," *Washington Post*, July 23, 1986.

15. Richard G. Hutcheson, Jr., *Mainline Churches and the Evangelicals* (Atlanta, GA: John Knox Press, 1981).

16. See Joel Carpenter, "Geared to the Times, But Anchored to the Rock," *Christianity Today*, November 8, 1985, pp. 44-7; "The Fundamentalist Leaven and the Rise of an Evangelical United Front," in Leonard I. Sweet (ed.), *The Evangelical Tradition in America* (Macon, GA: Mercer University Press, 1984), pp. 257-88; and *The Renewal of American Fundamentalism, 1930-1945* (Ph.D. diss. Johns Hopkins University, 1984). In this chapter we have relied heavily on Carpenter's excellent and thorough doctoral dissertation for many of the details that we present on fundamentalism during the 1930s and 1940s.

17. Ibid., 1984, p. 145.

18. Richard G. Hutcheson, Jr., p. 5ff.

19. Carl F. H. Henry, *The Uneasy Conscience of Modern Fundamentalism* (Grand Rapids, MI: William B. Eerdmans, 1947), p. 19.

20. Joel Carpenter, p. 47.

21. Carl F. H. Henry, p. 28.

22. Richard Quebedeaux, *The Worldly Evangelicals* (San Francisco: Harper & Row, 1980), p. xi.

23. Robert C. Liebman, "The Making of the New Christian Right," in Robert C. Liebman and Robert Wuthnow (eds.), *The New Christian Right* (New York: Aldine, 1983), p. 235

24. Bruce Shelley, "The Pioneers at Fifty," *Christianity Today*, November 8, 1985, p. 42.

7. In My Father's House . . .

Epigraph: Jerry Falwell, "Excerpts from the Rev. Jerry Falwell's News Conference," *Charlotte Observer*, April 28, 1987, p. 10A.

1. Marshall Frady, *Billy Graham: A Parable of American Righteousness* (Boston: Little, Brown, 1979), p. 225.

2. Interview with Rex Humbard on "In the Name of God." Post-Newsweek Stations, Inc., 1985.

3. Megan Rosenfeld, "Heritage USA & The Heavenly Vacation," *Washington Post*, June 15, 1986.

4. Michael Isikoff and Art Harris, "New Officers Unable to Account for $12 Million in PTL Funds," *Washington Post*, May 23, 1987.
5. Doug Finke, "The Gospel According to Bakker," *Charlotte Observer*, July 14, 1980.
6. Marshall Frady, p. 314.
7. Pat Robertson (with Bob Slosser), *The Secret Kingdom* (Nashville, TN: Thomas Nelson, 1982), p. 44.
8. Ibid., pp. 108-9.
9. Oral Roberts, *Miracle of Seed-Faith* (Tulsa, OK: Oral Roberts Evangelism Association, 1974), pp. 27, 21.
10. Razelle Frankl, "Television and Popular Religion: Changes in Church Offerings," in David G. Bromley and Anson Shupe (eds.), *New Christian Politics* (Macon, GA: Mercer University Press, 1984), pp. 133, 137.
11. John Whitt, "Isn't It Wonderful What God Can Do?" *Richmond Times-Dispatch*, December 8, 1985.
12. "LBF: Planting Churches to Meet the Needs," *Moral Majority Report* (November 1985).
13. Pat Robertson, *Shout It from the Housetops* (Plainfield, NJ: Logo International), 1972.
14. Jeremy Rifkin (with Ted Howard), *The Emerging Order* (New York: Ballantine Books, 1979), p. 97.

8. Is Anybody Listening? The Great Audience-size Debate

Epigraph: Ben Armstrong, *The Electric Church* (Nashville, TN: Thomas Nelson, 1979), p. 7.

1. Peter V. Boyer, "TV Turning to People Meters to Find Out Who Watches What," *New York Times*, June 1, 1987.
2. Ben Armstrong, *The Electric Church* (Nashville, TN: Thomas Nelson, 1979), p. 9ff.
3. Ibid., p. 122.
4. Jeffrey K. Hadden and Charles E. Swann, *Prime Time Preachers: The Rising Power of Televangelism* (Reading, MA: Addison-Wesley, 1981), p. 47.
5. William C. Martin, "The Birth of a Media Myth," *The Atlantic*, June 1981, pp. 7, 10-11, 16.
6. Ibid., p. 11.
7. Jeffrey K. Hadden and Charles E. Swann, p. 50.
8. William F. Fore, "A Critical Eye on Televangelism," *Christian Century*, September 23, 1981, p. 940.
9. See Jeffrey K. Hadden and Razelle Frankl, "Star Wars of a Different Kind: Reflections on the Politics of the Religion and Television Research Project," *Review of Religious Research*, 29/2 (December) 1987, pp. 101–110.
10. George Gerbner et al., *Religion and Television: A Research Report by the Annenberg School of Communications*, University of Pennsylvania and The Gallup Organization, April 1984.
11. The Gallup Organization report was coauthored by Harry E. Cotugno and Robert Wuthnow.
12. William F. Fore, "There is No Such Thing as a TV Pastor," *TV Guide*, July 19, 1980, p. 15.

13. William F. Fore, "Religion and Television: Report on the Research," *Christian Century*, July 18-24, 1984, p. 711.
14. David W. Clark and Paul H. Virts, "Religious Television Audience: A New Development in Measuring Audience Size." Unpublished paper presented at the annual meeting of the Society for the Scientific Study of Religion, Savannah, GA, October 25, 1985. William Behanna discussed the methodology of the study for A. C. Nielsen Company.
15. Reported in *Washington Post*, "TV Ratings," November 13, 1985.
16. George Gallup, Jr., "Demand for Fundraising Disclosure," *Washington Post*, May 23, 1987.
17. Data provided by the Arbitron Company.
18. Alvin D. Sanoff, "Zapping the TV Network," *U.S. News & World Report*, June 1, 1987, p. 56. Data source: Capital Cities/ABC Inc.
19. Arbitron figures reported here and below are based on the authors' research utilizing syndicate program analysis books in the Arbitron library in New York City.
20. The Nielsen/CBN data reported here are courtesy of CBN.
21. *People*, April 13, 1987, p. 46.

9. Politics As the Instrument of a New Ecumenical Movement

Epigraphs: All from Vern McLellan, *Christians in the Political Arena* (Charlotte, NC: Associates Press, 1986), pp. vi, 97.

1. Jerry Falwell, "Ministers and Marches." Sermon delivered at Thomas Road Baptist Church, Lynchburg, VA, March 21, 1965.
2. Jerry Falwell, *Listen, America!* (Garden City, NY: Doubleday, 1980), p. 6.
3. Ibid., p. 19.
4. Ibid., p. 18.
5. Robert N. Bellah, *The Broken Covenant: American Civil Religion in Time of Trial* (New York: Seabury Press, 1975), p. 1.
6. Harvey Cox, *Religion in the Secular City: Toward a Postmodern Theology* (New York: Simon and Schuster, 1984).
7. Richard John Neuhaus, *The Naked Public Square* (Grand Rapids, MI: William E. Eerdmans, 1984).
8. Michael Harrington, *The Politics at God's Funeral: The Spiritual Crisis of Western Civilization* (New York: Holt, Rinehart and Winston, 1983).
9. Irving Kristol, "Don't Count Out Conservatism," *New York Times Magazine*, June 14, 1987, p. 32.
10. Kenneth Burke, *Permanance and Change: An Anatomy of Purpose* (New York: The Bobbs-Merrill Company, Inc., 1965).
11. Leo P. Reibuffo, *The Old Christian Right: The Protestant Far Right from the Great Depression to the Cold War* (Philadelphia: Temple University Press, 1983), p. 241.
12. Flo Conway and Jim Siegelman, *Holy Terror*. (Garden City, NY: Doubleday, 1982), p. 82.
13. Ibid., p. 342.
14. Ibid.
15. Ibid., p. 341.
16. Ibid.
17. Ibid.
18. Ibid., p. 345.

19. Tina Rosenberg, "How the Media Made the Moral Majority," *Washington Monthly*, May 1982.
20. Donald E. Wildmon, *The Case Against Pornography* (Wheaton, IL: Victor Books, 1986), p. 7.
21. Jerry Falwell, quoted in *Liberty Report*, January 1986, p. 3.
22. Ibid.
23. Mary McGrory, "Falwell By Any Other Name," *Washington Post*, January 7, 1986.
24. Jeffrey K. Hadden and Charles E. Swann, *Prime Time Preachers: The Rising Power of Televangelism* (Reading, MA: Addison-Wesley, 1981), p. 165.
25. Ibid., p. 164.
26. Robert C. Liebman, "Mobilizing the Moral Majority," in Robert C. Liebman and Robert Wuthnow (eds.), *The New Christian Right* (New York: Aldine, 1983), pp. 49-73.
27. Jeffrey K. Hadden, Anson Shupe, James Hawdon, and Kenneth Martin, "Why Jerry Falwell Killed the Moral Majority," in Ray B. Browne and Marshall W. Fishwick (eds.), *The Godpumpers* (Bowling Green, OH: The Popular Press, 1987), pp. 101–15.
28. Interview with author, June 9, 1986.
29. Telex message, Jim Bakker to Jerry Falwell, printed in *Charlotte Observer*, April 28, 1987.
30. Transcript, press conference following PTL/Heritage USA board meeting, April 28, 1987. Printed in *Charlotte Observer*, April 29, 1987.
31. "Jones Assaults Moral Majority," *Moral Majority Report* (July 14, 1980), p. 7.

10. Pat Who?

Epigraph: Pat Robertson, "The 700 Club," 1979, cited in Jeffrey K. Hadden and Charles E. Swann, *Prime Time Preachers: The Rising Power of Televangelism* (Reading, MA: Addison-Wesley, 1981).

1. Undated direct-mail fund-raising letter from the Democratic National Committee and signed by Paul G. Kirk, Jr.
2. Paul Weyrich, "Conservatism's Future: Pat Robertson," *Conservative Digest*, August/September 1985. Unpaginated offprint.
3. Tom Wicker, "Bet-a-Million Bush," *New York Times*, August 8, 1986.
4. Hugh McDiarmid, "Bush Foes Win Fight, But War's Not Over," Detroit *Free Press*, February 22, 1987.
5. Hugh McDiarmid, "Dust Hasn't Settled on GOP Brawling," Detroit *Free Press*, April 26, 1987.
6. George Weeks, "Robertson's Edge Upsets GOP Leaders," *Detroit News*, April 26, 1987.
7. Results of the A. C. Nielsen special audience study were reported by CBN in David W. Clark and Paul H. Virts, "Religious Television Audience: A New Development in Measuring Audience Size." Unpublished paper presented at the annual meeting of the Society for the Scientific Study of Religion, Savannah, GA, October 25, 1985.
8. Pat Robertson (with Bob Slosser), *The Secret Kingdom* (Nashville, TN: Thomas Nelson, 1982), pp. 13-14.
9. Ibid., p. 196.
10. Ibid.

11. "The 700 Club," September 27, 1985.
12. "The 700 Club," June 11, 1986.
13. "Meet the Press," December 15, 1985.
14. Jim Castelli, "Pat Robertson: Extremist." Unpublished manuscript (Washington, DC: People for the American Way, August 1986), p. 26.
15. William Safire, "The Poli-preachers," *New York Times*, June 9, 1986.
16. From a broadcast of "The 700 Club," cited in Jeffrey K. Hadden and Charles E. Swann, *Prime Time Preachers: The Rising Power of Televangelism* (Reading, MA: Addison-Wesley, 1981), p. 161.
17. Senator John Warner, cited in a brochure distributed by American Coalition for Traditional Values, 1986.
18. R. Emmett Tyrrell, Jr., "Rev. Pat Robertson: Neoliberal Pundits Frightened—They Think He's Got a Chance," *Peoria Journal Star*, June 15, 1986.

11. The March of Folly

Epigraph: Leon Festinger, Henry W. Riecken, and Stanley Schachter, *When Prophecy Fails* (New York: Harper & Row, 1956, p. 3.)

1. William Miller, *Apology and Defense*. Cited in Leon Festinger, Henry W. Riecken, and Stanley Schacter, *When Prophecy Fails* (New York: Harper Torchbooks, 1964), p. 13.
2. Ibid., p. 15.
3. Ibid.
4. Barbara Tuchman, *The March of Folly* (New York: Alfred A. Knopf, 1984), p. 386.
5. Ibid., p. 7.
6. Louis Wirth, Preface to Karl Mannheim, *Ideology and Utopia* trans. by Louis Wirth and Edward Shils (New York: Harcourt, Brace & World, 1936), pp. xxii-xxiii.
7. Rodney Stark and William Sims Bainbridge, *The Future of Religion* (Berkeley: University of California Press, 1985), p. 1.
8. Michael Schudson, *Discovering the News* (New York: Basic Books, 1978), p. 194.
9. Ibid., p. 155.
10. Cited in ibid., p. 154.
11. S. Robert Lichter, Stanley Rothman, and Linda S. Lichter, *The Media Elite: America's New Powerbrokers* (Bethesda, MD: Adler and Adler, 1986).
12. Ibid., p. 293.
13. Ibid., p. 294.
14. Ibid., p. 30.
15. Ibid., p. 47.
16. George Gallup, Jr., *Religion in America. 50 Years: 1935-1985* (The Gallup Report, May 1985, No. 236), pp. 27, 40.
17. S. Robert Lichter, Stanley Rothman, and Linda S. Lichter, p. 295.
18. Ibid.
19. Ibid., pp. 295-6.
20. Ibid., p. 297.
21. Ibid., p. 296.
22. Leon Festinger, Henry Riecken, and Stanley Schachter, p. 26.
23. S. Robert Lichter, Stanley Rothman, and Linda S. Lichter, p. 55.
24. Ibid.

12. Is There Not a Cause?

Epigraph: Barbara Tuchman, *The March of Folly.* (New York: Alfred A. Knopf, 1984, p. 384.)

1. Quoted in William K. Stevens, "Margin of Vote is Called Key to Abortion Decision," *New York Times,* June 12, 1986.
2. Ibid.
3. Ibid.
4. Chief Justice Warren E. Burger, Excerpt from Dissenting Opinions, *New York Times,* June 12, 1986.
5. Quoted in Phil Gailey, "Abortion Foe Sees Hope in Mortality of Justices," *New York Times,* June 14, 1986.
6. Quoted in ibid.
7. Eleanor Smeal, undated direct-mail letter, 1986.
8. Ibid.
9. Ibid.
10. *New York Times,* August 8, 1980.
11. *The Connecticut Mutual Life Report on American Values in the '80s: The Impact of Belief* (Hartford, CT: Connecticut Mutual Life Insurance Company, 1981).
12. Ibid., p. 92.
13. *New York Times,* February 23, 1986.
14. *General Social Surveys, 1972-1985: Cumulative Codebook* (Chicago: National Opinion Research Center, 1985), pp. 215-17.
15. *Newsweek* poll conducted by The Gallup Organization, *Newsweek,* January 14, 1985, p. 22.
16. *Los Angeles Times* poll, July 1985 (Question #53).
17. *Newsweek,* January 14, 1985, p. 22.
18. *General Social Surveys;* ibid., p. 216.
19. *Newsweek,* ibid.
20. *General Social Surveys;* ibid., p. 216.
21. *Human Life Federalism Amendment.* Report Together with Additions and Minority Views of the Committee on the Judiciary, United States Senate S.J. 110. Washington, DC: U.S. Government Printing Office, p. 50.
22. *Time,* April 6, 1981, p. 20.
23. *Connecticut Mutual,* p. 128.
24. Ibid., p. 132.
25. Ibid., p. 151.
26. Patrick H. McNamara, "Conservative Christian Families and Their Moral World: Some Reflections for Sociologists," *Sociological Analysis* 46 (Summer), 1985, pp. 93-9.
27. *Connecticut Mutual,* p. 97.
28. *General Social Surveys,* p. 223.
29. *Connecticut Mutual,* p. 94.
30. *General Social Surveys,* p. 224.
31. *Los Angeles Times* poll, July 1985 (Question #55).
32. Park Elliott Dietz, "Personal Statement," *Report of the Attorney General's Commission on Pornography* (Washington, DC: Government Printing Office, 1986).
33. *General Social Surveys,* p. 225.
34. Ibid., pp. 224-5.

35. *Newsweek* poll conducted by The Gallup Organization, *Newsweek*, March 18, 1985, p. 60.
36. Ibid.
37. Ibid.
38. *Connecticut Mutual*, p. 104.
39. Cited in *Public Opinion* 8 (June/July), 1985, p. 32.
40. *Newsweek* poll, op. cit.
41. Ibid., p. 33.
42. Ibid.
43. Ibid.
44. Undated brochure entitled, "What is the Moral Majority?"
45. *Los Angeles Times* poll, July 1985 (Question #51).
46. Richard M. Smith, "The Plague Among Us," *Newsweek*, July 16, 1986, p. 15.
47. Kenneth D. Wald, *Religion and Politics in the United States* (New York: St. Martin's Press, 1987), p. 172.
48. Gallup Organization polls cited in *Public Opinion* 8 (June/July), 1985, p. 36.
49. Jerry Falwell, *Listen, America!* (Garden City, NY: Doubleday, 1980), p. 205.
50. Gallup Organization polls cited in *Public Opinion* 8 (June/July), 1985, p. 36.
51. Ibid.
52. Ibid.
53. Frederick Edwards and Stephen McCabe, "Getting Out God's Vote: Pat Robertson and the Evangelicals," *The Humanist* May/June 1987, pp. 5-10, 36.
54. *Los Angeles Times* poll, July 1985 (Question #49).
55. "Special Survey on Church and State," conducted for the Christian Broadcasting Network by The Gallup Organization, September 1984.
56. The *Los Angeles Times* poll was conducted July 9-14, 1986, and was reported in *Los Angeles Times* articles by George Skelton ("U.S. Voters in No Mood to Launch Moral Crusade," July 20, 1986) and Russell Chandler ("Believers' Views Differ on Doctrine, Sex, Afterlife, Public Policy," July 26, 1986). Some of the data reported here were provided by Russell Chandler.
57. George Skelton, July 20, 1986.
58. Ibid.
59. "Meet the Press," December 15, 1985.
60. Pat Robertson, *America's Dates With Destiny* (Nashville, TN: Thomas Nelson, 1986).

13. The Road to the White House

Epigraph: Pat Robertson, interview with *Sojourners*, September 1979. Cited in Carol Flake, *Redemptorama* (New York: Penguin Books, 1984).

1. David H. Everson, "The Decline of Political Parties," in *Proceedings of the Academy of Political Science*, 3414, 1982, p. 52.
2. Larry Sabato, *The Rise of Political Consultants* (New York: Basic Books, 1981), p. 285.
3. Ibid., p. 7.
4. Ibid., pp. 268-9.
5. Ibid., p. 286.
6. Cited in ibid., p. 12.
7. Nelson Polsby, "The News Media as an Alternative to Party in Presidential

Selection," in James I. Lengle and Byron E. Shafer (eds.), *Presidential Politics* (New York: St. Martin's Press, 1983), p. 141.
8. Interview with authors, August 7, 1986.
9. James W. Davis, *Presidential Primaries: Road to the White House* (Westport, CT: Greenwood Press, 1980), pp. 78-110.
10. Larry Sabato, p. 356.
11. James W. Davis, p. 78.
12. Interview with authors, August 8, 1986.
13. James W. Davis, p. 91.
14. Ibid., p. 96.
15. Jeff Gerth, "Tax Data of Pat Robertson Groups Are Questioned," *New York Times*, December 10, 1986.
16. Reid, T. R., " 'Too Late' to Seek Presidency In 1988, Schroeder Decides," *Washington Post*, September 29, 1987.
17. James W. Davis, p. 84.
18. Ibid., p. 104.
19. Ibid., p. 108.
20. Interview with authors, August 7, 1986.

14. A Strategy for Victory

Epigraph: Pat Robertson, Transcript of Speech to The Economic Club of Detroit, September 22, 1986.

1. Ronnie Dugger, "Does Reagan Expect a Nuclear Armageddon?" *Washington Post*, April 8, 1984.
2. William C. Martin, *The Atlantic*, June 1982. Cited in Dugger, April 8, 1984.
3. Pat Robertson, *America's Dates With Destiny* (Nashville, TN: Thomas Nelson, 1986), p. 19.
4. Ibid.
5. Ibid.
6. Interview with authors, August 7, 1986.
7. "How God Speaks to People Today," nationwide poll conducted by The Gallup Organization for the Christian Broadcasting Network, October 1986.
8. Ibid.
9. Quoted in "Idea of God's Guidance Accepted," *Charlottesville Daily Progress*, December 9, 1986.
10. The first survey was published in 1975: Andrew Greeley, *The Sociology of the Paranormal: A Reconnaissance* (Beverly Hills, CA: Sage Publications). Preliminary results of the follow-up study appeared in an article by Father Greeley in *American Health*, "Mysticism Goes Mainstream," January/February 1987, pp. 47-49.
11. Ibid., p. 49.
12. Ibid., p. 48.
13. Ibid., p. 47.
14. Bob Arnebeck, "FDR Invoked God, Too," *Washington Post*, September 21, 1986.
15. Ibid.
16. Ibid.
17. Robert Dugan, in *Washington Insight*, 8 (November), 1986. Newsletter of the National Association of Evangelicals Office of Public Affairs.
18. Interview with authors, December 18, 1986.

19. National Association of Evangelicals news release, April 29, 1986.
20. Clifford Goldstein, "The Christian Right: Will It Bring Political Pentecost to America?" *Liberty* 81 (November/December), 1986, p. 5.
21. Henry Klingeman, "I Just Called to Say I Love You," *National Review*, November 7, 1986, p. 29.
22. Address to Virginia Republican Party Leadership Advance, December 6, 1986, Staunton, VA.
23. Ellen Hume, "Voters Seek a Leader Who is Both Strong and Straightforward," *Wall Street Journal*, May 22, 1987.
24. Jim Castelli, "Pat Robertson: Extremist." Unpublished manuscript (Washington, DC: People for the American Way, 1986).
25. Dick Daebney, "God's Own Network," *Harper's*, August 1980, pp. 33-52.
26. Robert Dugan, in *Washington Insight*, 8 (November), 1986. Newsletter of the National Association of Evangelicals Office of Public Affairs.

15. The American Cultural Revolution: The Next Step

Epigraph: Paul Weyrich, "The Cultural Right's Hot New Agenda," *Washington Post*, May 1986

1. Alex Gage, "The 1986 Mid-term Elections: A Departure From Historical Patterns?" *Marketing*, Fall 1986, p. 1 (newsletter of Market Opinion Research).
2. Address to National Religious Broadcasters convention, January 30, 1985, Washington, DC.
3. Ibid.
4. Address to prayer breakfast, Reunion Arena, Dallas, August 23, 1984.
5. National Religious Broadcasters news release, January 1987.
6. For examples of such projections, see Kenneth C. W. Kammeyer and Helen Ginn, *An Introduction to Population* (Chicago: Dorsey Press, 1986).
7. Cited in Jonathan Peterson and Robert A. Rosenblatt, " 'Boomers' Face a Brave New World," *Los Angeles Times*, December 30, 1986.
8. Norman H. Nie, Sidney Verba, and John R. Petrocik, *The Changing American Voter* (enlarged ed.) (Cambridge, MA: Harvard University Press, 1979), pp. 263ff.
9. See, for example, Sidney Verba and Norman H. Nie, *Participation in America* (New York: Harper & Row, 1972), p. 145.
10. George Gallup, Jr., *Religion in America. 50 Years: 1935-1985* (Princeton, NJ: The Princeton Religious Research Center, 1985), pp. 18-20, 40-44.
11. David Roozen, William McKinney, and Wayne Thompson, "The Big Chill Warms to Worship: Family Cycle and Political Orientation Effects on Increases in Worship Attendance From the 1970's to 1980's." Unpublished paper presented to the annual meeting of the Religious Research Association, Washington, DC, November 1986.

Index